1001 Questions Answered About Insects

BY ALEXANDER B. KLOTS
AND ELSIE B. KLOTS

WITH PHOTOGRAPHS BY ALEXANDER B. KLOTS
AND DRAWINGS BY ELSIE B. KLOTS AND SU ZAN SWAIN

DOVER PUBLICATIONS, INC., NEW YORK

To

Christopher

Published in Canada by General Publishing Company, Ltd., 30 Lesmill Road, Don Mills, Toronto,
Ontario.
Published in the United Kingdom by Constable
and Company, Ltd.

This Dover edition, first published in 1977, is an
unabridged and unaltered republication of the
work first published by Dodd, Mead & Company,
New York, in 1961.

International Standard Book Number: 0-486-23470-3
Library of Congress Catalog Card Number: 76-48590

Manufactured in the United States of America
Dover Publications, Inc.
180 Varick Street
New York, N.Y. 10014

PREFACE

It would be presumptuous on our part to think that we could answer in one volume all of the questions that might be asked about insects. Anyone with the slightest awareness of the numbers of insects and the diversity of their structures and habits knows that would be impossible. In this book we have included many questions about the general biology of insects and about the activities of the group as a whole. We have tried to include questions whose answers are hard to find in the usual textbook or field book, and questions that treat with relationships not usually discussed in such books; yet at the same time we have tried to give a comprehensive story of insect life. It has been impossible, except in a few instances, to include questions about specific insects. The reader is referred to the bibliography, which lists a few of the books that deal with special aspects of insect life or with particular groups.

Rather than clutter up the answers with many cross references we have made a detailed index. *The reader is urged to use this index constantly.*

We have included a few questions on Spiders and related Arachnids, by special request.

ALEXANDER BARRETT KLOTS
Pelham, New York   ELSIE BROUGHTON KLOTS

INTRODUCTION

Since questions regarding the naming of animals and the categories used in their classification have been answered in a previous volume of this series (*1001 Questions Answered About Birds,* by Allan and Helen Cruickshank)*only a few have been included here. We remind our readers that all plants and animals are named according to the system established by Carolus Linnaeus in the tenth edition of his *Systema Natura* (1757). Each animal has a Latin name of two parts, called a binomial. This name is always italicized. The first part of the binomial is capitalized; it is the genus or group name. The second part is the name of the species. Thus, one widespread native North American butterfly, the Mustard White, is *Pieris napi;* while the common European Cabbage Butterfly (introduced into North America) is *Pieris rapae.* The fact that both of these species are placed in the same genus, *Pieris,* indicates that they have many similar characteristics and are quite closely related. They are considered distinct species, *napi* and *rapae,* since they differ in other characteristics, and do not normally interbreed. The dual name system, then, both identifies the distinctive interbreeding species and indicates its relationship with other distinct but closely related species. Sometimes species are divided into subspecies when geographically or otherwise separated populations show some constant differences from each other. A "trinomial" is used for naming subspecies, such as *Pieris napi oleracea* of eastern North America and *Pieris napi pseudonapi* of the Rocky Mountains.

All insects belong to the Insecta, or Hexapoda, a class of the

*Paperback edition published by Dover Publications, Inc., in 1976.

phylum Arthropoda (one of the twenty-one divisions of the animal kingdom). A class is made up of smaller groups called orders, which, in turn, are made up of families. A family is a group of genera. A complete classification of the Monarch Butterfly would then be:

Kingdom—Animalia
 Phylum—Arthropoda
  Class—Insecta
   Order—Lepidoptera (moths and butterflies)
    Family—Danaidae (Milkweed Butterflies)
     Genus—*Danaus*
      Species—*plexippus* (Linnaeus)

The name Linnaeus after the species name *plexippus* indicates that he first described that species, so is called the author of it. The parentheses around his name show that he described it as belonging to a genus other than *Danaus*.

Occasionally systematists use *super-* and *sub-* as prefixes to these divisional names in order to show still more detailed relationships. Thus you may encounter the term *superfamily*, which means a group of families that does not include the whole order; or *subgenus*, which means a group of species that does not include all of the species of the genus. Such names, although useful in showing relationships, are used chiefly by professional students of classification.

The giving and the recognition of the scientific names of animals is controlled by an International Code of Zoological Nomenclature.

CONTENTS

PHOTOGRAPHS
(Following page 142)

I. AN INTRODUCTION TO INSECTS AND THEIR RELATIVES

1. What are the distinctive characteristics of insects? Insects are so numerous and so varied that there are scarcely any characteristics that distinguish all insects from all other animals. Furthermore, immature insects often differ greatly from the adults of the same species,

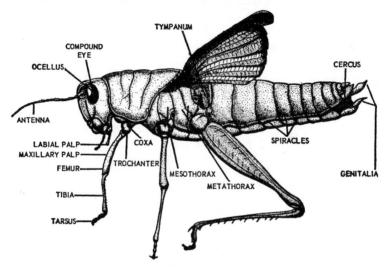

Figure 1. Diagram of lateral view of a Grasshopper.

and may not show important characteristics until they have matured. In general, one can say that insects are composed of segments that are grouped into a head, thorax, and abdomen; and that they have three pairs of legs and usually two pairs of wings.

2. What are the characteristics of the head? It bears a pair of segmented antennae (see questions 120–126), a set of mouthparts (see questions 127–142), and a pair of compound eyes and usually two or three simple eyes.

3. Of how many segments is the thorax composed? Three: the prothorax, the mesothorax, and the metathorax.

4. What characteristic structures are on the thorax?   Each segment of the thorax bears a pair of legs. (See questions 143–159.) The second and third segments bear, in addition, a pair of wings (see questions 160–193) when wings are present.

5. Of how many segments is the abdomen composed?   Typically it is made up of eleven segments. In many insects these have become so fused that there seem to be fewer.

6. Do insects have any internal body system that is distinctive? The respiratory system is characteristic. (See question 208.) Air is sucked in through several pairs of spiracles and carried to the internal parts through air tubes, the *tracheae*.

7. How many different kinds of insects are there in the world? Nearly 700,000 species of insects have been described. There may be two or three, or more, times that many since some of the very large groups have been little studied, especially in tropical regions. Some estimates put the total number, known and unknown, as high as 10,000,000 species.

8. How does this compare with the number of species of other animals?   This is over twice the number of species of all other animals combined, plus all of the plants.

9. How many species of insects have been described from North America?   Nearly 90,000 species of insects have been named from North America north of Mexico. There are certainly many thousands as yet unrecognized, as is shown by the large numbers of new species continually being named.

10. Why are there so many different species of insects?   Insects have become adapted to practically every possible type of land and fresh-water environment, and to utilizing every possible source of food and way of getting it. In doing this they have tended to become narrow specialists, each species supporting itself in a very particular way. Thus, in a genus of tiny moths whose caterpillars excavate mines in plant tissue, one species will be found only in Maple leaves, another only in Hickory, another only in certain Oaks, and still another only in certain other Oaks. Another group of species of the same genus may dig their mines only in the epidermis of twigs, each species in its particular species of tree or shrub. The relatively small individual size of most insects facilitates such narrow specialization.

11. Do insects live in all kinds of environments?   As a group, insects live practically everywhere on land and in fresh waters. Individual species, however, are usually very restricted environmentally, each living only in the very limited habitat for which it is adapted, and where its special foods occur. There are insects that live only on glacial snowfields, while others occur in hot deserts. Some are found only in subterranean caves, others in deep lakes, and still others in fast mountain streams. Some are found only in the water inside hollow leaves of specialized plants, others on stalactites, or in Penguin rookeries or in the nostrils of the Reindeer.

12. Are insects important to plants?   Scores of thousands of species feed only on plants. In fact, there is scarcely any part of any land plant that is not the source of food of some insect. Even fungi and lichens are thus attacked by special insects. In this way insects do an enormous amount of damage to plants. In great numbers of cases, however, other insects greatly benefit plants by cross-pollinating their flowers, by feeding upon other plant eaters, and by enriching the soil upon which they grow. Certainly plant life in anything like the quantity and variety in which it exists today could not survive the sudden extermination of all insects.

13. Are insects important to other animals?   So abundant and widespread in every environment are the insects that they vitally affect the lives of nearly every other land and fresh-water animal. The plant-eating insects serve as food for thousands of species of animals. Parasitic insects live at the expense of other animal groups and not infrequently are serious carriers of their diseases. But if all insects were suddenly exterminated many thousands of species of other animals would promptly follow them into extinction; and those which survived, including man, would have to adapt to terrifically disrupted conditions.

14. Are insects of great importance to man?   The plant-eating insects annually cost man billions of dollars' worth of food, timber, and other necessities, in addition to the great expense of fighting them. Still other insects live as parasites that suck his blood, carry some of his most serious diseases, and attack his domestic animals. On the other hand, man's agriculture benefits enormously from the work of pollinating insects; and the advantages gained from predatory and parasitic insects are worth far more to man than all of the expensive and dangerous insecticides that he uses. And, of course, without insects, man would lack silk, shellac, honey, beeswax, and many other products. If all insects were suddenly exterminated man would survive, but he would be able to do so only by drastically changing his whole economy.

15. What is the smallest insect?   Some of the Hairy Winged Beetles of the family Trichopterygidae are barely one-hundredth of an inch in length. They can easily crawl through the eye of a needle. Some of the Fairy Flies, family Mymaridae, that live as parasites in the eggs of Hymenoptera are probably as small.

16. What is the largest insect?   As far as bulk is concerned the largest is probably one of the Goliath Beetles of Africa (Cetoniinae) or an Elephant Beetle of South America (*Dynastes*); but for measurements we suggest the Stick Insect *Palophus titan* of Australia which is ten inches long and has a wing expanse of ten inches. The Atlas Moth (*Attacus*) of India may have a wing expanse of twelve inches; the Great Owlet Moth of South America (*Thysania zenobia*) has a slightly greater wing expanse but the over-all wing area is not as great.

17. Is this tremendous size range of insects significant?   It is significant when one realizes that the range is much greater than in any other group of animals. It speaks for the potential adaptability of the insects.

18. Is large size an indication of progress?   Excessive size, within the range of one's group, is considered to be a sign of the imminent extinction of the species. In general, the small size of insects has been of great benefit to them. The fossil evidence shows that many of the early species were very much larger than their present-day relatives. A Phasmid from the Carboniferous was nearly nine inches long; a

Dragonfly from the Permian of Kansas had a wing expanse of thirty inches; they, and their many large contemporaries, have become extinct.

THE RELATIVES OF THE INSECTS

19. What are the insects' nearest relatives? The insects belong to the great phylum Arthropoda, all of whose members have paired, jointed appendages and a more or less hard, durable, protective exoskeleton, which covers all parts of the animal except for the flexible joints. Other than the insects, the Arthropoda comprise four prominent classes (and a number of smaller, less-known ones). These are: the Crustacea, Diplopoda, Chilopoda, and Arachnida.

20. What are Crustacea? The best-known groups are those of the Lobsters, Crayfish, Shrimps, and Crabs; the Water Fleas and Beach Hoppers; the Sowbugs and Pillbugs; and the Barnacles.

21. How can we recognize a Crustacean? The group is so large and varied that it is difficult to characterize it briefly. Most Crustaceans have two pairs of antennae on the head, several pairs of appendages that serve as mouthparts, and from five to ten pairs of legs or other body appendages. Respiration is usually by means of blood-gills. The great majority are aquatic; and many more are found in salt water than in fresh water. Relatively few live on land.

22. What are the land-dwelling Crustacea? The best known are the small, flattened Sowbugs, Pillbugs, and Woodlice, often abundant in damp environments in humus and leaf mold and in rotting wood. People sometimes confuse them with insects. They have, however, no obviously distinct head, thorax, and abdomen, and usually have seven pairs of legs. They mostly scavenge on dead and decaying plant matter.

23. What are the Diplopoda? These are the Millipedes, or "thousand-leggers." All live on land. Most of them have rather long, cylindrical, wormlike bodies that are composed of many segments, each of which appears to bear two pairs of short, jointed legs. In some groups there are only a dozen or so pairs of legs; others have more than a hundred pairs. Many of them roll themselves in a spiral when disturbed and "play dead." Many secrete poisonous or repellent substances that afford them protection from predators. They feed on plant tissues and dead organic matter.

24. What are the Chilopoda? These are the Centipedes, or "hundred-leggers." They live on land, in crevices, under stones and logs, or burrowing in loose soil or leaf mold. Like the Millipedes they are long and slender, but usually have fewer segments (although some have nearly two hundred), have only one pair of legs on each apparent segment, and are more or less flattened. The front pair of legs, which are large, strong, and sharp, are used in injecting a dose of poison into their prey. The Common House Centipede, *Scutigera forceps,* scurrying around in search of prey, is a beneficial creature and should be left undisturbed. The largest species, which is found in Asia, is a foot or more long.

25. What are the Arachnida? This is a rather large and varied group, most of which live on land. The best known are the Spiders, Scorpions, Ticks, and Mites. The great majority of these are predatory on insects and other small animals, but many of the Mites feed upon plant matter, living or dead; and most of the other Mites and the Ticks live as parasites on larger animals. In nearly all Arachnids the head and thorax are joined, forming a "cephalothorax"; the abdomen is distinct from this. The head bears no antennae, and usually has two pairs of mouthparts and a number of simple eyes. The thorax, except in rare instances, has four pairs of legs. The abdomen usually is not distinctly segmented and bears no paired, jointed appendages.

A Spider, then, differs most markedly from the insects in having *four* pairs of thoracic legs, and no antennae or "feelers" on the head.

26. Is the Horseshoe Crab a real Crab? No. It is an Arachnid, but a most unusual one that lives in shallow waters along the oceanic coasts of eastern North America; four other species live similarly in Asia. They appear to have descended, with no fundamental changes, from the Eurypterids, a group of large Arthropods that flourished in the ancient Paleozoic seas, but is now extinct. To biologists the Horseshoe Crab, *Limulus,* is a classic example of what are often called "living fossils"—organisms that have survived, relatively unchanged, for enormous periods of time.

II. ARTHROPOD AND INSECT ORIGINS

27. From what did the Arthropods evolve?   The Arthropods share many fundamental features with the phylum Annelida, the segmented worms. It is believed, therefore, that they arose from a group of ancient Annelid-like animals. The structures and other features of a very small, interesting phylum, the Onychophora, strengthen this belief since they, "living fossils" in many ways, are in some features intermediate between the Annelids and the Arthropods.

28. What are the direct ancestors of the insects?   We do not know. Certainly it was a group (or perhaps, more than one group) of ancient Arthropods. The Trilobites, Paleozoic Arthropods known only from fossils, could have been ancestors, a belief based on their combination of general structures; but there is no actual proof, or even good evidence, that they were.

29. Where did insects originate?   Again, we do not know. They probably evolved in many different parts of the world more or less simultaneously, but over a period of scores of millions of years. We have no fossils to give satisfactory evidence.

30. How many species of fossil insects have been described? About twelve thousand. Many of them, however, are very incompletely known.

31. Why have not more insect fossils been found?   To be preserved an animal must be buried or encased so as to be protected from the air and from disintegration, by being silted over in the water or covered over on the ground. Conditions for trapping insects were not as common as for many other invertebrates, most of the fossil insects discovered having been caught in mud or in the resin that dripped down the bark of trees and then changed to amber. Insects were comparatively soft-bodied and would have decomposed more quickly than animals with shells or bones. Many insect fossils are known only from the wings, which, being harder, had a better chance of preservation.

32. How long have insects existed?   Insects have certainly populated the earth widely for 175,000,000 years. Unmistakable insect fossils have been found in the rocks of the Upper Carboniferous dating back possibly 250,000,000 years. Since these have fully developed wings they must have been evolving for many millions of years even then.

33. Are the insects in those ancient rocks similar to present-day forms?   Six orders of insects have been described from the Upper Carboniferous but, although they resemble orders living today, they are all extinct except one. That one includes the family Blattidae, or Cockroaches. The Dragonflies of the Carboniferous resemble the Dragonflies of today; but the differences are sufficient to cause entomologists to place them in separate orders. By the end of the Permian, however, all of the present-day orders had become established.

34. Where have these fossil insects been found?   They have been found in about 150 localities in various parts of the world. Dr. Frank M. Carpenter estimates that approximately nine-tenths have been collected in about twelve places. The oldest ones come from the Commentry shales of central France which date from the Upper Carboniferous. Large numbers are from the Tertiary shales of Florissant, Colorado (dating back about 30,000,000 years). Another important Tertiary source is the Baltic Amber of Germany and regions around the North Sea. The Permian limestones of central Kansas and northeastern Oklahoma have also provided many species.

35. Have fossil insects been found anywhere else in the United States?   Yes. A few of the important sources have been the coal mines of Rhode Island, Illinois, Pennsylvania, and Ohio, and the Tertiary shales of Wyoming.

36. Are new species being formed today?   Certainly the process of evolution is going on today. Many species are splitting into two or more different ones just as has happened since life began. Such changes do not come about overnight, of course, but may require many years or centuries.

37. Are any species becoming extinct? Undoubtedly many species are becoming extinct just as many always have.

38. What are the different ways in which a species may become extinct? The most obvious is for all members of a species to die, leaving no descendants. A less obvious way is for the species to change into one or more quite different species. The original ancestral form then exists no longer, although many of its characteristics persist in its changed descendants.

39. How is man affecting the evolution of species? By the relatively enormous changes in environment that man is causing, the survival of scores of thousands of plants and animals is vitally affected. Due to such man-made changes as widespread agriculture, deforestation, and city building, many species have been unduly favored and have increased enormously in numbers. Others have been handicapped and have been forced to adapt to the changed conditions if they were to survive. The industrialization of large areas, and the accompanying deposits of chemicals upon surrounding vegetation, is producing changes in some species that are providing opportunity for much study and research into the formation of new species.

40. Are the numbers of insects increasing? On the whole they probably are. Man has tended to break up large areas of one type of environment into many smaller areas of mixed environments. For example, what was once almost solid forest is now mixed areas of trees, shrubs, grasses, and herbaceous plants. This is advantageous to insects that are adapted to life in mixed areas. But there is no danger of insects ever reaching a state of abundance where they will become a serious threat to man's position of "supremacy."

III. AN OUTLINE OF INSECT CLASSIFICATION

41. How many orders of insects are there?   Opinions differ as to how many orders should be recognized as distinct, ranging from 22 upward. We have tended to be fairly liberal in this and recognize 32.

42. How many families of insects?   The number of families recognized varies even more than the number of orders, according to the specialist enumerating them. There are probably more than 700 families.

43. What are the orders?   See answer to question 44.

44. Approximately how many families and species are there in each order?

A GROUPING OF INSECT ORDERS, WITH
APPROXIMATE NUMBER OF FAMILIES AND SPECIES *

CLASS INSECTA—Insects
   SUBCLASS APTERYGOTA—primitively wingless insects
      Order   1. Thysanura—Bristletails
               2 families, 350 species
      Order   2. Diplura—Twintails
               3 families, 400 species
      Order   3. Protura—Telsontails
               3 families, 90 species
      Order   4. Collembola—Springtails
               10 families, 2,000 species

* Numbers of families vary according to the system of classification used and the specialist followed. The numbers given here agree in most cases with those given by A. D. Imms, *A General Textbook of Entomology,* 9th ed., revised by O. W. Richards and R. G. Davies (London: Methuen, 1957). The numbers of species have been based on those given by Curtis W. Sabrosky in "Insects," *The Year Book of Agriculture* (Washington, D.C.: U.S. Department of Agriculture, 1952). However, many additions have been made to include the approximate number of new species added since that time. Since in no case can we hope to have achieved complete accuracy, numbers are given in round figures.

SUBCLASS PTERYGOTA—advanced, winged insects

Division Exopterygota

Order 5. Ephemeroptera—Mayflies
13 families, 1,500 species

Order 6. Odonata—Dragonflies and Damselflies
23 families, 4,870 species

Order 7. Plecoptera—Stoneflies
7 families, 1,490 species

Order 8. Grylloblattodea—Grylloblattids
1 family, 5 species

Order 9. Orthoptera—Grasshoppers and Crickets
15 families, 15,200 species

Order 10. Phasmida—Walking Sticks and Leaf Insects
3 families, 2,000 species

Order 11. Dictyoptera—Roaches and Mantids
2 families, 5,300 species

Order 12. Dermaptera—Earwigs
8 families, 1,100 species

Order 13. Embioptera—Embiids or Web Spinners
7 families, 149 species

Order 14. Isoptera—Termites
5 families, 1,715 species

Order 15. Zoraptera—Zorapterans
1 family, 19 species

Order 16. Psocoptera—Bark and Book Lice
17 families, 1,100 species

Order 17. Mallophaga—Biting Lice
5 families, 2,675 species

Order 18. Anoplura—Sucking Lice
6 families, 250 species

Order 19. Hemiptera—True Bugs
50 families, 23,000 species

Order 20. Homoptera—Cicadas, Hoppers, Aphids, etc.
46 families, 32,000 species

Order 21. Thysanoptera—Thrips
12 families, 3,170 species

Division Endopterygota

Order 22. Megaloptera—Dobson Flies and Fish Flies
2 families, 200(?) species

Order 23. Raphidiodea—Snake Flies
1 family, 80 species

Order 24. Neuroptera—Net-Winged Insects
16 families, 4,500 species

Order 25. Coleoptera—Beetles
199 families, 280,000 species

Order 26. Strepsiptera—Twisted-Wing Flies
6 families, 300 species

Order 27. Mecoptera—Scorpion Flies
7 families, 350 species

Order 28. Trichoptera—Caddis Flies
22 families, 4,450 species

Order 29. Lepidoptera—Butterflies and Moths
89 families, 113,000 species

Order 30. Diptera—Flies
81 families, 86,000 species

Order 31. Siphonaptera—Fleas
12 families, 1,000 species

Order 32. Hymenoptera—Sawflies, Wasps, Ants, and Bees
73 families, 105,000 species

IV. INSECT DISTRIBUTION
AND GENERAL ECOLOGY

45. Are insects found everywhere? Insects are found in nearly every part of the land and fresh-water worlds, from the Arctic and Antarctic to the equator, on every continent and on practically every oceanic island.

46. How did insects become so widely distributed? Their powers of flight enabled them to fly or be wind-borne for great distances. Others may have been carried on floating drift. Parasites on birds and mammals were transported by the movements of their hosts. And many others have been carried by man, usually unintentionally, but sometimes on purpose.

47. Do the insects of different continents differ from each other? In detail they do. All of the important orders and most of the important families are well represented in all of the continents. But fewer genera are common to all continents, and very few species. The differences and similarities have given rise to the recognition of what are termed the "faunal regions" or "biotic regions" of the world.

48. What are the faunal regions? The land regions of the world are divided into four faunal regions, two of which are in turn subdivided. These are:

Faunal Region	*Extent*
Holarctic	The Mediterranean fringe of Africa, Europe, north and central Asia, North America
Palearctic	The Old World parts of the above
Nearctic	The New World parts of the above
Ethiopian	Africa, southward from the Sahara
Indo-Australian	
Indian or Asiatic	Southern Asia, and most of the Malay Archipelago
Australian	New Guinea, Australia and many of the islands of the Pacific
Neotropical	Tropical Mexico, the Antilles, Central and South America

49. Do any animals and plants occur in more than one faunal region?   Many groups of animals and plants occur in more than one faunal region; but each faunal region has many genera and species characteristic of it alone.

50. What are the origins of North American insects?   The larger part are fairly closely related to groups also found in Europe and northern and central Asia, i.e. to Palearctic groups. In some instances these groups appear to have originated in the Palearctic and migrated into North America by way of Siberia and Alaska. In others, they originated in North America and migrated the other way, from North America across what is now Bering Strait into the Old World.

51. Is there any evidence of insects having moved between North America and Europe across the Atlantic, via Greenland and Iceland?   Some people believe that this happened in a few instances but most scientists think not. Certainly it did not happen very often.

52. Are the insects of Alaska and Eastern Siberia very similar?   They are (as are the plants and other animals). A large proportion of the fauna of each region occurs on both sides of Bering Strait. There is clear evidence that the two were connected by solid land a number of times at intervals over a period of many millions of years.

53. Is it true that the great northern glaciation had something to do with the land bridge across Bering Sea?   Yes. During the most recent geologic period, the Pleistocene, there were apparently four great glacial periods, with warm (sometimes warmer than today) interglacial periods between them. When so much water was locked in the great continental ice sheets the oceans stood at much lower levels than they do today—low enough at times to expose great land areas where the Bering Sea now exists. It was probably during the most recent of these periods that most (if not all) of the ancestors of the American Indians entered in many waves from Asia.

54. Where did the remainder of the North American insects (and other animals) come from?   A large percentage (perhaps 40 percent) appear to have originated somewhere in the Neotropical regions and to have worked northward into North America. Probably there were great waves of northward movement during warm interglacial periods, and waves of recession southward during the colder periods of northern glaciation. Most of the movements were on the mainland of Central America, through Mexico; but there has also been quite a lot of insect migration along the island chain of the Antilles.

55. Did any insects originate in North America and stay here? A lot of insects appear to have done this, but few groups as large or as important as families. Of course a majority of our species and genera, which originated more recently than families, are found in North America alone. The families and orders, however, which must have developed far, far back in time, are mostly found also in other continents.

56. Do we owe any of our insect fauna to Africa and southern Asia? Very few, chiefly isolated genera and species that either may have been blown across the South Atlantic from Africa to South America, or similarly may have strayed across or around the borders of the Pacific.

57. Is there any evidence of former land connections between Europe and eastern North America or between Africa and eastern South America? There is some evidence, partly geologic, that such a connection may have once existed, at least between Africa and South America. Perhaps these two continents were once joined and then split away and drifted apart. Some scientists believe this was the case, but the majority do not and would like to see much more evidence.

58. Do North American insects show many differences in our different climatic regions? They do, indeed. In the northern regions the vast majority are those closely related to the insects of northern Asia and Europe; and the farther north we go the greater is the similarity. In the Arctic almost all of the species and genera are found right across Siberia to arctic Scandinavia. The farther south we go the more relatively abundant are the tropical-descended species and genera. Finally, when we get down to southern Texas, New Mexico, Arizona, and California, we find the great majority of the animals and plants identical with, or very closely related to, the species that occur in Mexico, and Central and South America. To a somewhat lesser degree the same is true for extreme southern Florida.

59. Do any Arctic insects occur normally very far southward?   A considerable number of far-northern species of insects, as well as of plants and other animals, occur far southward on high mountains. In the Alpine zone, above timberline on Mount Washington, New Hampshire, we find a truly arctic butterfly, *Oeneis melissa semidea,* whose closest relatives, merely slightly different subspecies, occur no nearer than other peaks above timberline in the Rocky Mountains and in the tundra north of timberline in the true arctic. On Mount Katahdin, Maine, is another, similar *Oeneis* (*O. polixenes katahdin*). Quite a number of moths, flies, Bumblebees, and other boreal insects, as well as many plants and other animals, show the same sort of distribution.

60. What is the explanation of these Arctic-Alpine similarities? Of course high mountaintops have cold climates and short growing seasons like the Arctic. But this merely explains how the arctic plants and animals can survive there, not how they got there in the first place. The great continent-wide glaciers of the Pleistocene, encroaching from the north, almost literally pushed the arctic plants and animals southward. Then, as the glaciers retreated northward, the arctic plants and animals followed them closely, keeping in the cold, tundralike areas where they could survive. But many individuals, instead of moving northward, simply followed the retreat of the glaciers upward on the high mountains. All of these movements took many thousands of years. Eventually the glaciers disappeared from the mountains, leaving areas of arctic tundra on the highest of them. In these the arctic plants and animals have survived, cut off by hundreds or thousands of miles of hotter lowlands from their nearest cousins.

61. Where are these Arctic-Alpine populations to be found?   There are three places in the Appalachian mountains: Mount Washington,

New Hampshire, Mount Katahdin, Maine, and two or three peaks in the Shickshock Mountains in the Gaspé Peninsula of Quebec. There are many in the Rocky Mountains, the southernmost being the high peaks of northern New Mexico near Santa Fe. In the West Coast ranges there are quite a few areas above timberline, such as Mount Rainier, Washington, Mount Hood, Oregon, and Mount Whitney, California; but these mountains have on the whole a curiously impoverished Arctic-Alpine life.

62. Are any of the Arctic-Alpine areas readily accessible?   Since there are good automobile roads up Mount Washington, and Mount Evans and Pikes Peak, Colorado, one may drive right up to this zone and enjoy studying and collecting many Arctic-Alpine insects. The best season for this is usually early to middle July.

63. How are the North American distribution zones classified?   A system of life zones was worked out chiefly by C. Hart Merriam and other workers of the U.S. Biological Survey. These were based largely on temperature averages and so followed a North-South sequence. Here is a list of these zones, with their mean annual temperature ranges.

Zone	Annual Temperature Range
Arctic-Alpine	Less than 50° F.
Hudsonian	50–57° F.
Canadian	57–64° F.
Transition	64–72° F.
Austral	
Upper	72–79° F.
Lower	More than 79° F., but with occasional frosts
Tropical	More than 80° F., with no frost

In the West, where aridity is great and where there are also many different plants and animals for other reasons, the Upper and Lower Austral zones are called Upper and Lower Sonoran zones.

64. Do the other more northern zones extend southward along the mountain chains the way the Arctic-Alpine does? They do, even more prominently. Hudsonian zone occurs on many mountains not quite high enough or cold enough for Arctic-Alpine. Canadian zone, characterized by Spruce-Fir forests, occurs in very large areas southward in the Appalachian Mountains even to Georgia; in the Rocky Mountains to southern New Mexico and Arizona and even into northern Mexico; and in the Sierras to southern California.

65. Where are the life zones most noticeable? On high mountains that rise from hot lowlands the life zones are most sharply delimited and obvious. One can start in a desert, in Lower Sonoran zone; work up through Upper Sonoran zone grasslands and Transition zone Scrub Oak, Juniper, and Pine forests; then pass into Canadian zone Spruce and Fir forests; and end up above timberline (passing through the borderline "Hudsonian zone") surrounded by fundamentally arctic plants and animals—all this within a horizontal distance of but a few miles.

66. Is any exact comparison of altitude and latitude possible? It has been calculated that, as an over-all average, climbing 500 feet is the equivalent of going northward 100 miles. This is subject to many local variations, since the south side of a mountain is likely to be hotter than the northern, and one side may be much drier than the other because of the direction of the prevailing winds. But it is a good standard to work from.

67. Are there any other systems of classifying environments? Many biologists prefer to use a system that recognizes units called *biomes,* feeling that the life-zone system is based too much on temperature averages. In many areas the biomes coincide quite closely with the life zones. The classification of the biomes is based primarily on the types of plants that are most enduring (the "plant climax") in the area, correlated with the most characteristic animals. The biomes have the great advantage of being recognizable all over the world. A dozen or more have been named; we give below only those most extensive in North America.

The Main Biomes	Index Plants and Animals	Corresponding Life Zones
Tundra	Heaths, Lichens; Reindeer, Muskox, Lemmings	Arctic-Alpine
Boreal Forest (Taiga)	Spruces, Firs; Moose, Varying Hare	Canadian
Deciduous Forest	Oak, Hickory, Beech, Maple; Virginia Deer, Gray Squirrel	Transition, Upper and Lower Austral
Grasslands (Steppe)	Bluestem, Grama, Bunch Grasses; Pronghorn, Prairie Dog	Upper Sonoran
Desert	Creosote Bush, Mesquites; Desert Fox, Antelope Jackrabbit	Lower Sonoran
Tropical Forest (Selva)	Canopy Trees, Lianas; arboreal animals, e.g., Coati	Tropical

68. Are many insects found in more than one of the biomes? A great many insects and other animals occur in two or more biomes. By no means all of the area of a biome will be occupied by the dominant types of plants. In what is essentially a forest region, for example, there will always be some open spaces occupied by shrubs, grasses, and herbaceous plants. These occur where something, such as fire, flood, or hurricane, has happened to destroy the forest in the area, permitting these other plants to get established. Or, perhaps, a local area will be too dry, or too wet, or too rocky for the forest trees. A great variety of plants will then occupy such an area, sometimes only temporarily, sometimes for a very long time. In such areas insects typical of grasslands, or of marshes, or of other special areas will exist as long as their special environment endures. If the area grows back to forest, they will disappear and be replaced by insects best adapted to the forest. Thus an insect adapted to grasslands may be most at home in the Grassland biome but may also exist in the scattered areas of grassland in Boreal Forest, Deciduous Forest, and Desert biomes as well.

69. Are many insects restricted to a single biome? A great many are, particularly the types that live and feed only in the dominant plant formation of the biome. Thus, in Coniferous Forest there are a large number of insects that feed only on Spruces and Firs, and other characteristic plants. They may be species that feed only on the leaves (needles) or buds, or in the growing shoots; they may burrow beneath the bark or feed on the seeds or on the pollen. But (unless man has mixed things up by planting the host trees in other regions) they will be strictly limited to the Coniferous Forest biome.

70. Are all insects restricted to particular environments?   The great majority are. Such species are known to the ecologist as *stenokous* species (Greek, *stenos*—narrow, *oikos*—home).

71. Do many insects live in a number of different environments? Not a great many. Those that do are called *eurokous* (Greek, *euros*—broad, *oikos*—home). A great many insects, however, live in a very restricted environment that may occur in nearly all biomes and all continents. The Drone Fly, *Eristalis tenax,* lives as a larva in foul liquids where much organic matter is decaying. Such an environment is a common one everywhere except in exceedingly cold regions or in exceedingly parched deserts. The adult flies visit any available flowers and suck nectar. It is as nearly cosmopolitan as any insect.

72. Are there many cosmopolitan insects?   There are relatively few naturally cosmopolitan ones, not a tenth of 1 percent of all insects. Probably the majority of the cosmopolitan ones have been transported by man; many of them are parasites of man, like the human Lice and Fleas, or household insects, like the Housefly. The Painted Lady Butterfly, *Vanessa cardui,* occurs on every continent, sometimes abundantly. It is a powerful migrant. Its caterpillars feed on thistles and many related plants and on some quite unrelated ones. A small, drab moth, *Nomophila noctuella,* of the family Pyralididae, which also feeds as a caterpillar on a variety of herbaceous plants, is another cosmopolite.

73. Has man introduced many insects from one continent to another?   He has, indeed, to the number of several thousand species. Most of the introduction has been unintentional. A great many of such introduced species have proven to be serious pests, like the European Gypsy Moth in North America and the Colorado Potato Beetle in Europe.

74. Are native insects ever serious pests?   A great many of them are, such as the Colorado Potato Beetle and the Spruce Budworm, both indigenous species in North America.

75. What are indigenous species?   They are species that originated in the region they now inhabit.

76. Why do more insects not spread to new regions?   The great majority cannot do so because they have become so minutely adapted to life in a certain environment, and so dependent on certain food, that they cannot survive changed conditions elsewhere. Many others which could survive such a change are unable to get started in a new region because another species, indigenous and well established there, may give them too much competition.

77. How is it, then, that in former times so many insects were able to spread widely?   Two features were chiefly responsible. In the first place, insects were the first group of animals in their size range to invade the land widely; and so, during some hundreds of millions of years, they were ever pushing out into unoccupied niches, where there was no established competition. In the second place, great waves of population movement accompany changes of climate and environment, such as have occurred many times in geologic history. The insects already established in a region would have been greatly weakened, driven out, or even exterminated; and the region would then be open for immigrants from elsewhere.

78. What is a niche?   The ecologist uses the term *niche* in the sense of a way of life, usually chiefly referring to the type of food an animal eats and how it gets it. In the community of animals that live, for example, in rotting oak logs, some species eat the wood. That is their niche. Others eat only the fungi that are breaking down the wood. That is their niche. Still others eat the wood eaters. They are predators, of a small size. That is their niche. The term does not refer so much to place, its usual use in ordinary language, as to how a species supports itself in a certain place.

79. Is size important in determining an animal's niche?   It is extremely important, especially regarding predators. A Tiger Beetle is a voracious predator, killing and eating other insects. But it can profitably feed only on prey within a certain range of size; it cannot profitably hunt very small creatures and it cannot master ones that are too large. And, of course, it never encounters animals that live in different environments, i.e., in different communities. In its environment, however, larger predators, such as foxes, that feed on animals within a very different size range, may coexist. And in the same environment may be cougars that feed on animals of a much greater size. To understand how the animals in a given unit of environment affect each other, we must know not only on what they feed, and how they do it, but the range in size of what they eat, and of what eats them.

80. What is a community?   The ecologist uses this term to refer to all of the species of plants and animals that affect each other in a unit of environment. In a dead oak log would be found many animals which eat both the wood, and the fungi and bacteria that are using it for their growth. In turn the plant-eating animals would be attacked by many predaceous and parasitic animals, and very likely these, in turn, would be victims of other predators and parasites. The basic plant food thus nourishes a whole succession of animals before eventually, through the activity of decay bacteria, it may pass into the soil and perhaps be utilized by another green plant. The whole group of species that thus are based on the original source of food, form an ecological community.

81. What are some of the actual insects and other animals of such a community?   The plant eaters in the log would include Millipedes and Sowbugs; the larvae of many families of plant-eating and wood-boring beetles such as June Beetles and Rhinoceros Beetles (Scarabaeidae), Click Beetles (Elateridae), Darkling Beetles (Tenebrionidae), and Pleasing Fungus Beetles (Erotylidae); and termites (Isoptera). These in turn would be fed on by such predators as Centipedes, the larvae and adults of many Ground Beetles (Carabidae), Flat Bark Beetles (Cucujidae), and Checkered Beetles (Cleridae); and all of them, both plant eaters and predators, are voraciously attacked by many parasitoid wasps (Ichneumonidae, Braconidae, etc.) and flies (Tachinidae). Then the Woodpeckers, and later, Shrews and Salamanders, may burrow into the log and eat any or all of its inhabitants.

82. What is the place or area in which an ecological community lies?   Such an area is termed a *biotope*. The log, with its contained community of life, is a biotope. So also would be the dead body of an animal, with its community of scavengers and the animals that feed on them. The term is often used quite flexibly. The dead-log biotope is a part of the larger forest-floor biotope. A single species of tree, supporting a whole little world of life, is a biotope; and it in turn may be regarded as a part of the far larger forest biotope. An isolated cave is a biotope. So is an acorn, containing acorn-eating insects, predators, and parasites and scavengers.

83. Where are insects most abundant?   The number of species and genera is by far greater in the tropical regions. In numbers of individuals, however, the Temperate zone insects may well exceed those of other regions, especially if we exclude the termites and ants, which are extraordinarily abundant in the tropics.

84. Do tropical insects, in general, have any distinctive characteristics?   They tend to exceed those from other regions in both size and brilliance of color. The matter of size can be correlated with the generally higher and more uniform temperatures in the tropics, which are especially favorable for the growth and survival of invertebrates. But the matter of color, although very definite, cannot be explained, although there are many theories.

85. Do Temperate zone insects, in general, have any comparable characteristics?   Their colors tend to run more to browns and grays, which are pigment colors, than to the bright structural colors of so many tropical insects. Perhaps the browns and grays match the shades of dead leaves and other vegetation, which are a greater environmental feature in the temperate regions where decay is slower.

86. Do Arctic and Alpine insects, in general, show any distinctive features?   They show a high incidence of both hairiness and dark colors. Both are adaptations to the relatively low temperatures of the environment. Hairiness to some degree prevents heat loss. Dark colors, on the other hand, promote heat absorption from the sun. Both are vital factors for cold-blooded animals such as insects.

87. What is meant by cold-bloodedness?   Most animals do not have highly efficient heat-production and body-temperature mechanisms like those of the birds and mammals. Their body temperature tends to become greatly lowered when the environment is cold, and raised when it is hot. They are, therefore, much more affected by environmental temperatures.

88. Is cold-bloodedness always a disadvantage?   In many ways it is advantageous. An insect merely slows down in all of its activities as it becomes colder, and thus during the cold period uses up much less food as a source of heat. It can often withstand very long periods of cold and then resume activity quickly when it becomes warm again. The bird or mammal, on the contrary, usually must keep going at the same rate, using up much food at a period when food may be hard to get, and dies much more easily from a lowering of the body temperature. Each type of activity has its advantages and disadvantages.

89. Do insects of the hot deserts tend to have special characteristics?   They generally tend to be light colored, although this is more a matter of matching the light tones of desert environments. Of course there are many exceptions to this generality, for in deserts animals tend to lead underground and nocturnal lives as a way of escaping the great heat and dryness of the desert day—and thus their color matters less. Desert species of insects, like the desert plants, often have a dense covering of hair, or a coat of wax, to reduce the evaporation of water. Beetles often are more spherical in shape than their Temperate zone relatives, and have an air-filled space between the forewings (elytra) and the body.

90. Do many insects do anything about controlling or regulating their environment?   A large number do this in one way or another. Special cases, cocoons, and nests do a great deal to protect the insect from environmental conditions. Few insects do much more than this, however. Hibernating insects such as Ladybirds often spend the winter in dense clusters of many thousands, the temperatures within which are considerably higher than about the edges. Honeybees cluster together in the same way during the winter. In hot weather some wasps spray their nests with water to cool them; and social wasps and bees fan the nests vigorously with their wings. Ants and termites dig their nests deeper during cold seasons or in very dry periods; and some underground termite nests have special ventilation shafts.

91. Are any insects found in salt water?   A good many species live in brackish water, but relatively few in the actual ocean. One family of Water Striders, the Halobatidae, live on the surface of the ocean, often far from land. The Tide-Pool Springtail, *Anurida maritima,* lives on the surface of tide pools and along beaches. Some flies of the family Ephydridae are called Brine Flies because they live in the very concentrated brine about salt mines and salt works; others live in very salty inland lakes, such as Great Salt Lake, and still others along oceanic coasts. The larvae of two species of mosquitoes, *Aedes detritus* and *Culex fatigans,* have been found living in water three times as salty as the sea; and other mosquitoes such as the American *Aedes taeniorhynchus* and *A. sollicitans,* among our worst pests, breed in tidal water in salt marshes. Midges (Chironomidae) live in Lake Bulack near the Caspian Sea where the water is 285 parts salt per thousand.

92. How does the insect population of Antarctica compare with that of the Arctic?   In the Arctic there are approximately four hundred species of plants, so Sawflies, Bumblebees, Coleoptera, and Lepidoptera can live in numbers as far north as the plants go; and Mosquitoes and Black Flies live wherever there are warm-blooded animals upon which to feed. But in the Antarctic there are practically no flowering plants, no ferns, and only a few lichens, mosses, and algae. A few Springtails and one wingless Midge are the only insects, although in places there are many Mites. Fleas and Lice are to be found on mammals and birds the world over.

93. What are snow fleas?   Several species of insects have been called snow fleas or snow insects. In very early spring Springtails of several species rest on the snow, often swarming at the bases of tree trunks, and tumbling into sap buckets. Several species of Stoneflies creep about on the snow all winter. A Scorpion Fly (Mecoptera), sometimes called the "snow-borne Boreus," several Crane Flies (Tipulidae), and one Winter Gnat (*Trichocera*) may be seen about tree trunks or under stones and loose boards. Most species feed on molds, green and blue-green algae on the tree trunks or the pollen of evergreen trees. Some of the Springtails feed on sap and one species in Canada is carnivorous.

94. Do many insects live in caves? Many species of insects can be found wandering about in caves or living near the entrances; but there are some species that have become truly cavernicolous, living permanently in caves. Most of these belong to the Coleoptera, families Carabidae, Staphylinidae, and Silphidae. There are many Collembola and Thysanura, however, as well as a few Orthoptera, Corrodentia, Diptera, and isolated examples of several other orders.

95. Do cave insects show any special adaptations? They are strongly negatively phototropic. Many of them have reduced or completely degenerated eyes, the degeneration of the eyes increasing the deeper they live within the caves. They tend to be lighter in color, thinner skinned, and often more hairy. Their tactile organs are usually better developed.

96. What do cave insects eat? Some are predaceous on the Collembola and other small organisms; some are parasitic; and many feed on decomposing organic matter, refuse from bats and other animals, and substances brought in by underground streams. The Collembola probably feed on colloidal substances in the water that seeps in.

97. Are there many insects, other than ants and termites, that live in the soil? Some species from most of the orders have become adapted to a subterranean existence for some part of their life. Many lay their eggs in the soil; the larvae of countless beetles, flies, and Hymenoptera live there; many pupae find protection there, often over the winter.

98. Are subterranean insects locally abundant? They are most abundant in forest areas and least abundant in the desert. Forest populations have been recorded as high as 65,000,000 per acre. Wireworms alone sometimes are numbered as high as 198,650 an acre. Serious infestations of particular insects may result in even higher counts in certain localized regions: Japanese Beetle larvae may be found 175 per square yard, and in one golf course were reported to be 1,531 per square yard; Asiatic Beetle larvae counts have reached 4,500 per square yard.

99. How are insects adapted for underground life?   Many have developed fossorial legs for digging which may be broad and shovel-like or stoutly spined, or adapted for shearing roots as in the Mole Cricket (*Gryllotalpa*). The wireworms (Elateridae), on the other hand, have very short legs and hard, glabrous bodies that can slip through the soil; and dipterous larvae are completely legless. Sub-terranean pupae are usually spined to assist them in working up to the surface for transformation.

100. Do any more insects live in such very unusual environments? The larvae of many families of flies live in putrefying liquid environ-ments such as sewage plants, septic tanks, and privies; those of one species live in barrels and tanks of highly corrosive and poisonous formaldehyde solutions that are used for preserving and embalming biological specimens. They feed on particular molds that grow on the surface of the formaldehyde. A relative of the Brine Fly is the Petroleum Fly, *Helaeomyia petrolei,* which lives in pools of crude petroleum in California and Cuba.

V. INSECT STRUCTURES
AND FUNCTIONS

SKIN AND SKELETON

101. Do insects have a skeleton?   Insects, like other Arthropods, have a skeleton on the outside of the body. It is called an *exoskeleton.*

102. Has the exoskeleton affected the insects' way of life?   It has been, probably, the most important single factor in determining the insects' way of life. In the first place an external skeleton automatically gives a great deal of protection to the body, acting as a suit of armor. But this is not wholly an advantage since to afford real protection an exoskeleton must be very heavy—so heavy, in fact, as to prevent fast movements and swift flight. Aquatic Arthropods are not affected very much by this weight, for a few gas chambers will give them buoyancy. But to a terrestrial Arthropod the weight of the exoskeleton is a serious factor.

103. Is the insect skeleton as heavy as that of other Arthropods?   It is lighter, containing much less lime than the skeleton of such as the Lobster and Crab.

104. Does an exoskeleton have any distinct advantages?   It acts to prevent evaporation of water from the body surface. This is a great advantage to a land animal, especially to a small one, since excessive desiccation is an ever-present danger. Also, it provides a place of attachment for muscles, giving a much greater mechanical efficiency in the matter of leverage than does the internal skeleton. This is a factor in the apparent greater muscular strength of insects.

105. Where on the skeleton are the muscles attached?   They are attached to internal projections of the skeleton, called *apodemes,* as well as to the internal surface in general.

106. Does an exoskeleton have disadvantages?   It has several. One is that it makes the outer surface of the body relatively insensitive to touch stimuli. Another, and perhaps the chief one, is that the exoskeleton, once formed and hardened, is not elastic. The insect can not grow much larger without the skeleton becoming too tight.

107. How have the insects met these disadvantages of the exoskeleton? They have met the first by evolving a great many sensitive touch-hairs which protrude outwardly, and are connected internally with sensory nerve endings. They have also evolved many special receptor structures, located in tiny pits in the skeleton, which detect changes of heat, light, and chemical factors of the environment. They have met the second by periodically shedding the essentially dead shell, which they cannot "let out," and by forming a new larger one. This is wasteful of materials, however. Furthermore, it subjects the insect to considerable danger during the molt and until the new larger exoskeleton has hardened.

108. How is the exoskeleton formed? It is formed by the hardening and toughening of secretions formed by glands in the true living skin, the *hypodermis*. The exoskeleton itself, which lies outside of this, is known as the *cuticula*.

109. What are the chief substances in the exoskeleton? There are three chief ones: *chitin, sclerotin,* and *waxes,* as well as a host of minor ones.

110. What is chitin? Chitin, chemically a nitrogenous polysaccharide, is the characteristic substance of Arthropod skeletons. It is very resistant to most chemicals and very tough and flexible.

111. What is sclerotin? Sclerotin is a complex mixture of proteid substances allied to the materials of our hair and nails. It is dark in color, and hard and rigid. It gives mechanical strength and hardness to the exoskeleton.

112. Are chitin and sclerotin uniformly distributed throughout all parts of the exoskeleton? Chitin occurs throughout all parts. Sclerotin is almost absent in the parts between segments and between other units that must be flexible. It occurs in greatest proportion in such structures as the mandibles and other hard mouthparts, in claws and strong spines, and in the internal muscle attachments, the apodemes.

113. What part do the waxes play?   Waxes, permeating most of the exoskeleton, furnish most of the waterproofing.

114. How has an insect retained any freedom of movement?   By having a large number of flexible, unsclerotized joints.

115. What are the units of the skeleton?   The units are known as *sclerites*. They correspond roughly to the bones that make up our own skeleton.

116. How are the sclerites arranged?   On the appendages they usually form ringlike segments connected by the thin flexible regions that largely lack sclerotin. On the segments of the body, which were primitively ringlike, there are typically four sclerites: a *tergum* (or *notum*), extending across the dorsal (top) surface; a *pleuron* covering each side; and a *sternum* extending across the ventral (bottom) surface. This primitive arrangement has become greatly modified in most insects, each of the fundamental sclerites being divided into a number of smaller ones. Thus the notum of each segment of the thorax may be divided (anterior to posterior) into a *prescutum, scutum,* and *scutellum.* Each pleuron may be divided into an *episternum* and an *epimeron,* and these may be subdivided into upper and lower parts. Each sternum may be divided (anterior to posterior) into as many as four parts, although in most insects there are only two, the *sternum* and *sternellum.* Practically every group of insects differs distinctively from all others in some pattern of subdivision, shape, or arrangement of these parts. On the abdomens of most insects the pleura are membranous or not recognizable, only the terga (dorsal) and sterna (ventral) sclerites being evident.

117. Can the skeletal units be seen on the head?   They cannot, for the head, originally evolved from six (or five) segments, is a tightly fused, hollow capsule with most traces of even the original segmentation lost. Instead, certain main head regions are visible. These are: in front, the *frons* or face; on top, the *epicranium,* at either side of which is one of the compound eyes, when they are present; on either side, a *gena* or cheek; and in many insects an *occiput* posterior to the epicranium, and sometimes, low down on each side, a *postgena.* There are often small cervical sclerites in the neck, or *cervix,* and sometimes above the upper lip, a *clypeus.*

APPENDAGES

118. What are the chief appendages of insects?   The head bears a pair of antennae and the mouthparts, some of which are true appendages. The thorax has three pairs of legs and two pairs of wings. The abdomen has a number of pairs of vestigial legs (present in primitive Apterygota only) and two pairs of reproductive appendages at the posterior end. In addition to these the abdomen may bear various paired projections and gills and sometimes a median appendage at the posterior end.

119. What was the origin of these appendages?   Most of them originated from the single pair of jointed, leglike appendages found on each segment of primitive Arthropods. These are referred to as "true" or "primitive" appendages. Some mouthparts, the wings, miscellaneous abdominal projections and gills, and the median posterior abdominal appendage did not evolve from true appendages, but arose as outgrowths of the body wall.

ANTENNAE

120. What are the antennae?   The antennae are a pair of segmented appendages modified chiefly as sensory receptors.

121. Do any insects lack antennae?   The antennae are lacking in the order Protura, but are present in all other adult insects.

122. Do antennae differ greatly in size?   In most insects they are simple, segmented, tapering, threadlike structures. They may, however, be short and bristlelike; or they may be as long or longer than the entire body of the insect. They tend to be smaller in insects having very good eyesight, as in Dragonflies. In most immature insects they are short, or may be absent.

123. Do antennae differ in shape in different insects? Great variation in form is to be found. Sometimes they have many side branches like the teeth of a comb (*pectinate*) or may even look like wide feathery plumes (*plumose*). Sometimes the terminal part is greatly

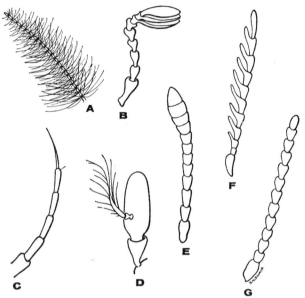

Figure 2. Types of Antennae. A, Plumose; B, Lamellate; C, Setaceous; D, Aristate; E, Clavate; F, Pectinate; G, Filiform.

swollen so that the antenna is clublike (*clavate*). Sometimes, as in the Scarabaeid Beetles, the terminal part may bear large flat plates (*lamelliform*). Or sometimes the whole antenna may be greatly shortened and swollen, as in many flies (*aristate*).

124. Is there any value to such peculiarly shaped antennae? Anything that increases the surface area of the antennae increases the possible number of sensory organs, making the antennae more sensitive as receptors.

125. Do insects hear with the antennae? Not in the way we think of hearing. But the antennae often are very sensitive to the vibrations of any surface that they are touching, and of course such vibrations can be caused by sound waves.

126. For what are antennae used? Insects are often seen "exploring" their environment with waving antennae. The sensations which they receive are primarily those of smell. The antennae of the males of many insects (especially those of the Emperor Moths and of Mosquitoes and Midges) are broadly plumose or feathery, enabling the males to sense the females from far off. The antennae of some male Oil Beetles are used for grasping the female during mating. The antennae of some male moths bear special plumes of scent scales (*androconia*), or hairs which are used in courtship.

MOUTHPARTS

127. What are an insect's mouthparts? They are a set of structures that surround the mouth opening in such a way as to enclose a space, the *cibarium,* just external to the actual mouth opening. Counting from the anterior to the posterior, in a relatively primitive insect such as a grasshopper they are: *labrum, mandibles, first maxillae, hypopharynx,* and *labium.*

128. What is the labrum? It is a flat flap hanging down from the lower part (*clypeus*) of the face, just anterior to the mouth. It is movable by muscles and acts as a front or upper lip. It is not derived from appendages.

129. What are the mandibles? They are the chief jaws. The pair of them lies a little anterior to the mouth, one on each side. Being derived from a pair of appendages they move sidewise against each other. They may be stout and strong with large grinding surfaces; or they may become elongated and sickle-shaped or drawn out into needlelike stilettos.

130. What are the first maxillae? They lie just behind the mandibles and like them are sidewise working appendages. They serve chiefly for picking up and holding food, sometimes for spooning or biting it. Typically each consists of a basal portion from which arise three separate structures: a spoonlike *galea,* a sharp, bladelike *lacinia,* and a jointed *maxillary palpus.* These, too, become greatly modified in many insects.

131. What is the hypopharynx? It is a single sensory structure lying centrally behind the mouth opening. It is an outgrowth of the head, not derived from paired appendages. It varies in size and form but is usually quite inconspicuous although in the Euglossid Bees it is very long, trailing along under the body and out behind when in flight.

132. What is the labium? It is a broad, posterior lower lip which closes the rear of the circle of structures around the mouth. Although usually a single structure, it originated from a pair of true appendages, the *second maxillae,* which more or less fused together and moved behind the mouth. It is typically rounded and spoonlike, sometimes with two or four lobes, and bearing on each side a jointed, sensory palpus, the *labial palpus.* It helps hold food in the cibarium and serves as a tasting organ.

133. Are the mouthparts of all insects alike? By no means. There are two main types, those adapted for biting and chewing, and those adapted for sucking. Each order has its own modification of one of these types, or a combination of them.

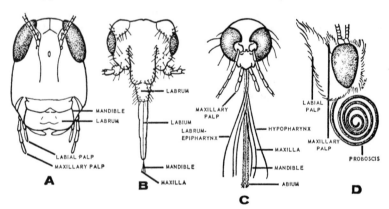

Figure 3. Types of Mouthparts. A, Typical biting and chewing mouthparts of a Grasshopper; B, Piercing and sucking mouthparts of a bug; C, Piercing and sucking mouthparts of a Mosquito; D, Sucking proboscis ("tongue") of a butterfly.

134. How are sucking mouthparts formed? The same basic parts are present as are in the biting type but considerably changed. The change consists of an elongation outward of the ring of mouthparts around the mouth opening. These parts fuse or lie together, forming a tube through which liquids are sucked up into the mouth. In each of the orders with tubular, sucking mouthparts this tube, or beak, is differently formed and is used in a different way.

135. What are the different ways in which tubular mouthparts are used? In some the tube is used for sucking up exposed liquids. In others it is equipped with piercing structures as well. In still others it has lapping structures at the tip.

136. Do any insects have both biting and sucking mouthparts? Yes, this is a specialty of the bees. They have the separate labrum, mandibles, and maxillae; but the labium is more or less elongated with its edges rolled down to form a tube through which liquids, such as flower nectar, can be sucked. Another peculiar mouthpart combination is found in neuropterous insects such an Ant Lions and Aphis Lions. The mouthparts look like regular biting ones with long, slender, piercing mandibles. These mandibles, however, are grooved or hollow. When prey is captured and pierced it is held in such a way as to permit the blood to run down the mandibles into the mouth.

137. Do immature and adult stages of the same insect ever have different mouthparts? This is the case in several orders, such as the Odonata, the Lepidoptera, and the Diptera.

138. How are the mouthparts of Dragonflies peculiar? Immature Dragonflies and Damselflies have a very highly specialized labium. This is elongated and hinged across the middle. It has a pair of strong, grasping jaws at the tip. Normally it is carried folded back, with the scoop-shaped front portion held masklike over the face; but it can be shot far forward to grasp prey some distance ahead. The adults have relatively normal biting mouthparts.

139. What kinds of mouthparts do immature and adult moths and butterflies have? The caterpillars have relatively ordinary chewing mouthparts. The adults, however, have a part of each maxilla greatly elongated, forming half of the long coiled tube through which nectar and other liquids are sucked. This proboscis is incorrectly referred to as the "tongue."

140. How do the mouthparts of immature and adult Mosquitoes and flies differ?   Mosquito larvae and the larvae of primitive flies usually have paired biting mouthparts. The larvae of the more specialized flies have lost most of the mouthparts and, in fact, most of the head. A pair of strong mouth hooks serves for tearing and shredding the food. Adult Diptera have, for the most part, well-developed sucking mouthparts.

141. Are any insect mouthparts so reduced as to be useless?   The adults of a number of large groups of insects have the mouthparts so reduced that the insect can take in neither water nor food. The adult instar lives upon the nourishment consumed by the immature instar. This is true of Mayflies, Midges (Chironomidae), and certain families of moths and other smaller groups.

142. Are mouthparts used much in identifying and classifying insects?   One of the first things to look at in identifying an insect is its mouthparts. Biting mouthparts are usually easily told from the tubular, sucking ones, which look like beaks, even with the naked eye. There are some tricky ones, however, such as the Scorpion Flies (Mecoptera) and the Weevils (Coleoptera), which have small biting mouthparts on the end of a long beak.

LEGS

143. Do any insects have more than six legs?   None have more than six (three pairs) on the thorax. Many, however, have various paired appendages on the abdomen that were, in a far distant ancestral stage, legs; but these appendages no longer function as walking, climbing, or swimming legs, having either degenerated or been converted to other uses. Many larvae have leglike structures on the abdomen that do act as legs but they are probably not derived from ancient ancestral ones.

144. Are all insects' legs alike?   All have a common pattern, consisting of five divisions. From the body outward these are: *coxa, trochanter, femur, tibia,* and *tarsus.*

145. How do these different parts function?   The coxa acts as the ball of a ball-and-socket joint by which the leg is attached to the body.

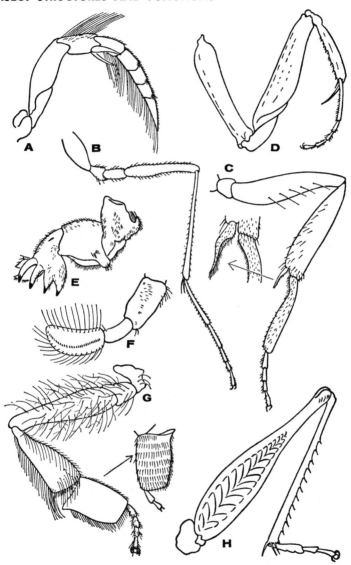

Figure 4. Legs of insects to show variety. A, Swimming leg of Diving Beetle; B, Walking leg of Ichneumon Wasp (after Metcalf and Flint); C, Ant leg to show antennae cleaner; D, Raptorial leg of Preying Mantis; E, Fossorial leg of Mole Cricket; F, Food-gathering leg of Water Boatman; G, Pollen carrying leg of Honeybee; H, Jumping leg of Grasshopper.

The trochanter is a very small segment connecting coxa and femur. The femur is usually the largest segment, packed with muscles. The tibia tends to be long but slender. It often bears spines and, at or near its outer end, movable *spurs* which often give the insect traction. Finally the tarsus, or foot, typically five-jointed, bears a pair of strong *claws* at the tip, various pads or glands that secrete sticky substances, and other minor structures.

146. Do any insects use their legs for other than walking or running?   A great many do. In one or another group of insects legs are modified and used for such special tasks as swimming, leaping, digging, scooping up prey, seizing and killing prey, courtship and mating, making sounds, hearing, soaring and gliding, spinning silk, carrying food, modeling and sculpturing, cleaning the eyes and antennae, and tasting.

147. How are some insects' legs adapted for swimming?   The hind legs of the adults of several groups of aquatic insects are more or less lengthened, flattened, and furnished with a row of long, close-set hairs along each edge. They thus serve as oar blades. This is most marked in the Giant Water Bugs (Belostomatidae), Backswimmers (Notonectidae), and Water Boatmen (Corixidae) of the order Hemiptera; and the Diving Beetles (Dytiscidae) and Water Scavenger Beetles (Hydrophilidae) of the order Coleoptera.

148. What insects have the legs especially adapted for leaping? The champion jumpers among insects are the Locusts (Locustidae), Meadow Grasshoppers (Tettigoniidae), and Grouse Locusts (Acrididae) of the order Orthoptera; the Flea Beetles (Halticinae) of the order Coleoptera; and the Fleas (order Siphonaptera). In such insects the hind legs have greatly swollen femora containing powerful muscles.

149. What insects have legs especially adapted for digging?   The chief groups are the Mole Crickets (Gryllidae) of the order Orthoptera, the nymphs of the Cicadas (Cicadidae) of the order Homoptera, and many Dung Beetles of the family Scarabaeidae. In all of these it is the forelegs that are especially strong and flattened, serving as shovels and rakes. The Mole Crickets also have a special process on each foreleg that acts as a pair of shears with which rootlets are cut.

150. How are legs adapted for scooping up prey?   The legs of adult Dragonflies and Damselflies are long and slender, with a row of stiff bristles along each side. When in flight they are held slanting forward to form a basket by means of which small flying prey are scooped out of the air and held until the jaws can grasp them. These insects are probably the most accomplished aerialists of any animals.

151. Do many insects seize and kill their prey with their legs?   A great many do, many of them having the front legs adapted for quick and powerful grasping. In most instances the fore tibia can be snapped back against the femur. Often both tibia and femur are set with sharp teeth or spines that pierce and hold the prey. Or the tibia may be

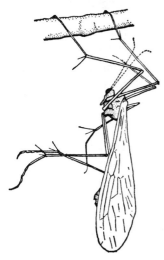

Figure 5. *Bittacus*, a predaceous Scorpion Fly, hangs by its two front legs from a twig, or even from a clothes line. This individual was photographed as it hung by the first two legs of one side.

curved and bladelike, and fit into a groove along the femur. The legs are often greatly lengthened so that the insect can reach far forward to grab the prey. Among the best-known groups with legs like this are Preying Mantids (Mantidae) of the order Dictyoptera; Giant Water Bugs (Belostomatidae), Creeping Water Bugs (Naucoridae), and Ambush Bugs (Phymatidae) of the order Hemiptera; and Mantis Flies (Mantispidae) of the order Neuroptera. A most unusual family of the Neuroptera, the Bittacidae, hang from twigs by the forelegs and seize with their long hind legs small insects flying past.

152. How are legs especially used in courtship and mating?   The males of many insects have legs, usually the fore pair, especially adapted for various sexual functions. Often, as in many Owlet Moths (Noctuidae), the legs bear dense brushes of scent hairs which, when spread, waft the products of special gland cells to the female. In some of the Long-legged Flies (Dolichopodidae) the males have cup-like structures on the forelegs that fit over the eyes of the females during mating. In some of the Diving Beetles (Dytiscidae) the males have suction disks on the forelegs by means of which they can hold on to the slippery bodies of the females.

153. What insects make sounds with their legs?   The males of many locusts "stridulate" (produce sounds by rubbing two surfaces together) by rasping especially roughened areas of the hind legs against similar areas in the wing bases. Other Orthoptera stridulate by rubbing the wings together. The larvae of Passalid Beetles (Passalidae) have a special stridulating apparatus on the hind legs. It is believed that groups of these larvae and of their parents keep together in the rotting logs in which they live by means of the sounds thus produced.

154. How can insects hear with their legs?   The Long Horned and Meadow Grasshoppers, Katydids, and Crickets have a true hearing organ, a chordotonal organ, on the tibia of each foreleg. Some termites and Stoneflies have similar structures on the tibiae; some Diving Beetles (Dytiscidae) and Chafers (Scarabaeidae) have them on the tarsi. Other insects that have hearing organs have them on various parts of the body.

155. How do insects soar and glide by means of their legs?   In one very unusual group of insects, the Phantom Crane Flies (*Bittacomorpha*), the tarsi are broad, flat, and hollowed beneath. The flies, which have proportionately rather small wings, spread the legs like the spokes of a wheel, thus gaining considerable buoyancy from the surfaces of the tarsi. Rising air currents often are enough to keep them in the air.

156. What insects actually spin silk with the feet? The members of the small order of the Embiids (Embioptera) have silk glands in the fore tarsi of both the nymphs and adults. These produce silk with which they line the tunnels of their underground nests.

157. How are legs adapted for food-carrying? The hind legs of most (but not all) bees have the tibia and the basal segments of the tarsus enlarged and provided with long, stiff hairs. This makes a very efficient apparatus for forming and carrying a large ball of pollen accumulated from flowers.

158. How are legs adapted as special cleaners? The front legs of many insects have a notch with a movable spine fitting over it, through which the antennae can be drawn and scraped clean. Many butterflies, especially the Brush Footed Butterflies (Nymphalidae), have small, hairy front legs which are quite useless as legs but very efficient as brushes with which to clean the surfaces of the compound eyes.

159. What insects taste with their feet? Probably many groups do. The butterflies, in particular, have very sensitive taste structures on the soles of the feet. When a butterfly alights on a flower, the petals of which are faintly sweet, this taste mechanism on the feet causes the tubular proboscis of the mouth to uncoil and to probe down into the nectary of the flower.

WINGS

160. Why is the insect wing said to be a unique organ of flight? The insects are the only animals that have wings originally evolved for flight, since bird and bat wings are modifications of pre-existing limbs.

161. How did insect wings originate? They are believed to have originated as flat expansions of the sides of the thoracic segments. They were probably useful in gliding.

162. Were there originally two pairs? Originally there were three pairs, one on each thoracic segment; but later the first pair dropped out and the second and third developed in a greater degree and became jointed at the bases.

163. Have any insects been found with three pairs of wings?
Fossil species of the order Palaeodictyoptera, as well as a few others, show large leaflike expansions on the prothorax, in addition to the two well-developed pairs on the other two thoracic segments.

164. Do immature insects ever have wings?   Full-sized and functional wings occur only in adult insects with the one exception of the Mayflies. However, developing wings may be seen as small, fleshy pads on the thorax of immature insects (nymphs) of the orders of the Exopterygota, and in the pupae of most Endopterygota.

165. What are the thickened lines and ridges on insect wings?
They are the *veins*.

166. Is there any name for the areas of the wing membrane between the veins?   They are called the *cells*.

167. How do the wings develop?   Each wing develops as a flattened, saclike fold of the body wall. As this grows larger and broader the two broad surfaces of the sac come to lie close together, gradually fusing. The fusion is not complete, however, the upper and lower walls remaining separate along several long lines.

168. How do the veins develop?   Into the hollow spaces that are left when the wing membranes fuse, a trachea pushes its way outward from the body. The walls of the hollow spaces then thicken and become sclerotized; they thus form the main veins. As a trachea grows outward it will form various branches; cross veins will develop, linking main veins.

169. What is the function of the veins?   After the emergence of the adult, air is pumped through the tracheae of the veins into the developing wings in order to expand them; and blood circulates in the vein spaces around the tracheae. In addition to this circulatory function, which largely dies down after a while, the veins give strength to the wing without giving it too much rigidity, the cross veins acting as struts to give further support at strategic places in the wing.

170. Of what importance are the wings in identifying and classifying insects?   There is no other set of structures of more significance in studying insects. Each order has its characteristics of wing shape and venation. Most families and even many genera have distinctive features. In many cases even species may be distinguished from each other by differences of color and pattern on the wings, and by venation.

171. How is wing venation studied? One must first learn the main veins each of which arose along the path of a main tracheal branch. Each has its characteristic way of branching, as well as position, and can be recognized and compared in the different groups of insects.

172. What are the main veins and their characteristics? The main veins are shown in Figure 6. The names of the veins and their standard abbreviations, given below, follow the Comstock-Needham system as worked out by Professors J. H. Comstock and J. G. Needham of Cornell University. This is the most generally followed system.

TABLE OF WING VEINS

Costa (C)
Subcosta (Sc)
      branches: *Subcosta—one* (Sc_1)
                  Subcosta—two (Sc_2)
Radius (R)
      branches: *Radius—one* (R_1)
                  Radial sector (R_s)
                          branches: *Radius—two* (R_2)
                                        Radius—three (R_3)
                                        Radius—four (R_4)
                                          Radius—five (R_5)
Media (M)
      branches: *Media—one* (M_1)
                  Media—two (M_2)
                  Media—three (M_3)
                  Media—four (M_4)
Cubitus (C)
      branches: *Cubitus—one* (Cu_1)
                  Cubitus—two (Cu_2)
First Anal (1A)
Second Anal (2A)
Third Anal (3)

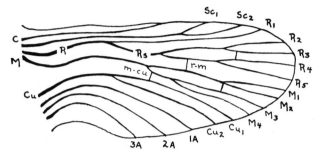

Hypothetical wing, labeled.

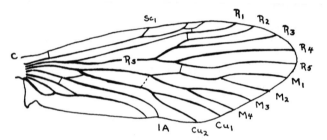

Relatively primitive wing, F. W. of Caddisfly (*Rhyacophila*). This is not unlike ancestral wing, although there has been some fusion of anal veins.

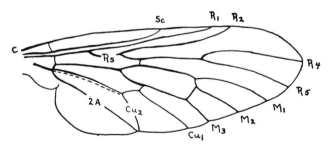

Advanced wing, Snipe Fly (*Leptis*). Here several fusions of veins have taken place, and some veins have dropped out.

Figure 6. WING VEINS.

173. Do any insects' wings resemble this hypothetical ancestral type? Some do fairly closely, as that of the Caddisfly in Figure 6.

174. How can the veins be identified when they have evolved many differences from the ancestral type? This has been done chiefly by studying the development of the wings in the immature stages and seeing how and where the tracheae branch. Series of fossil wings have also been studied. The comparison of large numbers of related insects, both fossil and extant, enables one to arrange a series that shows the steps through which venation may have evolved.

175. Are the wings flat? Most insect wings have a series of folds or corrugations. Sometimes this is a result of the folding of the wings when not in use, but this is not the case in the Dragonflies where the corrugations are quite deep at the base of the wing.

176. Do all insects fold their wings at rest? No, indeed. Dragonflies and some Damselflies rest with their wings spread out horizontally. Some moths, notably the Geometridae, do the same. Caddisflies, Stoneflies, Alder Flies, Lacewings, and the Homoptera hold their wings sloped rooflike over their backs. A few moths wrap their wings around their bodies. Many flies and most butterflies close their wings together straight upward over the back.

There are many interesting exceptions; for example, one species of butterfly, *Hamanumida didala* of Africa, holds its wings out horizontally to show the gray top surface when it rests on rocks of the same color, but elsewhere folds them over its back. Earwigs and beetles fold the hind wings both lengthwise and crosswise before tucking them up under the front wings. Cockroaches and Grasshoppers fold their hind wings fanwise.

177. Can any insects hover in one place as a helicopter does? Dragonflies, Sphinx Moths (Sphingidae), many flies such as Bee Flies (Bombyliidae) and Flower Flies (Syrphidae), and some wasps and bees are expert fliers that often hover in one position, in front of flowers or when seeking prey.

178. Can any insects fly backward? All of the above-mentioned groups, and various others, can fly backward for at least short distances.

179. Is the shape of the wings correlated with the type of flight?
It often is, the best-flying insects tending to have long, slender wings.
In many of the Sphinx Moths the fore wings are large and sharply
pointed, forming with the small hind wings a triangle that is very
suggestive of the wings of the modern, very fast airplanes. A more important correlation is the great size and power of the flight muscles.

180. Do many insects soar and glide? None soar or glide without
occasional strokes of the wings, but many insects do a great deal of
soaring, interspersed with power flying. Some of the butterflies are
especially adept at this, having relatively large, broad wings and
small, lightweight bodies. The Monarch, *Danaus plexippus,* of North
and South America, has been known to cross both the Atlantic and
Pacific Oceans; undoubtedly it soars and glides much of the distance,
not having the endurance to fly continuously for so great a distance.

181. How efficient is the insect wing aerodynamically? In the
powerfully flying insects the wings are most beautifully adapted for
the stresses and aerodynamics of flight. The veins are thicker, stronger,
and closer together at the base, gradually tapering toward the outer
margin. They are similarly much stronger and closer together toward
the front edge (the "leading edge") and further apart, thinner, and
more flexible toward the rear edge (the "trailing edge"). This makes
the wing an excellently constructed "airfoil," capable of exerting
both propulsion and lift, and largely avoiding drag.

182. How are insects' wings moved? The wings are not moved
simply by muscles pulling in turn at the base, as one might think. Instead, they are so hinged to the thorax that when the shape of the
thorax is changed the wings automatically move. Thus, when verti-
cally aligned muscles in the thorax contract, making it flatter and
wider, the wings are raised upward. Other muscles, having the opposite effect, make the thorax higher and narrower and cause the wings
to drop downward.

183. How are the wings moved at different angles? This is accomplished by other muscles pulling on a number of small *axillary
sclerites* that touch or fasten to the wing bases. When they are moved
to various positions the moving wing is twisted. When the front edge

slants downward on a down stroke, forward propulsion is gained. Owing to its differential flexibility and this twisting, the tip of a wing on one up-and-down stroke during flight follows a horizontal figure-8 course.

184. How are the front and hind wings coördinated? In many insects this is done merely by moving them simultaneously. Such insects are seldom very good fliers. In other groups the front and hind wings of each side overlap broadly so that the friction tends to keep them together. But in some insects the wings are actually locked together.

185. How is the coupling of the wings in flight contrived? Most moths have a seta or a group of setae, the *frenulum,* at the base of the front margin of the hind wing, which catches into a fold on the base of the front wing. A few moths and Caddisflies have a projection, the *jugum,* on the rear margin of the front wing which fits into a fold on the front margin of the hind wing. Many bees and wasps have a series of recurved spines, the *hamuli,* on the front margin of the hind wing which hook onto the rear margin of the front wing.

186. Is the mechanical coupling of the wings an advantage to the insect? It seems to be. In insects having such a coupling the four wings beat as a single pair. In this connection it should be noted that in two very highly successful orders, the Diptera and the Coleoptera, only one pair is used in flight. In the Diptera the second pair has been replaced by a pair of rodlike *halteres* that act as stabilizers. In the Coleoptera it is the first pair, the *elytra,* that are no longer used actively in flying.

187. The Dragonflies move the two pairs independently and yet they are excellent fliers. How is this explained? The Dragonflies time the stroke of the hind pair so that they meet the oncoming air before it has been disturbed by the front pair of wings. The wings thus operate in antiphase. The locust *Schistocera* has solved the problem in yet another way by beating the hind pair in greater amplitude so that they are in advance of the front pair during much of the stroke.

188. Do insects ever fly upside down?   If a Dragonfly is lighted from beneath while flying it will fly upside down. This does not prove that insects do it in nature but it shows that Dragonflies can.

189. How do insects steer when flying?   Steering is done by the wings and not, as one might expect, by the legs or abdomen. The movement of the wings may be compared to the feathering of oars in turning a boat when there is no rudder. The long, slender abdomen of the Dragonflies and Damselflies is undoubtedly used to maintain balance.

190. How fast do insects fly?   It is difficult to estimate the speed of insects in flight. Many exaggerated tales have been told and retold. The figures that are now most widely accepted for their speed under controlled circumstances are those of Magnan who lists some of them as follows, in miles per hour: Aeschna Dragonfly, 15.6; Hornet, 12.8; Hummingbird Hawk Moth, 11.1; Horsefly, 8.8; Syrphid Fly, 7.8; Bumblebee, 6.4; Honeybee, 5.7; Housefly, 4.4; Damselfly, 3.3; Scorpion Fly, 1.1. But there is little doubt that in nature they may go somewhat faster, the Dragonflies possibly making 33 miles per hour.

191. How fast do insects beat their wings?   Recordings made in the laboratory show that not only does the wing beat vary in different species but that it varies in one individual at different times. In general, the frequency is dependent upon the ratio between the power of the wing muscles and the resistance, or weight, of the load. (This is a fact long known to physicists.) According to Professor L. P. Chadwick, large-winged, light-bodied butterflies may have a wing-beat frequency of 4–20 per second, whereas small-winged, heavy-bodied flies and bees beat their wings more than 100 times a second, and Mosquitoes 988–1,046 times a second. A table prepared from a number of sources by Imms lists the following wing-beat frequencies in strokes per second: Honeybee, 250; Housefly, 190; Bumblebee, 130; Syrphid Fly, 120; Hornet, 100; Horsefly, 96; Hummingbird Hawk Moth, 85; Cockchafer, 46; Aeschnid Dragonfly, 38; Scorpion Fly, 28; Damselfly, 16; Large White Butterfly, 12.

192. How are these wing-beat frequencies obtained?   Nearly one hundred years ago studies were made of wingbeat frequencies of flying insects by comparing the sounds made by their vibrating wings with an instrument of known pitch. Another method used at that same time was that of permitting the wing tip of a fastened insect to brush against the smoked surface of a disk revolving at a known speed. Recently the former method has been revived by Sotavalta (Roeder, 1953) who has had a musical training and has an ear for absolute pitch. Remarkable results have been obtained by Chadwick and Edgerton with high speed photography and stroboscopic techniques. Various other methods have been used also, all of which have combined to give us considerable knowledge regarding all aspects of the aerodynamics of insect flight.

193. How high in the air have insects been found? Collections made 2,000 feet over England included Aphids, small Flies and Chalcid Wasps, Leaf Hoppers, and small beetles. But these were probably blown up or else drifted up with air currents. The strong fliers are seldom, if ever, found so high.

ABDOMEN

194. Are there any true appendages on the abdomen? The cerci and the external genital appendages are the only ones in Pterygote insects.

195. What are the cerci? These are the true paired appendages of the eleventh (the last) segment of the abdomen. In primitive insects they are a pair of short, jointed spurs, but in Stoneflies, Earwigs, and some Roaches they are quite prominent, and in the Mayflies trail out behind as two long filaments.

196. What is the function of the cerci? They have a tactile sense.

197. How are the cerci of Earwigs unusual? They are very large and strong, forming a pair of sharp forceps blades and are capable of giving a firm pinch. These are used by the Earwigs as a defense.

198. What are the external genitalia? These are the appendages of segments eight and nine, which have become greatly modified. In the males they form part of a set of structures that clasp the female during mating. In females they form a set of structures concerned with the laying of eggs, and are therefore called ovipositors.

199. How do the ovipositors work? As the eggs are laid the ovipositor mechanism places them in some particular location. In many of the more primitive orders the ovipositors are separate and paired, being used merely to tuck the eggs into crevices or cement them to some object. In many orders, however, they form a tube and a sheath. The tube can be thrust into some plant or animal tissue, or into the soil, and the eggs thus laid deeply within.

200. How long are the ovipositors? In some insects they are absent or rudimentary, but when present they vary greatly in size. In Meadow Grasshoppers and many parasitic wasps the ovipositor may be longer than the rest of the body and trail out behind in flight. The females of some of our large Ichneumon Wasps of the genus *Megarhyssa* have a set of ovipositor tubes that are as much as three inches long. With these they can pierce two inches of wood, laying their eggs in the tunnels of wood-boring Sawfly larvae, the hosts of their species.

201. What is a sting? The sting of wasps, ants, and bees is the ovipositor of the female, which has become adapted as a weapon. A set of glands secretes two poisons, one acid and the other alkaline, which are injected into the victim through the ovipositor.

THE MUSCULAR SYSTEM

202. How many muscles does an insect have? In the year 1760 someone described a Goat Moth as having 4,041 muscles. This number has never been verified. The Goat Moth caterpillar has more recently been reported to have 1,647. Insect muscles are very small and a complete count is difficult. Suffice it to say, they have many more than man has.

203. Are insects strong muscularly? Insects seem to perform astonishing feats of physical prowess. Many are able to pull 20 times their own weight; a *Donacia* Leaf Beetle once pulled 42.7 times its own weight and a Stag Beetle pulled a load 120 times its own weight. This same beetle, when suspended by its jaws, held a weight of 7 ounces. Termites build nests 30 feet high; Fleas jump 13 inches (their legs are only .1 inch long). We might go on and on giving statistics as to their seemingly remarkable performances.

204. Are insects stronger than man?　From the figures given above it would look as though they were. Comparisons have been made showing that if a Flea were the size of a man it would be able to jump 450 feet; or if a Stag Beetle were the size of a man it could lift 10 tons. This is specious reasoning, however, and such comparisons should never be made except in fun. The strength of a muscle is proportional to the area of a cross section of the muscle. As it grows in size its strength increases in proportion to the square of a linear dimension, but the volume or weight increases as the cube of the linear dimension. Thus strength does not increase proportionately with size. A large animal does not have the proportionate strength of a small one. If an insect were to become as large as a man its strength would not have increased proportionately.

205. Do insects get tired?　Of course they do. But they show a remarkable resistance to fatigue. A Drosophila Fly has been known to fly continuously for 6.5 hours, and a Schistocerca Locust for 9 hours. Wing muscles have made more than one million successive beats before tiring. This, however, does not tell the whole story because a worker Honeybee may tire after 15 minutes of flying.

206. What is the explanation of an insect's resistance to fatigue? A human, during exercise, increases his oxygen consumption about 29-fold. An insect, in flight, is able to increase it up to 100 times. This is made possible by the efficiency of the tracheal system which takes oxygen directly to the cells, and the presence in the muscle cells of an enzyme for cell respiration.

207. What happens to the muscles when an insect molts?　They become detached from the old exoskeleton at each molt and then reattached to the newly forming one.

RESPIRATION

208. How does an insect breathe? Air enters the body through small openings called *spiracles,* which are on the sides of the body. It then passes through a system of branching tubes, the *tracheae.* Each trachea becomes increasingly smaller until the tiny closed branches, the tracheoles, at the end are less than .1 millimeter in diameter. Oxygen diffuses through the fluid that partly fills the trachea, through the walls of the tracheoles, and into the body cells. This type of respiration is the open, or *holopneustic,* type.

209. Do insects have internal air sacs similar to those of the birds? Some winged insects do. The Honeybee has two large ones that occupy a large portion of the abdominal cavity. The June Beetle has hundreds of small ones. The alimentary canal of adult Mayflies, which do not eat, forms a large air sac. Such air sacs, by reducing the specific gravity, increase the insects' buoyancy.

210. How many spiracles does an insect have? It is believed that the archetypal, or primitive, insect had a pair (one spiracle on each side) in each segment. The maximum number known among living insects is ten pairs: two on the thorax, and one on each of eight abdominal segments. The number is reduced in many species.

211. Do spiracles open and close in respiration? In Fleas, Houseflies, and many caterpillars they open and close rhythmically. In most insects their opening is synchronized with movements of the body. Spiracles are provided with special valvelike devices which keep out dust and water.

212. Do spiracles have any function other than respiration? During expiration considerable water leaves the body through the spiracles, just as it does in the human breath. This water loss is not regulated with any efficiency. In fact, high temperatures force the spiracles open, so at such times water loss is greatly increased. Many desert insects have much smaller spiracles than their relatives elsewhere, which may be a direct adaptation to their arid, hot environment.

213. Are the tracheae simple tubes? No. They have a unique, characteristic spiral thread in their lining.

214. Do oxygen and carbon dioxide enter and leave through the same spiracles? There is usually a division of function: the last six pairs of spiracles tend to serve for the expiration of carbon dioxide. The action is reversed at times.

215. Does an insect require air? Insects can get along on very little air. Grain weevils can even survive for some time in pure carbon dioxide. Some insects seem to get oxygen from the breakdown of carbohydrates and fats within their body.

216. How do insects that are parasitic within the bodies of other animals get their oxygen? Many obtain it by diffusion through the body wall, drawing it from the semifluid environment in which they live. Others have tubelike structures, sometimes developed from the eggshell, which maintain a respiratory connection (like a snorkel) with the outer world.

CIRCULATION

217. Does an insect have blood? Yes, but it is a combination of blood and lymph, called *haemolymph*. It is very different from human blood and probably does not carry oxygen.

218. Does the blood have red cells? No. The plasma contains amoeboid, colorless cells of which thirty different types have been found. The plasma, itself, is colorless or pale yellow, greenish, or sometimes reddish. This color is determined largely by the food the insect has eaten. Larvae of some Chironomid Midges (called Bloodworms), of one aquatic genus of Backswimmers, *Buenoa,* and of the Horse Bot Fly, *Gastrophilus,* have bright red plasma which contains true hemoglobin.

219. Do insects have a heart? The dorsal blood vessel is the major pulsating organ. It lies along the dorsum of the abdomen, sometimes extending up into the head. The portion that lies in the abdomen is called the heart; the rest of it is known as the *aorta.* Sometimes it is a simple tube with paired openings and sometimes it is divided into a series of chambers ranging in number from one to thirteen. It is open at the front end but usually closed at the rear. It is held in place by fan-shaped, suspensory ligaments.

220. What is the rate of the heartbeat?   The rate is so affected by general metabolism, stage of development, and temperature that no accurate figure can be given. Figures range from 29 beats per minute in the larvae of the White Butterfly *Pieris brassicae* to 160 in the Thysanuran *Campodea*. The majority of figures are below 90 beats per minute.

221. What are accessory pulsating organs?   Many insects have additional pumping organs in various parts of the body, even in the legs and wings. They may beat at a different rate from the dorsal blood vessel and may even cease beating at times.

222. Do insects have arteries and veins?   The insect blood system is an open one, that is, the blood does not remain in closed vessels. The blood, after leaving the dorsal blood vessel through its open anterior end, flows through the cavities of the body, some of the larger of which are definite sinuses, enclosed by membranes. From these the blood works its way back into the openings of the heart. Thus the insect has no arteries, except for the dorsal aorta, and no veins.

223. Are insects warm-blooded or cold-blooded?   The internal body temperature of insects varies with the surroundings. They are therefore "cold-blooded." Studies have shown that the pigmentation of their body affects the amount of heat they absorb: the black form of a Locust has a higher body temperature, and therefore a higher rate of activity, than the green or brown form. Insects often orient the body so as to get the greatest amount of heat possible from the sun in the cool of the day. When the temperature of the body reaches its optimum for that species the insect is most active, slowing down again when the temperature of the environment drops.

THE NERVOUS SYSTEM

224. Do insects have a brain?   The insect brain is the dorsal ganglionic center lying just above the esophagus. It normally is composed of three parts: a *protocerebrum,* a fused pair of ganglia that innervates the compound eyes and ocelli; the *deutocerebrum,* a fused pair of ganglia that includes the antennary and olfactory lobes; and the *tritocerebrum,* the fused ganglia that receive nerves from the front of the head. Actually the insect brain shows as great a range in size and complexity as does the vertebrate brain, that of the locust being as different from that of a wasp as a frog's is from a man's.

225. How big is the insect brain?   The brain of a Dytiscid Water Beetle is about $\frac{1}{4,200}$ of the volume of the beetle, but that of a Honeybee is about $\frac{1}{174}$ of the volume of the bee's body, and that of a *Formica* Ant is $\frac{1}{280}$ of its body volume.

226. How does the comparative size of the insect brain compare with that of man?   It is hard to make the comparison in terms of volume. The average weight of a man's brain is 3 pounds; that of a woman's is a few ounces less, which would make them about $\frac{1}{40}$ to $\frac{1}{60}$ of the body weight.

227. How does an insect behave if its brain is removed?   It is comparatively inert, being unable as a rule to initiate acts. It will feed if food is placed in contact with the mouthparts, but it cannot find food for itself. However, some insects have been able to copulate and lay eggs after decapitation.

228. Of what beside a brain does the insect nervous system consist?   The central nervous system includes, in addition to the brain, a cluster of fused ganglia lying just beneath the esophagus and connected with the brain by circumpharyngeal connectives; and a series of paired, usually fused ganglia lying along the ventral side of the body, three in the thorax (sometimes fused into one) and a variable number in the abdomen. All of these ganglia are connected by paired longitudinal nerves, making up the ventral nerve cord. There is also a visceral, or sympathetic, system, and a peripheral system.

FOOD AND DIGESTION

229. Is the digestive system similar to that of higher animals?
Yes. It is a hollow tube extending from one end of the body to the

other, made up of the following regions: mouth, pharynx, esophagus, crop, gizzard, mid-intestine, and hind intestine. A variable number of blind pouches, called caeca, are attached to the beginning of the mid-intestine, thereby increasing the surface area of its wall.

230. What is the crop?   It is an enlargement of the intestine, just behind the esophagus, which has a number of uses. Blood-sucking insects, which have to take advantage of a good source of blood, use it to provide additional capacity. Grasshoppers actually digest food in it. Bees, in making honey, mix salivary enzymes and nectar in it. Some insects store air in it, the air they have swallowed and with which they will extend the body at the time of molting. The crop is absent in a few insects.

231. What is the gizzard?   It is the portion of the intestine behind the crop; it is sometimes called the *proventriculus*. In some insects it is very small, being little more than a valve that prevents regurgitation. In other insects, as in the Cockroach, it contains powerful teeth that crush and grind the food.

232. Can an insect be starved into eating anything that it does not ordinarily accept?   Normally an insect will die when it does not have its usual food. However, experimental work has shown that when breeding is carried on for long periods of time, and thousands of individuals tried out on new plants, an occasional individual may accept a new plant and become accustomed to it. Insects when placed in new environments with new species of plants sometimes adopt new foods.

233. Can insects go without food for long periods of time?   Predatory and blood-sucking insects often go for long periods of time without food. A newly emerged Flea has been known to live for 2,108 days without a meal. The Tsetse Fly larva turns into a pupa without ever eating, being sufficiently nourished by the rich blood consumed by the female parent. Adult Mayflies never eat, and adult Stoneflies eat little, if at all, since the year or years which they spend as larvae actively feeding beneath the surface of the water have satisfied their nutritional requirements. These, of course, are exceptional examples and are not a good answer to the question. Leaf-eating caterpillars, left without fresh leaves of their host plant for only a few hours, will sicken and die; adult insects can live longer.

234. Do insects need vitamins? Most species require the B vitamins. Vitamin C does not seem to be essential, although at least one insect, the Cockroach, synthesizes it.

235. Do insects require water? Although insects are often seen sipping from drops of water on foliage and at mud puddles they can usually get sufficient water from their food. Many that feed on dried cereals and stored grains are able to get along with only the water metabolized from their food. Such insects as Honeybees and flies that have liquid excrement do have to drink often.

236. Are any insects cannibalistic? Cannibalism, the practice of dining on one's own species, is commonly practiced among some species of termites. The wounded, crippled, and possibly the old are eaten. Lacewing larvae (Chrysopidae) are said to be cannibalistic, a reason often given for the long filaments on which the eggs are placed. The larvae of Ascalaphids are at times cannibalistic and so are the carnivorous larvae of some Blue Butterflies (Lycaenidae). Dragonfly larvae in captivity eat smaller individuals of their own species but whether they do this under natural conditions is doubtful. The most startling example of cannibalism among insects is probably the female Mantid's custom of devouring the male for her wedding breakfast.

EXCRETION

237. What are the Malpighian tubules? They are filamentous structures that are attached to the alimentary canal at the junction of the mid and hind intestine. They vary in number from 2 to 150 or more.

238. What is the function of the Malpighian tubules? They are primarily excretory in function, taking substances from the body cavity, mixing them with the urine which they secrete, and discharging the whole into the hind intestine to be passed out in the feces. The tubules have a very large surface area to aid them in this function; the cockroach has 60 tubules with a surface area of 132,000 square millimeters; in certain moths with 6 tubules their surface area is 209,000 square millimeters.

In some species the tubules have an accessory function such as supplying a substance to cover the egg chambers or to make the spittle (in Cercopidae) more durable; or manufacturing silk; or collecting lime for use in making shells, tubes, and tunnel linings.

GLANDS

239. Do insects have glands?   They have many glands, some unicellular, others multicellular and complex. They have salivary glands, hair glands, scent glands, stink glands, adhesive glands, froth glands, wax glands, and silk glands, to mention only a few.

240. Do they have endocrine glands?   Endocrine glands secrete hormones that play a very important part in an insect's life. Their presence has not been conclusively demonstrated in all species but experimental work has recorded the following types in some insects: (1) *neurosecretory cells* in the brain that terminate diapause in the pupa, control yolk formation in the egg, and regulate molting; (2) the *corpus cardiacum* lying behind the brain, which is concerned with molting and also works with the prothoracic gland and possibly with other of the endocrines; (3) the *corpus allatum,* known as the juvenile gland because if removed from a partly grown caterpillar the caterpillar will pupate prematurely. Later the hormone of this gland stimulates egg formation. It may also be concerned with respiration. (4) other head glands and prothoracic glands seem to be concerned with molting also. As in humans there is a complex interlocking mechanism involved with these glands and the way in which they act with and upon each other. A wide and interesting field of research is open in this area.

COLORS OF INSECTS

241. What produces the colors of insects?   Insect colors are either structural or pigment colors, or combinations of the two.

242. What are structural colors?   These are the colors that are produced, as are the colors of the rainbow and the prism, by the bending
or refracting of rays of light at different angles. When light passes
from one medium to another of a different refractive power, as in
passing from air through water or glass, it is bent. But each different
wave length, or color, is bent differently. So the reds will become
separated from the yellows, the yellows from the greens, and so forth.
In this way the "white" light of sunlight may be broken into its component colors.

The sky is not a beautiful mantle of blue stretched over our heads;
the waters of the sea contain no blue or green dye; but both sky and
sea appear to be colored because the rays of light coming from them
to our eyes have been bent or scattered by bouncing off an infinity of
tiny particles in the atmosphere or have been refracted in passing
through the shimmering sea. These, as well as the iridescence of the
oil slick on the road, are common examples of structural color.

243. Which colors in insects are structural?   All iridescence and all
metallic-appearing colors are structural. So also are most of the whites
and greens, and all of the blues and violets.

244. What are the structures that produce these insect colors?
The iridescence of the tropical *Urania* Moths is caused by the presence
of microscopically thin layers in the scales. These layers all lie parallel
to the plane of the scale and act as a refractive medium. The rich,
changeable blue of the *Morpho* wings (often used in "art" objects
and jewelry) is due to thin layers in the scale that lie at an acute
angle to the plane of the scale. In some insects the layers may run at
several different angles, or may be combined with one or more films
on the surface to produce patches of scintillating colors. Sometimes
the color is due to the presence of fine, raised ridges, or striae, in the
cuticle, which form what the physicist calls a "diffraction grating."
At other times minute particles diffuse the light, as the minute particles in the atmosphere diffuse the sunlight to give us the blue of the
sky; sometimes a thin overlying film in the outer part of the skin or
membrane will bend the rays of light in simple reflection.

245. How can one tell which colors are structural?   Purely structural colors are not soluble in any chemical solvent because there is

no colored pigment to be dissolved. But they disappear or change when stroked with a brush wetted with alcohol, benzene, lighter fluid, etc., returning when the surface dries out.

246. Are all structural colors permanent, since there are no pigments to fade?   Even structural colors may fade or change. This is due to shrinking of the color-producing structures as the specimen dies and dries. Some insects, such as "gold bugs," look brilliantly metallic when alive but change to dull objects within a few minutes after death. They may even change colors when alive under the influence of varying physical conditions.

247. What are pigment colors?   They are colors due to the presence of definite chemical compounds.

248. Where does the insect get these pigments?   They may be derived from the food the insect eats (the food eaten by the larva often producing pigments that are carried over into the adult) or they may be manufactured by the insect.

249. What are some of the insect pigment colors?   The green of green caterpillars, and of green insects such as Katydids and Stink Bugs, comes from the chlorophyll of the foliage upon which they feed. The reds and yellows of the Ladybirds are *flavones* obtained from their food. The bright red of Chironomid bloodworms is caused by *hemoglobin* formed from iron pigments in their food. (This color is actually in the blood and not in the cuticula.) All of the Whites, Sulphurs, and Oranges (Pieridae) form most of their pigment colors from *uric acid* wastes. Most of the browns and blacks are so-called *melanin* pigments formed by the oxidation of *tyrosin* in the presence of the enzyme *melanase*.

250. Do insects ever have a combination of pigment and structural colors?   Many insect colors are due to such combinations and thus add to the complexity of this subject. Some of the great *Morpho* Butterflies of the American tropics have brilliant structural blues, but very little pigment; they are pearly white or shimmering blue. Other *Morphos,* however, have brilliant structural blues underlain by deep brown or orange pigments; they have a much darker, richer blue appearance. In old specimens, long exposed to light, the pigments fade but the structural colors usually remain as bright as ever.

251. Are insects of one species always the same color? In many species color can be used as an identifying characteristic but in other species it may not be dependable because it shows such a range of depth, shade, quantity, and pattern. Some species show very great differences in different parts of their geographical range; some vary with the season; and in many there are differences between the sexes.

252. Does an individual insect change its color or its color pattern during its lifetime? Successive instars of an insect may be very different in color and pattern as well as form. The Swallowtail Caterpillars show a very striking change from deep brown when very young to bright green when mature. But all insects change some. An insect is always paler in color just after molting because the chief pigments and color-producing structures of the previous instar (257) were in the skin that has been discarded; it may be similar to the old or it may be different. Another type of color change comes as the adult matures. The newly emerged, or teneral, imago is much paler than it will be later. A few insects show quick changes in color as a response to the environment much the way Chameleons do, factors of temperature, humidity, and light being responsible. Other insects may be darker at night than during the day.

253. Are the male and female of a species ever different in color? Often. The males are frequently more brilliant than the females and are often differently colored and patterned as well. They are often further adorned with special structures, such as tails on the hind wings or patches of special scales. Sexual dimorphism is especially common among the butterflies, where there is more opportunity for a display of color, but it also occurs fairly often among Dragonflies, Grasshoppers, beetles, Tree Hoppers, and Sawflies. This is not unlike the sexual dimorphism in birds where the brilliant colors of the males, whose long survival is of less importance, are valuable in courtship, in establishing territorial rights, and in drawing attention from the more important females, who must lay their eggs and care for the young.

254. Do insects change color with the season?   One individual of a species does not change color with the season; but those that emerge in the spring may differ from those that emerge in the summer or fall. These differently colored individuals are referred to as *seasonal forms*. In some species the individuals that emerge in wet weather may be darker than those that emerge in dry weather. This difference is due to the moisture at the time of their emergence and does not denote a change in any one individual.

Temperature, moisture, and illumination have been shown to affect the development of color in insects. Larvae and pupae reared in temperatures colder than normal will transform into adults having more dark pigment, or melanin. In some species the adults that emerge in wet weather are darker in color than those that emerge in dry weather, giving rise to our recognition of *wet-season* and *dry-season forms*. However, if some of those individuals are removed from the brood and reared in opposite humidities they show a reversal of colors. The Migratory Locust, which is variable in color, will be bright green when raised on moist food or in a humid atmosphere. Pupae of the Cabbage Butterfly will have more black if the larvae are exposed to ultraviolet light just before pupation.

The examples given are only a few of the insects upon which a great deal of experimental work has been done. All of this work, done under controlled conditions, gives us explanations for many of the color variations found in species: spring and fall generations, wet- and dry-season forms, mountain and desert forms, and even why pupae on one side of a twig are different from those on the other.

VI. INSECT GROWTH AND DEVELOPMENT

255. Do insects grow in the same way that other animals do?
Their way of growing is peculiar to them and the other Arthropods, and quite different from that of other animals. Since they have an exoskeleton, which can neither be stretched nor added to, they can grow only a limited amount at a time. They then molt the old exoskeleton and make a new one. But before the new exoskeleton hardens the insect increases abruptly in size. Once the exoskeleton is hardened, further increase in size largely ceases until after the next molt.

256. Doesn't this make insect growth a jerky, start-and-stop process? It does; insect growth has been compared to ascending by a flight of stairs instead of going smoothly up a slope. It progresses in a series of stages.

257. What are these stages called? The act of molting is called *ecdysis*. The old exoskeleton that is molted is called the *exuvium*. The interval between ecdyses, largely spent in eating and storing foods and preparing for the next ecdysis, is called a stage, or *stadium*. The form of the insect during the stadium is called an *instar*.

258. What happens to the exuvium? Many insects with chewing mouthparts eat part or all of the exuvium. This is of course very thrifty, preventing the waste of the substances molted. However, the cast skins of many insects, especially of those emerging in great numbers like Mayflies and Dragonflies, may be left as untidy waste material.

259. How does molting take place? The cuticle becomes separated from its underlying hypodermis, the outermost layer of living tissues, by molting fluid. This fluid digests the inner layer of old cuticle and permits the expanse of the soft body, which then breaks through the weakened outer cuticle.

260. What determines the time at which an insect molts? Hormones produced by endocrine glands in the head and thorax are dispersed in the blood stream. An accumulation of these hormones initiates molting. The duration of the stadia usually decreases as the insect grows older. Perhaps in some cases the actual increase in size, and pressure of the old exoskeleton, has something to do with this.

261. Does an insect continue to molt throughout its entire life? Only until it reaches the adult stage. Further molting is then inhibited by the development of the reproductive glands, except in the case of a few Apterygota. The Mayfly molts once after the wings have attained their full growth but there is some question as to whether the instar that precedes the last molt is adult or nymphal; it is called a *subimago*.

262. Is there any growth of the adult after molting ceases? There is no true growth after the last molt, although there may be a slight increase in size. Honey Ant repletes that receive large stores of nectar from the workers become enormously swollen. The abdomen of a female often increases in size as her eggs mature. The most remarkable increase of this sort is that of the queen termite who, when her abdomen is swollen with eggs, may become seven or eight inches long and lies incapable of movement.

263. How many molts does an insect undergo? In some Thysanura there is but a single molt. Most insects, however, undergo from four to twelve, occasionally as many as forty. Inadequate nourishment prolongs larval life and in many species increases the number of molts. In Bedbugs, however, the immature instars, if starved or given only very small amounts of nourishment, will live long periods of time without molting.

264. How long does a molt take? Including a preliminary period when the insect must remain quiet without feeding, a molt may require from six hours to two or three days. During all of this time the insect is vulnerable to attack.

265. Does the molt perform any function other than permitting growth? It permits the change in form (metamorphosis) which is a striking characteristic of many insects.

266. Do males and females grow at the same rate? The males of some species may have one less instar and a shorter immature life. This permits them to emerge as adults ahead of the female. It also allows the female more time for eating and therefore for getting sufficient nourishment for the development and maturation of her eggs.

267. What determines the rate of growth during larval instars? Many factors, environmental as well as genetic. Some species normally complete larval growth in ten days or two weeks; others may take many years. But abnormal weather conditions may speed up or slow down these periods considerably.

268. What is Dyar's Law? It states that the hard larval head capsule, as well as other body parts of a caterpillar, grows in geometric progression, increasing in width at each molt by a ratio (usually 1:4) that is constant for the species. This holds true under all but extremely abnormal conditions.

A knowledge of this law is of practical use to people who are rearing insects, since by measuring and counting the head capsules they can tell how many molts have occurred, as long as the capsules show no gaps in the steady progression in size.

269. Do immature insects always keep growing provided they are not hindered by bad weather, lack of food, or other external adverse condition? No, many insects do not. Instead there will be a point during development when no further growth or development takes place, even though external conditions seem completely favorable. This sudden cessation of growth is known as *diapause*. It is basically caused by factors within the insect itself, characteristic of its species.

270. What is an example of diapause? Many Mosquitoes lay their eggs during late spring or early summer. The eggs could hatch, the larvae and pupae develop, and a new generation of mosquitoes emerge, if it were not for a diapause. As it is, the eggs lie inactive all summer, autumn, and winter until the next spring. Then and then only, after the lapse of many months and after being subjected to freezing, will the embryos in the egg develop. In some species the females lay their eggs on what is at the time dry ground, but which will be flooded when the snow melts the next spring.

271. Does the diapause ever occur in instars other than the egg? Diapause is known in a great many different insects and in all possible instars, i.e., egg larva, and pupa. (After an insect becomes an adult there is no more growth, of course.) In some arctic butterflies, for example, the eggs, laid in July, will hatch promptly. By early August the caterpillar is only half grown. It then goes into a diapause, remaining inactive until the next June. Even if brought indoors, warmed, and given proper food it remains inactive. Only after the long months of cold does the diapause mechanism break.

272. Has experimental work been done on diapause? A great deal has been done with some of the big Emperor Moths (Saturniidae) such as the Cecropia Moth, *Hyalophora cecropia*. These insects spend the winter as pupae, which were formed in the autumn. If the pupae are not chilled to 37.4°–41° F. for a month and a half or more, they will not transform to adults. If they are so chilled immediately after pupation and then warmed to 70° F. they will transform in a month or two, i.e., by November or December. Normally outdoors all winter, the pupae will not transform to moths until June.

273. Is the mechanism of diapause in these moths known? The first step is the production of a hormone secreted by a glandular part of the brain, when this has been warmed sufficiently after having been chilled sufficiently. This hormone, carried by the blood, stimulates an endocrine gland in the prothorax to secrete a different hormone. Distributed by the blood, this then stimulates the pupa to transform into an adult. In experimental work the blood from properly chilled pupae was injected into unchilled ones; the latter then transformed into adults.

274. What is the advantage to an insect of such a diapause? The diapause mechanism acts as a timer that prevents premature development of eggs, larvae, or pupae at seasons when they will not have a good chance of surviving. Furthermore, since the mechanism works uniformly for all individuals of a species, it ensures that the adults will all appear more or less simultaneously. This is essential for mating.

275. Does diapause affect only overwintering insects? There is much evidence that diapauses occur in insects subjected to just the opposite—to dangerously hot or dry periods, such as in desert weather.

276. What is the scientific value of our knowledge of the diapause mechanism? Through such experiments on diapause and growth we have found out much about the control mechanisms of insect growth and development, and of the changes from one instar to another; and of the effect of endocrine glands and their secretions, the hormones, upon these changes.

277. What are the insect endocrine glands that control growth and development? The protocerebral lobes of the brain produce a hormone that stimulates either a part of a ring gland around the pharynx, or prothoracic glands, or both. These then produce a hormone, or hormones, that stimulate the insect to grow and molt, and eventually to change into another instar. Another gland, the *corpus allatum,* produces a "juvenile" hormone that prevents, or inhibits, such change. The activities of the glands are, of course, controlled by many different hereditary factors. By learning about such features in insects we clarify our knowledge of the life processes of animals in general, including our own.

278. Is the knowledge of these insect hormones of any practical value? Work on these is being tried out in controlling harmful insects, with the idea of preventing them from maturing and reproducing. This is still largely experimental but may be of enormous direct value.

279. Do these hormones control the length of the period of development and of the adult life of an insect? They certainly play a large part in determining these, but of course many other inherited factors also are very important.

280. How long do insects live? Longevity in insects is a specific inherited factor, as in all animals, and therefore varies with the species. Some Mayflies spend two to four years as larvae and then live as adults only a few hours. Adult Honeybee workers live about six weeks.

Queen termites have been known to live and lay eggs for fifty years and may even live twice that long. The great majority of insects probably live less than a year. Females live longer than males, and unmated females longest of all.

281. Do insects grow at a different rate in different climatic regions?   Much experimental work has been done on this subject. It has been found that fluctuating temperatures will speed up growth as will increased periods of light and heat. For example, the Mediterranean Fruit Fly, *Ceratitis capitata,* takes twenty days to complete its life cycle at a temperature of 79° F. and a relative humidity of 70. In the region of Paris it has two generations a year; in Nice it has four; in Jerusalem, five; in Cairo, nine; and in Calcutta, twelve. That means that it reaches the adult stage and is able to reproduce more quickly in the warmer regions; it does not necessarily mean that the life span of the individual is shorter, although it usually is. Since this is a very destructive pest on fruits, such a knowledge is valuable in combatting it.

282. If an insect loses a leg or other part can it grow a new one?   Regeneration of organs takes place much less frequently in insects than in other invertebrates. It seldom occurs after the adult stage has been reached, except in the Apterygota where growth and molting may continue in the adult and may even be stimulated by an injury or amputation. But regeneration does sometimes occur in early stages, a part such as a leg being perfectly regenerated.

283. Is there any healing of wounds in insects?   Wound healing, which is a form of regeneration of tissues, is more easily accomplished the younger the stage, but is still possible to some extent in the adult.

284. What is autotomy?   It is self-amputation, usually of an injured leg and always at a definite place. It occurs frequently in immature Walking Sticks (Phasmidae) where, at the articulation of the trochanter and the femur, there is a two-layered membrane through which no muscles cross. It is a defense mechanism, often permitting the insect to escape attack with the sacrifice of only a leg, and a minimum of bleeding.

METAMORPHOSIS

285. What is metamorphosis?   Metamorphosis is the occurrence of one or more pronounced changes of form during the growth and development of an individual. The change from a polliwog to a frog is an example. The two are really the same individual but with radically different forms and ways of life.

286. Do many animals have a metamorphosis?   A great many do, from sponges and snails to frogs. Metamorphosis is particularly common among marine invertebrates. It is relatively uncommon among vertebrates, however, except in the Amphibians (Frogs, Toads, and Salamanders). A very interesting one is that of the eel, which first develops as a ribbon-shaped, almost transparent larva, drifting along in the Gulf Stream before it reaches the continent and develops its adult form.

287. Is a metamorphosis of advantage to an animal?   Development with metamorphosis is believed to confer more than one great advantage. One is that it enables the animal to specialize on different ways of life during the different stages. The caterpillar specializes on feeding and growing (with, of course, necessary adaptations for self-protection). It need do nothing else. After it has become an adult it may feed very little, and grows no more, living on what it ate as a caterpillar. It concentrates on finding a mate, and reproducing. Each stage can do its particular job better for not having to do any other major ones. The animal benefits from a division of labor between its various stages.

Another advantage is that when both the immature animal and the adult feed, they may feed on different foods, in different environments, and thus not compete with each other. The individual, during its dual life, is able to utilize more than one source of food—it has two sources of income—and is able to exploit each more efficiently.

288. What is an example of an insect seeking food in two different environments in its lifetime?   The immature Dragonfly, living in the water, feeds on other small aquatic animals there. It is very efficient at this, with specialized structures for capturing prey under water. After it has transformed to the adult it may range great distances away from the water; and it feeds on flying adult insects which it captures by specialized structures as well as by its remarkably swift and agile flight. Its flight also enables it to reach far-distant waters where it may mate and where its young will in turn feed according to their means.

289. Do all insects undergo metamorphosis? No. The primitive, wingless Apterygote insects develop with hardly any changes of form or habits, merely growing, from egg to adult.

290. If a young insect differs considerably from the adult but changes directly into an adult, does it have a metamorphosis? Yes. It has a *direct* or *incomplete metamorphosis.*

291. Is there a special name for the immature stage of an insect that has incomplete metamorphosis? It is called a *nymph.* Aquatic nymphs are called *naiads.*

292. How many insects have incomplete metamorphosis? The orders of the Exopterygote insects have an incomplete metamorphosis. They total about 96,500 known species.

293. What is complete metamorphosis? It is an *indirect* metamorphosis in which the immature stage does not change directly to the adult but passes through an intermediate form.

294. What is the immature stage of an insect having complete metamorphosis called? It is a *larva.*

295. What is the name of the stage intermediate between larva and adult? The *pupa.*

296. Do many insects have complete metamorphosis? The Endopterygote insects all have complete metamorphosis. They total nearly 600,000 known species. They are obviously in the great majority. Perhaps this is due, in part, to the advantages of complete metamorphosis.

297. Do any insects have more than one kind of larva during their metamorphosis? A few groups of insects with complete metamorphosis go through a complicated series of larval stages in which a very active young larva changes into an entirely different-looking, more sedentary form; this changes into a still different form, and this into still another form before the change to the pupa. This is called a *hypermetamorphosis*. It is best known in the Oil Beetles and Blister Beetles (Meloidae) in which it is correlated with a very specialized, parasitoid larval life.

EGGS

298. Do all insects lay eggs? The great majority do, and hence are called *oviparous*.

299. Is it true that some insects give birth to living young? A fairly large number of insects do this. In most cases the eggs are merely retained within the body of the female until they hatch, the embryo in the egg feeding only on the food materials stored in it. Such insects are called *ovoviparous*. This occurs regularly in various groups, such as some Thrips, Roaches, Muscoid Flies, and beetles.

300. Are any young insects nourished from maternal tissues before they are born? This condition, which is similar to that of mammals, occurs in some Aphids, Psocids, Twisted Winged Insects, and Roaches, and in such flies as the Tsetse Fly and a special group known as the Pupipara. These insects are truly *viviparous*.

301. Are viviparously produced larvae more advanced at birth than others? In many groups they are not. But in the Pupiparous Flies, of which there are several families, and in the Tsetse Flies, the larvae are fully grown, or nearly so, at birth, and change to pupae almost immediately. This condition is correlated with special parasitic habits of the adult females.

302. What do insect eggs look like? The shape varies greatly from one species to another. Some are very long and slender, others are flat and disk-shaped. The majority are oval or spherical.

Many are quite plain, but in some groups they are very irregularly

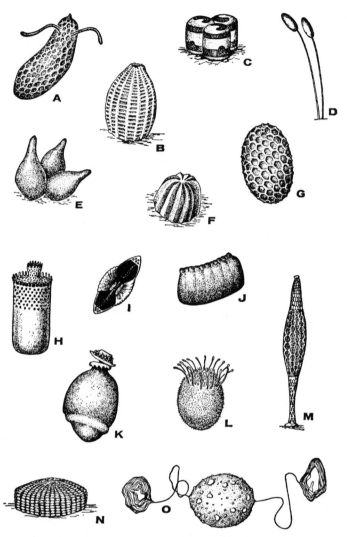

Figure 7. Eggs of insects to show variety. A, *Drosophila*, a Fruit Fly (after Comstock); B, *Pieris*, a butterfly (after Teale); C, Harlequin Bugs; D, Lacewings; E, Elm Leaf Beetles (after Gov't bulletin); F, *Apatura ilia*, an Emperor Moth; G, *Lithocolletes fragilella*, a Honeysuckle miner (after Metcalf and Flint); H, *Piezosterum subulatum* (after Comstock); I, *Anopheles*, a mosquito; J, A Cockroach "purse"; K, *Perla marginata*, a Stonefly (after Metcalf and Flint); L, *Podisus*, a Stink Bug (after Chu); M, *Hydrometra martini*, a Marsh Treader (after Comstock); N, Cotton Worm Moth (after Comstock); O, *Heptagenia interpunctata*, a Mayfly (after Metcalf and Flint).

shaped and ornately sculptured with raised ridges, grooves, pits, rows of spines, or knobs. The eggs of Stink Bugs have a crown of thorn-like spines forming a circle around the upper end, for example; and many butterfly eggs have longitudinal ribs with transverse groovings in between.

303. Are insect eggs usually colored? The majority are white or cream colored; but many of those that are laid on foliage are green. Some are patterned; those of the Harlequin Cabbage Bug are a bold black and white.

304. How large are insect eggs? The size varies enormously, depending upon the group. The eggs of the smallest insects, which, when full grown, are only about $\frac{1}{50}$ to $\frac{1}{100}$ inch long, are invisible to the human eye. The eggs of some large species are nearly $\frac{1}{4}$ inch long. The eggs of the common Housefly are relatively large, about $\frac{1}{25}$ inch long; the female who lays them is only about seven to eight times as long. The single overwintering egg of certain female Aphids is almost as large as the female herself.

305. How many eggs does each female lay? This also varies enormously with the species of insect. Perhaps an average number is 100–200.

The Sheep Ked Fly lays but a single, large egg. A female Housefly may lay from 800–1,000 during a lifetime of several months. A female Dobsonfly may lay 2,000–3,000 in a single mass. The females of the social insects, who may live and continue to lay eggs for many years, have an enormous lifetime production. A queen Honeybee may lay 2,000 a day for many weeks. The large queen termite *Bellicositermes natalensis* of Africa, who is about four inches long when her abdomen is swollen with ovaries, is said to lay as many as 36,000 in 24 hours, which is about 25 a minute, and 13,000,000 a year. Since such queen termites are believed to lived for fifty or a hundred years, the total egg production might well run over a billion.

306. What is the significance of the tremendous fertility shown by some insects? In most cases the production of a large number of eggs is correlated with a very high rate of mortality of the larvae from disease, predation, or parasitism. Many are produced, but very few mature. On the other hand we usually find that in the species where there are special adaptations that enable most of the offspring to live to maturity, the reproductive capacity is small. Each species has evolved a mechanism that more or less adjusts its reproductive capacity according to the chance of survival, and maintains a relatively stable population from year to year.

307. Are the social insects an exception to this?   They seem to be, at first glance. But if we realize that in a termite society or ant commune, there may be several to many million individuals, and that a single (or a very few) fertile females are responsible for maintaining the numbers of this horde, we see that the same rule holds.

308. How are insect eggs fertilized?   In the great majority of cases the female receives a large number of male sex cells, spermatozoa, at the time of mating. These are stored (and may multiply) in a special sac in her abdomen. As she lays her eggs the sperm meet them on the way out, entering the egg through a very small opening, or set of openings, the *micropyle*. Fertilization thus takes place just after the egg is laid.

309. Do insects ever lay unfertilized eggs?   It not infrequently happens that female insects in captivity will lay their eggs even though no male has been present.

310. Do unfertilized eggs ever develop?   Normally they never do. In certain groups of insects, however, the development of unfertilized eggs (*parthenogenesis*) is the regular thing. In the social Hymenoptera unfertilized eggs normally develop into males, fertilized ones into females.

311. What stimulates an insect to lay her eggs?   "Ovary pressure" is the important factor, of course. But often very specific external environmental stimuli must be present. Roaches lay only at night, or in the dark. A gravid Tiger Beetle will lay eggs if confronted with a hole resembling her normal tunnel in the ground. Many plant-eating insects will lay eggs only in or on the specific plant tissue that is the normal food for their larvae. Proper amounts of light and warmth are often essential. Humidity factors may be important, especially in ground-dwelling insects.

312. Do insects lay their eggs singly or in groups? Most insects lay their eggs in groups or clusters. Roaches and Mantids lay them in clusters covered by a secretion from special glands. These *oötheca* have a characteristic shape and size in each species. It is easier to distinguish the oötheca of the two large Chinese Mantids now naturalized in the United States (*Paratenodera sinensis* and *P. angustipennis*) than to identify the adults. Some moths and butterflies, such as the Tent Caterpillar Moths and the Mourning Cloak Butterfly, regularly lay the eggs in a collarlike layer around a twig. One African Swallowtail lays the eggs in strings hanging down from the food plant. Culicine Mosquitoes lay the eggs, cemented side by side, to form a neat floating raft.

313. Are the eggs laid in characteristic places? They are laid almost invariably in a consistent place by each species, usually on or near the food on which the larvae will feed, even though the adult may never feed on this, or even feed at all. Carrion-feeding insects lay the eggs in decaying meat or similar organic refuse. Parasitoid wasps and flies lay the eggs in, on, or near the particular host insect in which the larvae will live. Locusts dig a hole in the ground or in soft wood, thrust the whole abdomen into it, and then slowly withdraw the abdomen, laying the eggs and neatly packing them in the hole with the ovipositor appendages. Many butterflies lay the eggs only on the underside of a leaf of the larval food plant; but the Viceroy lays a single egg on the top of the very tip of a leaf. A few insects, on the other hand, scatter the eggs at random—Walking Sticks are noted for this. Many Dragonflies and Mayflies either drop the eggs while flying over the water or dip the tip of the abdomen into the water in flight, releasing the eggs through the surface film.

314. What is the insect eggshell like? The shell, known as the *chorion,* is often thick and heavily sclerotized, especially in most bug (Hemiptera) eggs and in species where the egg will overwinter or have to withstand great dryness. In perhaps a majority of insect eggs, however, the chorion is relatively thin and flexible, and is often quite transparent.

315. Are many insect eggs very delicate? Probably the majority are; but in species whose eggs may not hatch for several months, and must withstand extremes of heat, cold, or dryness, the eggs are remarkably resistant.

316. How are eggs attached to solid objects? A gland near the end of the female's abdomen secretes a cement that fastens each egg securely in place. Lice thus cement their eggs to the hairs of the host. In the Green Lacewings (Chrysopidae) the female draws the cement out to form a long thread, as much as $\frac{1}{4}$ inch long, from the end of which the egg dangles. Some midges suspend their eggs from a disk of silk on the surface of the water. And in many aquatic insects which drop the eggs into the water the egg has adhesive filaments that stick to water plants and keep the egg from falling to the bottom. Some of the nest-building Solitary Wasps and bees cement the egg to the side of a cell, near the top, where it will not be involved with the stored foods.

317. What kinds of protective coverings are formed over eggs? Many kinds. There is a basis of cement, which may be a simple layer, protecting the eggs. Or this may be whipped into a froth which hardens full of bubbles that give "dead air" insulation against heat and cold, as in the egg masses of the Eastern Tent Caterpillar. Again, the female may incorporate other substances in the cement covering, such as earth, dung, or even a thick felt of her own hairs. Water Scavenger Beetles (Hydrophilidae) cover the eggs with a silklike substance that forms a hard case about them.

318. Are many eggs laid within plant tissues? A great many insects cut slits or bore holes using the ovipositor, and tuck the eggs into these. Some of the Long Horned Grasshoppers, Tree Crickets, Cicadas, and Tree Hoppers occasionally damage twigs and canes of cultivated fruit trees and shrubs in doing this. Many of the wood-boring beetles bore holes in bark or wood in which to lay eggs.

319. How do Acorn Weevils lay their eggs in acorns? The Nut and Acorn Weevils (*Curculio*) have a very long curved beak as long as, or longer than, the rest of the insect. At the tip of this are the tiny, but powerful, mandibles. With these the female bores a deep hole into a nut or acorn and then turns around and lays an egg in it. It is said that the male has been seen accompanying her and helping her to get loose when her beak gets stuck in the hole. We have never witnessed this.

320. Do many insects lay their eggs in the bodies of other animals?
A great many do, especially among the parasitoid wasps, the females of some of which have ovipositors several times the length of the abdomen. These pierce the host and an egg is thus laid inside. A few aquatic insects and one European Coreid bug lay their eggs on the body of the male or on another species of animal.

321. How does the Human Warble Fly lay its eggs in man?   It doesn't, although its larvae bore in through the human skin and live beneath it. The female Warble Fly seizes a Mosquito (usually of the genus *Psorophora* that commonly attacks man) and cements her egg to the lower surface of the Mosquito. When the Mosquito alights on a human the fly egg hatches immediately and the fly larva bores in through the skin. No more specialized way of laying the eggs is known.

322. Do any flies try to lay their eggs in open wounds?   Blow Flies (Calliphoridae) of some species are said to do this. Certainly the Screwworm Fly (*Callitroga*) lays eggs in the wounds of animals and in sore eyes as well. The maggots start to feed in the wounds but soon invade sound tissue.

323. Do many female insects carry their eggs about after laying them?   Some Mayflies fasten two egg capsules to the posterior part of the body, releasing them only when they are over suitable water. Roaches often carry the egg capsule (oötheca) projecting from the genital opening for some time, finally depositing it in a suitable crevice.

324. Do any female insects brood or take care of their eggs?
Quite a few do, in the groups that are developing or have developed a social life based on the family. Thus, female Earwigs and Bark Beetles

care for the eggs, keeping them clean of mold. Queen ants and termites starting a new colony do the same, but after the first brood of workers emerge these take over this job.

325. How long do insect eggs take to hatch? This varies enormously, depending on the species and its particular specializations. In some flies the larvae may hatch in from eight to twelve hours, while in those species that hibernate as eggs this stage may last eight to ten months. In some insects, such as some Walking Sticks and Scorpion Flies, the eggs may last over a second winter and hatch twenty months or so after they were laid.

326. How do the young larvae get out of the eggshell? Those with biting mouthparts usually simply eat their way out, and frequently eat the shell. Some split the shell by bodily contortions. Some merely have to push open a lid or trapdoor with which the eggshell is furnished. Dragonflies and some Orthoptera have special expanding or pulsating organs that swell up and rupture the shell. Young Lice take in air through the porous head end of the eggshell, and by ejecting it at the rear, build up a pressure that literally blows them out.

LARVAE

327. What is a larva? A larva is any immature animal that differs markedly from the adult. Its occurrence is a widespread phenomenon in many animal phyla. Tiny, ciliated larvae, free-swimming or drifting, eventually settle down to grow and transform into adult Sponges, Sandworms, Snails, Sea Urchins, and Barnacles. They may have special names such as "planula," "trochophore," and "veliger"; but all are larvae. Similarly any immature insect that differs markedly from what it will be like as an adult is a larva.

A nymph is an insect larva that transforms directly into an adult. The fact that we give it a special name merely emphasizes its being a distinctive type of larva. The word was formerly used to mean a pupa, and is still so used at times, particularly in France. There are many different types of nymphs which have been named and classified by specialists.

A naiad is a nymphal type of larva that lives in the water, usually respiring by means of tracheal gills. Eventually it transforms directly into an aerial adult with a regular, tracheal air-breathing system. The name originated from the Greek word meaning "swimmer."

328. Are larvae ever given other names? A great many larvae with special forms or habits have been given various common or vernacular names, such as grub (beetles, bees, wasps), maggot (flies), caterpillar (butterflies and moths), inchworm (Geometrid Moths), cutworm (Noctuid Moths), wiggler or wriggler (Mosquitoes), doodlebug (Ant Lions, Tiger Beetles), and hellgramite (*Corydalis*). One special type of larva that has a scientific designation is the *triungulin* (Latin—three-clawed), a special type of small bristly larva that occurs in instances of hypermetamorphosis such as in Oil Beetles (Meloidae).

329. Do any larvae ever reproduce? Curiously enough there are a few instances where the animal never develops beyond the larval instar; it is therefore the larva that reproduces. This is known as *paedogenesis* (Greek—child reproduction). In some of the Gall Midges, *Miastor,* a female lays a few large eggs. These develop into larvae, in which develop other larvae, called *daughter nymphs,* who gnaw their way out of their mother's body. This may go on for several generations, after which appear more generations of normal, winged adults. Much the same sort of phenomenon occurs in many aphids.

330. Are larval insects more primitive than the adults? In general they tend to be, although of course many specialized larvae are highly advanced. As a rule the larvae show more of the primitive ancestral characteristics of a group than do the adults. The larvae of moths and butterflies, for example, have relatively primitive biting mouthparts, while the adults have highly advanced, tubular sucking ones. And, of course, no larval insects have functional wings, while most adults do.

331. Do all larvae have legs? Many larvae, especially those of flies, wasps, and bees, have no legs.

332. Do any larvae have more than three pairs of legs? Many larvae have additional appendages on the abdomen that look like legs. None of these are true, jointed legs, although perhaps some of them have evolved from parts of primitive jointed legs. The abdominal leglike appendages of larvae are known as prolegs. They are best developed in the larvae of most moths and butterflies and of Sawflies.

333. How does one distinguish between a caterpillar and the larva of a Sawfly?   Sawfly larvae have only a single tiny eye on each side of the head whereas caterpillars have from four to six. Sawfly larvae have a different pattern in the arrangement of abdominal prolegs;

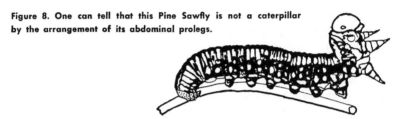

Figure 8. One can tell that this Pine Sawfly is not a caterpillar by the arrangement of its abdominal prolegs.

they may have none at all or they may have from six to ten pairs; whereas caterpillars usually have a pair on each of segments 3 to 6 and segment 10; or a pair on each of segments 5, 6, and 10; or on 6 and 10; but never on segments 7, 8, or 9.

334. Are there many different types of Endopterygote larvae? There are many of interest to specialists, but four chief types can be easily recognized by anyone. First is a generalized type with well-developed thoracic legs but no abdominal legs. They may be relatively short and broad, and often flattened, such as those of most Net-winged Insects (Neuroptera) and many beetles; or they may be quite long and slender, like the larvae of other beetles, such as the Wireworms and Mealworms, of flies, Scorpion Flies, and some of the primitive flies. They are called *campodeiform* larvae.

Another type, very common among beetles, in which the abdomen is very large and fleshy, and usually curved downward, bears no abdominal legs and only small thoracic legs. Such larvae are called *scarabaeiform* since they are best typified by the larvae of the Scarabaeid Beetles. They are usually burrowers in loose soil and in leaf or wood mold, dragging themselves slowly along, often backward. They are often called grubs.

Then there are the slender larvae with abdominal prolegs, or leg-like structures, as well as thoracic legs, that are typified by the cater-pillars of most moths, butterflies, and Sawflies. They are called *eruciform* larvae.

The larvae of most of the wasps, ants, and bees have well-defined, but very small heads; they lack legs, and have large, fat, smooth bodies. They are able to move about very little. They too are called

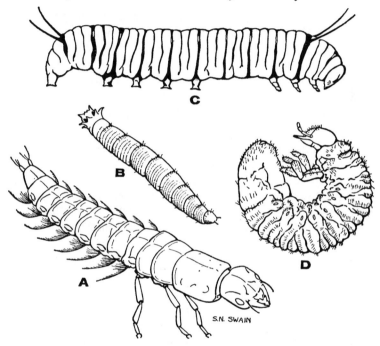

Figure 9. Types of Larvae. A, Campodeiform larva of an aquatic beetle; B, Vermi-form larva of a fly; C, Eruciform larva of a butterfly; D, Scarabeiform larva of a Scarab Beetle.

grubs and are described as *vermiform*. Finally, the larvae of the higher flies not only lack legs but have the head so small as to be hardly recognizable. They move about chiefly by elongation and shortening of the body and are truly *vermiform*. They are commonly called maggots.

Practically all of these larvae bear little or no resemblance to the adults into which they will transform. In the majority of cases they live in quite different environments and feed differently. These differences are a measure of the completeness of their metamorphosis.

335. What do larvae do primarily?   Feeding and growth are the chief occupations of the larvae. These are the tasks on which they concentrate, and are their contribution to the survival of their species.

336. How fast do larvae grow?   This depends on the length of life normal to the species. It also is influenced by weather and by the abundance or scarcity of food. Most insects, being short lived, grow at a rate much greater than those of such slow-growing animals as man. A Polyphemus Moth caterpillar increased its weight 4,140 times in 56 days. At such a rate a human baby weighing nine pounds at birth would weigh more than eighteen tons in less than two months.

337. How much do larvae eat?   This depends, likewise, on the duration of larval life, and also on the quality of food. Wood eaters, which develop slowly, must eat a great deal, since wood is not very nutritious. Leaf eaters need eat less. Seed eaters eat much less, since seeds contain highly concentrated and nourishing foods. The same is true of eaters of animal foods, which are both nourishing and quickly digested. On the other hand, eaters of animal foods may have much more difficulty in finding the food, and so alternate periods of intensive eating with periods of near starvation. The larva of *Scarabaeus,* the Sacred Scarab, eats dung, stored for it by its parent. It eats almost continuously, consuming more than its own weight of this dry food in each 24 hours. Larvae that feed on plant tissues that are largely water eat proportionately more. Those that feed on dried animal foods, such as Skin Beetles and Larder Beetles, eat much less. Some fly larvae, nourished within the body of their parent that has sucked rich mammalian blood, do not feed at all.

338. How much of their food do larvae digest?   A coefficient of digestion can be calculated by dividing the dry weight of the food eaten, minus the dry weight of the excrement, by the dry weight of the food. This figure comes to 25 percent for leaf-eating caterpillars such as the Silkworm and the Tortoiseshell Butterfly; to 36 percent for the larvae of the Cabbage Butterfly; to 46 percent for larvae of Mealworm Beetles, feeding on much more nutritious grain. A dairy cow, eating dry hay, scored 72 percent efficiency.

339. Do many larvae do all of the eating, the adult none? A great many do, the mouthparts of the adult being so degenerated as to be almost useless. In others the adults may take in water but no food; or they may take in a little food but not nearly enough to enable them to reproduce. In all such instances the energy and material used by the adults are largely or entirely derived from the food they ate as larvae.

340. What are some of the insects in which the adults never eat or drink? Among the more primitive orders, the Mayflies are exceptional in this. The nymphs, which may spend two or three years developing in the water, do all of the eating. The mouthparts of the adult are tiny and functionless and its digestive tract is largely transformed into an air sac that gives greater buoyancy in flight. The non-biting Midges (Chironomidae), closely related to the Mosquitoes, similarly neither eat nor drink as adults. The same is true of the Emperor Moths (Saturniidae), which is surprising because they are the largest of our moths, some with a wing span of a foot.

341. Are there any insects in which the adults do all the eating and the larvae none? There are a few rare examples of this, chiefly in the Pupipara, a group of parasitic flies in which the larvae develop full growth inside the mother.

342. What larvae digest their food before swallowing it? This is a very common and characteristic way of feeding practiced by larvae of the higher flies and various others such as those of Diving Beetles. In the fly larvae the head is greatly reduced and the mouthparts replaced by strong mouth hooks. With these the larva shreds the food around its head and mixes it with digestive fluids which it squirts out of its mouth. When the food has been digested, or at least liquefied, the larva sucks this in with what is left of its digestive fluids.

343. How do larvae feed that live in other insects? Some of them just eat their way along and kill and devour the host in short order. Others, however, which take perhaps from two weeks to a month to mature, are faced with a situation fraught with danger to themselves. If they should cause the death of the host long before they are ready to stop eating and pupate, the dead host would putrefy, and would most certainly cause their own death. Such larvae begin by eating tissues that are not essential to the life of the host, leaving the vital organs until last. As a result they have fresh food from beginning to end. The host may continue to eat and even to grow, making more food available to the larva living within. It is a common experience among collectors who have taken home small caterpillars to rear, to find that the caterpillar eats normally, grows well, and seems healthy until, just when it is reaching full size, there emerges from it the larva, or sometimes a number of larvae, of a Tachinid Fly or an Ichneumon, Braconid, or Chalcid Wasp. There will be practically nothing left of the host, the invaders having finished their job by dining last on its vital organs.

344. Do predaceous larvae have any special means of killing their prey? The majority have the usual weapons of predators, such as strong jaws and grasping legs. A number have poisonous secretions that numb or kill the prey, or make use of devices such as traps or snares.

345. What larvae make use of poisonous secretions? The most outstanding are the nymphs of predatory bugs. Thrusting its tubular beak into the prey, such a larva injects a drop of its special salivary secretion. This often acts very rapidly, enabling the bug to suck out the juices of its victim at leisure. We have seen Ambush Bugs (Phymatidae) less than a third of an inch long paralyze butterflies with a three-inch wing span; and the nymph of a predatory Stink Bug (Pentatomidae) only an eighth of an inch long master a Sphinx Moth caterpillar two inches long and several hundred times its weight. Giant Water Bugs, Backswimmers, Water Scorpions, and Assassin Bugs all do likewise.

346. What larvae make traps? The best known are the larvae of the Ant Lions (Myrmeleontidae). Short, stocky, and flat, they live in sheltered spots in loose, fine sand or dust. Shuffling around backward in a circle, the larva uses its head as a shovel with which to throw the sand outward. As it continues to do this a conical pit is formed which may be two inches or more in diameter with steep sides slanting down to the center. Here the Ant Lion lies with only its long, sharp jaws above the surface. Any small insect that falls into the pit will be seized. If the Ant Lion misses its first grasp, it hurls head-loads of sand at the prey, preventing its climbing the steep, loose slopes of the pit. Once seized, the prey is soon mastered and its blood extracted.

The larvae of three families of Caddisflies, the Hydropsychidae, Philopotamidae, and Psychomyiidae, spin silken nets in streams, and regularly attend these to seize small animals that have become caught, as well as to eat other particles of organic material. It is curious that none of the terrestrial insects has evolved a silken web as means of catching prey as the Spiders have.

347. What larvae dig holes and live in them? The best known are the Tiger Beetle larvae, sometimes (like the Ant Lions) known as "doodlebugs." The larva digs a cylindrical burrow in the ground into which it backs. Waiting with its head filling the entrance it seizes any small animal that passes nearby, drags it into the burrow, and devours it. The larvae of some Tiger Beetles excavate burrows in the stems of plants. They have hooks on the abdomen which aid them in holding fast to the walls of their burrow when struggling with their prey.

348. What larvae make and live within individual cases? Many groups of insects do this. Among the moths most of the Bagworms (Psychidae) and Case-Bearers (Coleophoridae) make tubular silken cases which they carry about as they feed. The larvae of many small Tineid Moths do the same, including those of the Case-Bearing Clothes Moth that is often destructive to woolen and silk fabrics and to furs. The cases of most of the Bagworms, some of which are three inches or more long, are elaborately camouflaged with bits of leaves, twigs, and debris. Other case-making larvae are those of various groups of beetles such as the Leaf Beetles (Chlamydinae) which make short cases composed largely of their own excrement; and the larvae of various of the Case-Bearer Moths that hollow out seeds as portable cases.

349. Do many aquatic larvae make cases? The majority of Caddisfly larvae make and live in portable cases. These are basically made of silk to which may be cemented all kinds of substances. Most commonly used are bits of leaves, bark, and twigs. Some however use grains of sand and small gravel. In one family, the Helicopsychidae, the larva makes a spiraled case of sand and gravel in the form of a Snail shell.

350. Why aren't cases of sand and gravel too heavy for the larva to carry around? They would be in air, but in water they weigh proportionately much less; and a bubble or two of air makes such a case, and the larva, actually lighter than water.

351. What larvae make communal nests? Quite a few do, although not nearly as many as make individual cases. The best known are the caterpillars of moths and butterflies, and of some Sawflies. These are not truly social, but merely gregarious. Among the moths the gregarious American Tent Caterpillars spin loose silken webs in the forks of shrubs and trees. Each caterpillar does its share of the spinning, but there is no other coöperation. When the caterpillars are full grown they scatter, spin individual cocoons, and pupate in them independently. The caterpillars of related species of the same genus (*Malacosoma*) do not make communal webs, although the European Lackey Moth (*M. neustria*) lives in a communal web in the very early larval stages. The Palearctic Processionary Caterpillars also spin dense webs, from which they go forth to feed; they also hibernate together in the webs. The larvae of moths of quite a few other families also make and live in communal webs.

The larvae of a number of butterflies spin webs. Those of the Mexican White (*Eucheira socialis*) make flask-shaped nests that are so dense that people sometimes use them as bags. The caterpillars of the eastern North American Baltimore (*Euphydryas phaeton*) live together during their first season in a communal web and hibernate in it. The larvae of some of the famous big, iridescent blue *Morpho* butterflies of the tropics live in groups in webs.

352. Do any larvae make individual shelters utilizing leaves still on the plant? Great numbers do. The commonest type is a nest made by folding or rolling a leaf or tying leaves together with silk. In this the larva lives, perhaps eating the folded part of the leaf, perhaps leaving this untouched while going out to feed. Such "leaf rollers" and "leaf tyers" are extremely common among the smaller moths, the so-called "microlepidoptera," especially in the families Olethreutidae, Tortricidae, and Pyralididae.

353. Do nymphs and larvae make special preparations for molting? Most of them do, at least by retiring to a sheltered spot where they are less likely to be disturbed or attacked. The larvae of many moths and butterflies spin a special silk carpet which their legs can grasp firmly during ecdysis, and many remain on this for a day or two until the molt is finished and the new exoskeleton hardened. Some spin a cocoon.

354. What is a cocoon? A cocoon is primarily a structure in which a larva encloses itself before it pupates. People sometimes confuse the cocoon with the pupa itself.

355. What are cocoons made of? The great majority have silk as a basis. Some are entirely silk, but most cocoons have other substances incorporated, either bits of leaves, wood, earth, and the larval excreta, or else other larval secretions. The commonest of the latter are the urinary secretions of the excretory organs, which harden to form a chalky deposit. Often the hairs of the larva are interwoven with the silk; in some cases these add appreciably to the bulk and the temperature insulation. Some cocoons are formed of little more than the compacted soil or humus around the larva.

356. Do all larvae make cocoons? Many do not, merely transforming to the pupa in the open or in a crevice or underground. This is even true of some of the largest groups of moths (Owlets and Geometrids), contrary to the popular idea that all moth caterpillars make cocoons.

357. Do any cocoons have a complicated structure? Many have such features as special lids or escape hatches at one end, or special valves that will allow the mature insect to escape but discourage the entrance of marauders. Many others lack such specialties and are almost completely airtight and waterproof.

358. Where are cocoons formed? Some are made in the loose upper layers of the soil; others are under loose bark or stones, or in crevices. Many are formed in rolled up leaves, in larval nests, or

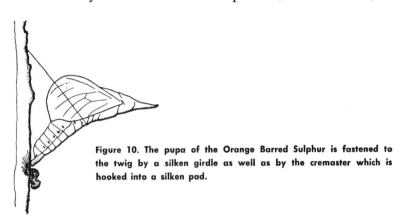

Figure 10. The pupa of the Orange Barred Sulphur is fastened to the twig by a silken girdle as well as by the cremaster which is hooked into a silken pad.

fastened to twigs and branches. Some, made in leaves still growing on a tree, fall to the ground in autumn. Others swing from twigs by silk girdles woven as a part of the cocoon-making job.

359. Do larvae make the cocoon and pupate where they have been eating? Many do; many do not, but may travel feet or yards away from their larval habitat. Many larvae, in fact, develop a wanderlust just before pupation and travel far and fast. It is common in the late summer and autumn to see caterpillars busily scurrying across roads on their way to pupation.

PUPAE

360. What is a pupa? A pupa is the stage in a complete metamorphosis into which the larva transforms, and which, in turn, transforms into the adult. The name comes from the Latin *pupa,* doll. The pupa apparently looked like a doll swathed in blankets.

361. What are the characteristics of a pupa? Although they differ enormously in size, shape, and details, practically all pupae have one thing in common: they are passive and immobile. They are sometimes referred to as the "resting stage."

362. What are the chief types of pupae?   Three chief types are recognized. An *exarate* pupa has the antennae, wings, and legs relatively free and loose, merely folded against the body. An *obtect* pupa is much more compact; the appendages and wings are quite visible

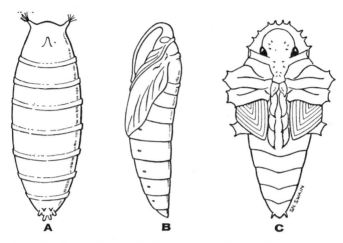

Figure 11. Types of Pupae. A, Coarctate pupa of a fly; B, Obtect pupa of a Sphingid Moth; C, Exarate pupa of a beetle.

but firmly attached to the body, not projecting free. A *coarctate* pupa is one formed inside the last larval skin, which makes a hard, smooth shell around it known as a *puparium*. Such puparia, although segmented, are cylindrical and barrel shaped, showing none of the pupal structures within.

363. What insects have each of these types of pupae?   The higher flies, in which the larva is a smooth, legless, and almost headless maggot, have a coarctate pupa. Most moths and butterflies, the more primitive Diptera, and most of the Rove Beetles (Staphylinidae) and Lady Beetles (Coccinellidae) have obtect pupae. The rest of the Endopterygote insects have exarate pupae.

364. Are pupae really resting?   Although it does not move about, or eat, and although it respires but very little, the pupa is really seething with internal activity. When first formed, the pupal shell (exoskeleton) contained the structures of the larva. These must be largely broken down and rebuilt into the adult organs. Thus, in a few days or weeks an almost complete reorganization takes place of all of the complex organs, tissues, and cells of the insect. (See question 376.)

365. Are pupae capable of any movement?   The pupae of a few groups, such as some of the Lacewings (Chrysopidae and Hemerobiidae), the Snake Flies (Raphidiodea), the Mosquitoes (Culicidae), and many Midges (Chironomidae) crawl or swim quite freely, chiefly as a means of avoiding harm. And many pupae are able to wiggle the abdomen and thus may work themselves out into open air, just before emergence, from a cell in the earth or a tunnel in wood.

366. Do any insects with externally developing wings have pupae? A few Scale Insects (Coccidae) and the Thrips (Thysanoptera) have a pupalike last larval instar.

367. How are the wings of pupae formed?   They develop as inwardly growing, internal sacs in the larva. When the larva transforms into a pupa these turn inside out, and thus lie on the outer surface.

368. What is the prepupa?   It is the last part of the last larval instar when the larva is preparing for pupation. In this it rests inactively while its larval tissues begin the change into those of a pupa. After a time the last larval cuticula is shed, exposing the pupa.

369. Do any pupae have unusual shapes?   Many butterfly pupae have very irregular shapes with projecting spines and other structures. The head may bear a single long horn projecting forward; or the thorax may have a large median process; or the abdomen may bear rows of projecting spines.

370. Do many pupae have bright colors?   Most pupae are quite plainly colored, at least at first. Some, however, are very brightly colored, often with iridescent or metallic patches or spots. In most exarate and obtect pupae the colors of the adult insect show through the pupal cuticula as they develop so that the older pupa may be brightly colored and patterned.

371. Why are some pupae irregularly shaped and brightly colored?
The majority of such pupae are those formed in the open, as are
those of most butterflies. Their unusual appearance, by making them
look different, prevents many birds and similar insectivorous animals
from recognizing them as edible. Many butterfly pupae greatly resemble crumpled leaves or bits of bark. One, *Feniseca tarquinius,*
looks like a monkey's head.

372. What is a chrysalis? The butterfly pupa is often called a
chrysalis (plural: *chrysalids*). The word comes from the Greek
chrysos—golden, and was originally used because of the metallic
golden spots on the pupae of some Brush-footed Butterflies (Nymphalidae).

373. Are any butterfly pupae enclosed in cocoons? Those of the
Skippers (Hesperioidea) and some Satyrs (Satyridae) are sometimes found in a very loose mesh of silk that might be called a
cocoon.

374. How are butterfly chrysalids fastened in place? Butterfly
chrysalids have a spike or bundle of hooklets at the rear end of the
abdomen, called the *cremaster*. In some families this catches in a pad
of silk woven by the caterpillar, and suspends the pupa head down.
In other families the pupa is held not only by the cremaster and pad
of silk, but also by a thin silk loop around the body. The pad and
girdle represent the last remains of the cocoon that doubtless was
spun by their ancestors.

375. How long does the pupal instar last? Here again, as with
other instars, one can only cite limits. The average pupal instar may
last from ten to twenty days, but with insects having very fast development (some have a generation every twelve to fourteen days) the
pupal stage may be of only four or five days' duration, whereas with
insects whose life cycle encompasses one or two years it may endure
for several months.

376. How do the internal changes of the pupa take place? Some
adult organs that began development in larval or embryonic life
carry on in the pupa. So do many small centers of cell growth known

as "rudiments" or "buds." A large part of the larval tissue breaks down, a process called *histolysis,* into many loose cells, or may actually be destroyed in special cells called *phagocytes.* At this time a pupa, if opened, seems to have relatively few solid structures internally and to be largely filled with slimy liquid. Then around the various organs and buds, cells form into tissues, and tissues into organs of the adult. The pattern is different in all groups of insects. To give one example: in beetle pupae the fore and hind divisions of the digestive tract persist with little change from larva to adult; in the higher flies however these regions largely disintegrate and must be built anew. It is impossible to generalize more than to say that the majority of larval organs disintegrate and are replaced by those of the adult.

377. Does the adult emerge from the pupal shell as soon as it is fully formed?   It will not emerge until external conditions provide the proper set of stimuli. Usually emergence, called *eclosion,* takes place only above a certain threshold of temperature. It is also affected by barometric pressure, a lower pressure often stimulating it. In many insects eclosion takes place in the early morning.

378. Does the pupa itself help the adult in eclosion?   It sometimes wiggles its way out of the soil or wood to be nearer the outside world; or it may cut the cocoon or cell with its mandibles.

379. How does the adult get out of the cocoon if the pupa has not cut it?   Adults with jaws can cut their way out. Those with soft, sucking mouthparts may have special cutting structures; many moths have hard, sharp spines, or bladelike cutters on their shoulders; most Fleas have cutters on the head. Others have special pressure organs or a means of dissolving the cocoon.

380. What insects dissolve the cocoon?   The best known are many of the moths, such as some of the Emperor Moths and Puss Moths. They secrete a liquid from the mouth that contains potassium hydroxide (caustic potash); with this they dissolve one end of the cocoon.

381. Do silkworms dissolve the cocoon? They do, and in so doing destroy the value of the silk. They are therefore killed in the cocoon before eclosion, by baking.

382. How do flies get out of their hard puparium? The higher flies (Cyclorrhapha) have a large bladder, *ptilinum,* in the front of the head. At eclosion this is blown up violently by pressure from within. It puffs out forward, cracks the puparium, and opens a channel in the soil through which the soft, fragile adult can crawl. As the adult dries out and its exoskeleton hardens, the bladder is withdrawn, leaving a U-shaped suture or line on the face of the fly to show where it was.

383. How do most adults get out of the pupal shell? First they rupture it, either by means of struggling within it or by contractions of the abdomen which force liquids and gases forward, expanding the thorax. This cracks the thoracic portion of the shell, usually in a line along the back. Through this opening the adult pushes out its head and thorax. It continues to push with the legs, keeping the abdomen contracted, until the head and thorax are extracted. As soon as the legs come out they catch on to something and pull. Within no more than a minute or so the adult is entirely out.

ADULTS

384. Is the newly emerged adult ready for flight or other activities? Its cuticle is still soft and flexible, its wings are not expanded, and it is still wet from the remains of the molting fluids that loosened it from the pupal cuticula. It usually must have a period during which it can dry out and become harder. The adults of some aquatic groups that pupate in the water spread the wings and take off in a second or two.

385. What does an insect have to do after eclosion? It must crawl up to where it can hang, back downward. It must expand the wings, which then must have adequate time to harden. Its exoskeleton must harden, not only externally for protection but internally for muscle attachment. It must dry off, clean itself of any remnants of pupal shell and molting fluid. It must also eject the urinary wastes that have accumulated during the pupal stage. All of this may take from a few minutes to several hours.

386. What is meconium?　This is the liquid waste, largely the products of the excretory organs, which could not be excreted by the pupa. These wastes usually form a thick, creamy fluid, at times brightly colored red or pink. While completing its transformation the adult, usually after its wings are fully expanded, voids a drop or sometimes several drops of the meconium.

387. What are "rains of blood"?　At times when great swarms of European butterflies, such as the Lesser Tortoiseshell, have emerged by the thousand, the bright red meconium drops will actually make a limited area look as though red rain had fallen from the sky. In medieval times when people knew nothing about butterfly development, these "red rains" were a source of wonderment; and there are records of their being a cause of panic as signs of some approaching disaster.

388. Is meconium poisonous or obnoxious?　Meconium is no more harmful to humans than the concentrated urinary secretions of birds. It will, however, stain and bleach fabrics. The amateur entomologist is therefore warned not to let moths emerging from pupae do so near curtains or upholstery.

389. Are newly emerged adults fully colored?　They usually are not, although the wing patterns and colors of butterflies and moths are as bright as they ever will be. Considerable time is needed for the cuticula to harden and darken normally. Its colors, both structural and pigment, may not develop for some days, or even weeks. Anyone rearing insects should therefore never be in a hurry to kill specimens that have just transformed to the adult.

390. What adult insects take the longest to develop their full colors?　In most Dragonflies the newly emerged adult, described as "teneral," may require one or two weeks to develop full color. In the widespread genus *Sympetrum,* some species of which are common nearly everywhere in Europe and North America, the teneral adults are pale yellow, and require two weeks or more to develop the full, bright-red color of the body. In other Dragonflies, such as *Libellula pulchella* and *Plathemis lydia,* the abdomen develops a bright, whitish-blue "bloom" only after some weeks of maturing, and the dark wing markings similarly require some time to attain their deepest shades.

391. Are there any bodily adjustments which adults have to make after eclosion? In the newly emerged moth or butterfly the tubular proboscis, or tongue, is seen to be composed of two separate parts, each of which represents a part of one of the paired maxillae. These must be fitted together for their whole length to form the tube. This can be watched while the insect is preparing itself after eclosion. Finally the two halves lock together and the resulting proboscis is coiled, like a watchspring, beneath the face. Other insects with tubular mouthparts must make similar, although lesser adjustments. The same thing must also be done at the rear end in many females with tubular ovipositors that are similarly evolved from paired appendages.

392. How long is it before the adult is ready for reproduction? In many species in which the reproductive organs develop fully in the pupa it is ready immediately. But in many others a period of several days may be necessary. Females may mate soon after eclosion but their eggs may not mature for several days or weeks.

393. What are insect "drinking societies"? In many insects, especially moths and butterflies, the young males may gather in swarms at wet earth, such as around mud puddles on roads, and sip water. It may be several days before they scatter and go in search of the females. Especially in tropical regions such mud-puddle clubs may number many thousands of individuals of many different species.

VII. INSECT SENSES AND COMMUNICATION

394. Do insects have the same senses that man has? They do, but the organs differ in structure, location, and sensitivity.

395. What are the insects' chief senses? They are touch, hearing, taste, smell, and sight. These concern stimuli or forces outside the individual. In addition, insects react to stimuli such as the force of gravity, i.e., they have a sense of balance or equilibrium; and they react to the positions of their own parts, i.e., they have a kinesthetic sense. (Just as we can "feel" that our arm is straight or bent, that our head is turned to one side, and so on.)

396. Do insects have any senses that man does not have? They do not appear to. However, their sense organs are differently located, enabling them to pick up sensations in a way that would be foreign to man; and the threshold of sensitivity of the different organs varies so much from man's that the resulting over-all picture sometimes appears quite dissimilar.

397. How does the difference in location of a sense organ affect the apparent feeling? Can a human imagine being able to taste something several feet ahead, or something that he has stepped on? Can a human imagine hearing with the forearms? or sensing light (not heat) with the skin of the back?

398. Why is it misleading to even speak of an insect "feeling" or "knowing"? These words are so linked in the human mind with conscious sensation that it is misleading to use them with respect to an insect. The human "sees" the difference between red and blue, or "is aware of" the difference between hot and cold, or "feels" the difference between a rough surface and a smooth one. He is conscious of these things in respect to himself. There is no indication that the insect has any awareness or consciousness of self.

TOUCH

399. Are insects sensitive to touch?   Insects are extremely sensitive to touch, far more extensively so than man. Reactions to touch often determine their entire way of life.

400. What are the touch receptors?   The touch receptors consist of setae, that is, hairs or bristles, with a movable base. An extremely slight stimulus to one of these causes a movement at its base and sets up a sensory nerve reaction.

401. Where are the touch receptors located?   They are most abundant on the antennae, but occur practically everywhere on the insect, even on the wings and the surfaces of the eyes.

402. Do the touch receptors have any other function?   They also serve in some insects for a simple sort of hearing, by responding to sound waves, especially of very low frequencies.

403. Do touch hairs play a part in any habitual way of life?   Many insects seek small cracks and crevices where they remain hidden during the day. The touch hairs on the upper and lower surfaces of a flat insect, or all around on a cylindrical one, stimulate the insect so that it remains in a confined space.

404. How do touch hairs keep some insects flying?   Certain insects, such as the migratory Locusts, have a special bundle of touch hairs on the head. When these are stimulated by an air-current flowing from the front of the insect they create a nerve stimulus that keeps the insect's wings beating in a flight motion. This motion intensifies the air-current so that as long as it is flying, it keeps flying. This is the mechanism that explains the very long-distance flights of such insects.

405. How can this flight stimulus be demonstrated?   A number of the locusts can be fastened around the edge of an easy-turning, horizontal wheel, all heading clockwise or counterclockwise. Each locust can be stimulated to start flying by blowing in its face. The combined flight movements make the wheel spin around, and will keep it spinning for hours.

HEARING

406. Do any insects have hearing organs similar to our ears?
In several orders of insects there are special hearing organs which, like our ears, occur in pairs, one on each side of the body. They are known as *chordotonal* or *tympanic* organs.

407. How does the insect tympanic organ function?   The fundamental structure is a thin, flat membrane, the *tympanum* or eardrum. This vibrates when sound waves strike it. From it cordlike *chordotonal sensilla* connect with an auditory nerve, transmitting the stimuli just as the chain of human earbones does.

408. What groups of insects have such tympanic organs?   Orthoptera, such as Locusts, Long Horned Grasshoppers, Crickets, and Cicadas, have well-developed ones; so also do the majority of moths.

409. Where are the tympanic organs located?   In Locusts they are on each side of the basal segment of the abdomen. In Long Horned Grasshoppers and Crickets they are on the tibia of each foreleg. In Cicadas they are located on the lower surface of the base of the abdomen. In moths they are on each side of either the rear of the thorax, or the front part of the abdomen.

410. Do any insects have hearing organs that are not eardrums?
Most insects have *hair sensillae* that react to vibrations in the air, including those within the frequencies of acoustics. In some caterpillars they seem to be scattered over the body. In the House Cricket and the Cockroach they are on the anal cerci. In the male Yellow Fever Mosquito a cluster of these hairs on the antennae has been named *Johnston's Organ.*

411. What is the range of hearing of insects?   Insects in general have a wide range of hearing. In Crickets, the hairs on the cerci respond to vibrations well below those commonly attributed to sound; their tympanic organs react to sound of 16,300 cycles per second.

Other insects show great variations also, but tympanic organs in general react to cycles of from 250 to 45,000 per second. A few Noctuid Moths react up to 80,000 cycles per second and some Grasshoppers up to 90,000.

412. How does insect hearing compare with man's? The human range of audition is approximately from 20 to 20,000 cycles per second. This means that some insects can hear lower frequencies than man can hear, and some can hear considerably higher ones. Some Grasshoppers, for example, can hear sound more than two octaves higher than man. Most insects require a louder sound than man does, however; in some frequencies a pressure 30,000 times that required to reach man's threshold of hearing is necessary; whereas in other frequencies the insect hears as well as man.

413. Are characteristics of sound other than frequency involved in insect hearing? Yes, which is one of the reasons why it is so difficult to compare their hearing with that of man. Overtones and modulation of frequencies affect the quality of insect sounds and correspondingly are involved in their audition. A Cricket can discriminate between the stridulation of another Cricket and an artificial sound made by the scraping of a file, even though both are of the same pitch. It can recognize a Cricket call transmitted over the telephone, even though the modulations make it unrecognizable to a man.

414. Of what value is supersonic hearing to insects? Frequencies in the stridulating sounds of Grasshoppers are equal to the highest ones in the range of tympanic sensitivity, so that it is apparent that hearing of this order is essential to an insect if it is to "hear the voices" of its own species. Furthermore, moths have been observed to drop suddenly into the grass upon the approach of Bats, indicating that they hear the supersonic sound emitted by the Bats, probably thereby gaining a certain amount of protection from the predation of these enemies.

SOUND MAKING

415. Do insects have voices? They do not have a true voice in the human or mammalian sense, but they do make definite and characteristic sounds. This they do by stridulating, which is the rubbing together of one part against another; by tapping; by vibrating some part of the body; or by forcing air out through the spiracles.

416. With what organs do insects stridulate?   Males of Short-horned Grasshoppers and Locusts rub the inner sides of the hind femora, each of which bears a row of eighty to ninety fine spines, against a projecting vein on the outside of each tegmen (the thickened fore wing). Longhorned Grasshoppers rub the two tegmina together, the right one having a hardened area or scraper, and the left one a prominent filelike vein. The Crickets do the same, but some of them have the file on the right wing cover instead of on the left. Dung Beetles rub a hind leg against a ridged area on the base of the second leg. The males of some Waterboatmen rub a field of pegs on the front femur across the sharp cephalic margin of the body.

417. How is the chirping of the male Snowy Tree Cricket produced? By scraping the left wing cover across the file on the right wing cover, while holding the wings nearly perpendicular to the body. While doing this the male exposes a scent gland on the upper surface of the mesothorax which secretes a substance greatly relished by the female.

418. Does the female Snowy Tree Cricket appreciate the chirping of the male?   All of the chirping is apparently wasted as far as the female is concerned; at least she seems to have no auditory organs with which to hear it. But the emission from the thoracic gland is not wasted, because scenting it, she crawls over the male's back to lap up the liquid secretion; then mating takes place.

419. Is it true that one can tell the temperature by the Tree Cricket's chirp?   Yes, if you are sure that you are listening to a Snowy Tree Cricket (*Oecanthus niveus*). A convenient formula to use is:

$$T = 50 + \frac{n - 40}{4}$$

(*n* being the number of chirps per minute). Another method is to count the number of chirps in 14 seconds and add 40. The temperature will be in degrees Fahrenheit.

If you are listening to a Katydid (*Cryptophyllus perspicalis*) the formula is:

$$T = 60 + \frac{n - 19}{3}$$

420. What insect is considered the noisiest of all insects? The Cicadas are usually considered the noisiest of all insects; but it has been said that the European Cricket (*Brachytrypes megacephalus*) is louder still and that its note can be heard a mile away.

421. How do Cicadas produce their noise? The male has a pair of shell-like drums with a complex series of resonators, located on the base of the abdomen. When the drums are vibrated the resulting sounds are modified by the resonators.

422. What insects make tapping noises? Some termite soldiers tap with their heads, this probably serving as a warning of the approach of danger. The Death Watch Beetle (*Anobium*), which burrows in old furniture or in beams and wooden paneling, taps against the sides of its burrows with the lower part of the front of the head. This tapping is possibly a sex call, but is thought by superstitious people to presage a death in the household. Larvae of Stag Beetles (Lucanidae) often tap as they work through decaying wood. Ants often click their mandibles and knock their heads against solid objects. Book Lice (Psocoptera) tap with a knob located near the tip of the abdomen.

423. How do bees and flies make their characteristic hum? The buzzing and humming of bees and flies is made by the rapid vibration of their wings. Some of them vibrate the thorax also; and the Syrphid Flies, when hovering or at rest, can hum by vibrating a membranous infolding of the lining of the tracheae.

424. Has the sound made by bees and flies been measured in the laboratory? It has been used in determining wing-beat frequencies. When a Housefly hums on the F above middle C it is an indication that its wings are beating 335 times a second.

425. What beetles commonly make sounds? Many beetles, especially the Flower Beetles, Cockchafers, and Dung Beetles, make quite

loud sounds, whirrings and buzzings, with their wings. The big June
Beetles can also make a sound by blowing air out through the spiracles. The large striped *Polyphylla* species, relatives of the June
Beetles found in western North America, squeak vigorously in this
way when disturbed. The big Horned Passalus (*P. cornutus*) have
stridulatory organs consisting of patches of minute denticles on the
back of the abdomen, across which similar patches on the lower surface of the wings scrape.

426. Do any butterflies and moths make sounds?   Many Sphinx
caterpillars squeak, and various Skipper (Hesperiidae) larvae make
grating noises by scraping their jaws across a leaf surface. Some pupae
make grating noises by wiggling their abdominal segments together;
some Hairstreak (Lycaenidae) pupae have filelike edges, probably
sound-producing, on certain abdominal segments. Adults of the
Death's Head Sphinx Moth make a high-pitched vibration by forcing
air out of the mouth; and some other moths and butterflies click their
wings when in flight. Charles Darwin, in *The Voyage of H.M.S. Beagle,*
describes the clicking of the Calico Butterfly, *Ageronia,* in the New
World tropics. In Australia the males of the Whistling Moth, *Heca-
tesia,* make a whistling sound during courtship, with a hollow structure on the wings.

427. Are insects ever kept in captivity for their song?   In Portugal,
China, and Japan, Crickets and Grasshoppers are kept in cages for
their songs.

428. What insects make sound by forcing air through the spiracles?
Some Diptera, the queen bee, and the June Beetles can produce sound
in this way. Lubber Grasshoppers do it too.

429. Is the ability to make sound of any value to the insect?
Much of the sound-making seems to be incidental to other activities.
The "music of flight" that comes from the vibration of the wings is
generally believed to be without function, merely reflecting the state
of activity. And yet it has been shown that wing-beat frequency, and
its resulting sound, in the female Mosquito is both a means of recognition and a powerful sexual stimulus to the male. A tuning fork
vibrating at the proper frequency will lure male Mosquitoes and evoke

sexual reactions. Sounds made by organs that have obviously evolved with that function alone almost certainly must be of some importance to the insect. They act as a warning, or so as to frighten away enemies, to call social insects together, or to attract the opposite sex.

430. Do insects sing more by day or night? This differs greatly, depending on the period of chief activity of each group of insects. Grasshoppers, for instance, sing only during the day; and Cicadas sing by day only when the weather is dry and warm. Crickets, on the other hand, sing both day and night. Katydids are chiefly nocturnal, tuning up at dusk. Some insects show diurnal rhythms in their periods of singing. Some Grasshoppers start singing twelve hours after the last period of darkness even when the period of illumination is reversed.

431. Do both sexes make sounds? As a rule only the males stridulate; but the humming that comes from wing vibrations in flight is made by both sexes.

432. Barking dogs don't bite (so it is said). Do humming Mosquitoes bite? Both male and female Mosquitoes hum, but only the females "bite." On the other hand, there are female Mosquitoes that bite consistently but that either do not hum or have hums above the range of human audition.

433. Is it true that there is a difference in the pitch of the hum of a male and female Mosquito? Yes. The wing-beat frequency of the female is less than that of the male, as is true with most insects. However, the temperature and the age of the insect also affect the frequency and therefore the pitch; and each species has its characteristic range of frequencies.

TASTE

434. Do insects have taste buds like ours? Insects have chemoreceptors that can be called receptors of taste. Their nature is not clear but they are probably thin-walled hairs; hence they are not similar to man's taste buds.

435. What are insects able to taste?   Many insects have a very delicate sense of taste although it may not be like ours in that what is sweet to us may not be sweet to them. Experiments with Honeybees and with Dytiscid Water Beetles indicate that they are sensitive to sweet, sour, salt, and bitter, the same four taste sensations that man distinguishes.

436. Where are the taste receptors located?   In the majority of insects they are located on the maxillary and labial palpi, in the mouth cavity, or on the antennae. However, in butterflies and some flies, as well as the Honeybee, they are on the tarsi of the legs; and in some Ichneumonid and Braconid Wasps, and in the Crickets, they are on the ovipositor of the female.

437. How sensitive is their sense of taste?   Most caterpillars probably react only to "pleasant" and "unpleasant" tastes, with a few gradations in between. But many insects show a distinct and delicate sensitivity to the four tastes, though in varying degrees. The Honeybees' threshold of sensitivity to sugar varies: they notice solutions of 34.2 percent on the mouthparts and tarsi, but only 2.5 to 3 percent on the antennae. Blowflies (Calliphoridae) react to sugar solutions when their tarsi are 3 millimeters away, but of course smell may be involved; however, they do react to sugar on the tarsi when the solution is as dilute as .002–.003 percent. The Milkweed Butterfly shows the greatest sensitivity of all of those tested; it reacts to sugar solutions of only .0003 percent, which indicates a sensitivity 2,408 times that of the human tongue.

438. Is the sense of taste of any value to insects other than in exploring for food?   Taste is most certainly tied in with smell in building up the bond between members of an ant colony. The almost continual licking and grooming that goes on is partly a food exchange, partly cleansing the larvae to keep them free of fungus infections, and partly a distribution of social hormones which regulate the development of the proper numbers of each caste; but the importance of the taste factor in this operation cannot be ignored.

439. What causes the uncoiling of the butterfly's proboscis?   This "tongue" uncoils like a paper-snake horn because of inflation brought about by a change in blood pressure. It is initiated by the taste receptors of the tarsi.

SMELL

440. Do insects have a sense of smell? Most insects have a very keen sense of smell, depending upon it for guidance in much of their behavior.

441. What are the insect olfactory organs? They are minute pore plates or thin-walled pegs or cones which in some cases are sunk in pits. All are covered by a thin cuticle and connected with sensory nerve cells that lead to the neurones.

442. Where are the olfactory organs located? They are primarily on the antennae although sometimes also on the maxillary and labial palpi. A drone Honeybee may have as many as 30,000 receptors on each antenna. The *Pieris* butterflies receive only about one-half of their smell stimuli with the antennal receptors, getting the other half with the palpi. The aquatic Hydrophilid Beetle seems to get all of its smell stimuli with the palpi (possibly because it uses its antennae for a special respiratory purpose).

443. How acute is an insect's sense of smell? Not all insects have an equally acute smell sense. It is difficult to compare it with man's because factors of nutrition, humidity, and pressure alter it considerably. In many cases insects show a vastly lower threshold of sensitivity to odors than does man, but this was brought out in experimental work with specific chemicals and did not take into account differences in age, nutritional state, sex, feeding habits, etc., of the insect, which in nature would be significant. However, the Honeybee can distinguish the essence of orange from forty-three other odors, so undoubtedly its olfactory sense is sufficiently acute to meet the demands of daily life.

444. Of what value is the sense of smell to insects? It is used by the insect in almost countless ways: as a means of recognition of its own kind or of an outsider; in the recognition of the opposite sex of its own species; in the search for food; in the search for the proper host upon which to lay its eggs; or in orientation and finding its way back to the nest.

445. How do insects use smell in the recognition of their own kind? In ants, for example, the sense of smell has become in many ways more important than the sense of sight. Each colony has its characteristic odor compounded of the basic odor of the insect, the elements of the soil, the food that has been brought in, and probably of something yet unrecognized by man. This smell becomes associated with each individual and determines its acceptance and inclusion in the group and the rejection of an individual from another colony.

446. What is an example of an insect using smell to locate the opposite sex? Male moths are particularly keen in spotting the location of a female of their own species. Forty or fifty of them have been known to gather around a box in which a virgin female had been concealed, even though she was no longer present. A male Saturniid has been known to react to the presence of a female a mile away within ten to twelve minutes of the time of her arrival; and there are even reports of one having sensed the female presence a full five miles distant.

447. Does the ordinary observer have an opportunity to see an insect in the act of smelling? If one has ever seen a Cockroach waving his antennae in the general direction of a piece of ham, one has seen the smell receptors in action. Scarab Beetles may be seen searching for dung with their antennae outstretched in front of them and with the clubs of the antenna spread apart so that each platelike component will offer full surface area to volatile particles in the air.

448. Do caterpillars have a sense of smell? Many caterpillars are drawn to odors not detectable by man. They use their sense of smell in finding their food plant and, in the case of gregarious larvae, in finding each other or tracing their way back to the nest.

VISION

449. What kind of eyes do insects have? Most insects have a pair of large *compound eyes* and a variable number of small, simple eyes, or *ocelli*.

450. Do any larvae have compound eyes? The larvae of those insects having incomplete metamorphosis, the Exopterygota, have compound eyes. The larvae of the Endopterygota have ocelli only, with the exception of *Corethra,* a small fly related to the Mosquitoes, and *Panorpa,* a Scorpion Fly.

451. What is the structure of the compound eye? It is composed of a group of separate units known as *ommatidia.* Each ommatidium has an outer cornea, or corneal lens, made up of three layers, each with a different refractive index; a crystalline cone lying behind the cornea; and, at the base, seven or eight elongated pigment cells called *retinal cells,* which are grouped around an optic rod, the *rhabdome.* A nerve leads from the basement membrane of each ommatidium to the optic nerve. An ommatidium is partly surrounded by pigmented cells, the *iris cells,* which prevent light from passing across from one ommatidium to another.

452. What are the tiny hexagonal areas one can see in the compound eye? Each is a tiny *facet* that makes up the mosaic of the surface of the eye. Each facet is the outer surface of a single ommatidium.

453. How many facets are there in an individual compound eye? The number varies. Some worker ants may have only 6 to 9; the Housefly has 4,000; a Dytiscid Water Beetle has 9,000; butterflies have from 2,000 to 27,000; and Dragonflies have 10,000–30,000.

454. Is the number of facets any indication of visual acuity? The number of facets seems to affect the resolving power, which means the ability to separate two lines so that they may appear distinct from each other.

455. Are the facets the same size in any one eye? Not always. In Tabanid Flies, especially the males, the facets over the top and front of the eyes are much larger. The same is true in Dragonflies. In some of the flies the line of demarcation between the two kinds of facets is very distinct; and in some beetles they have become partially or completely separated. The separation in several genera of Mayflies is so marked that the upper set of ommatidia are elevated much like a "stovepipe hat."

456. Is there any difference in the visual acuity of different-sized facets?   In some species there is evidence that the larger-sized facets are used for night vision, the smaller ones for day vision. The smaller facets below give more exact impressions.

457. To what range of radiant energy wave lengths is the insect eye sensitive?   It is sensitive to wave lengths ranging from 2,537 to to 9,000 Ångstrom units (Å.), which is a far broader sensitivity than that of the human eye.

458. Do insects have form perception?   Most insects have some form perception but it is not sharp. Many insects show a marked preference for vertical lines as is evidenced by flies alighting on vertical strings and cracks. It has been shown that bees cannot distinguish between solid squares, circles, and triangles; but if the figures are broken up into patterns the bees can discriminate, preferring the figure with the greatest number of subdivisions. This may not be due to their ability to recognize a pattern as much as it is a response to the "flicker effect" of the broken pattern.

459. Do insects have depth perception?   Depth perception of some sort is important to an animal who has to catch its prey; fortunately most insects have it to a degree. Although they do not have binocular vision that can be compared with man's, it is true that when one eye is covered their depth perception is markedly affected. The criterion of depth seems to depend upon the angle of simultaneous stimulation of corresponding points of the retina of the two eyes.

460. Do insects have color vision?   Most insects have true color vision, but one must remember that the ability to distinguish colors is not proof of color vision unless one is sure that colors are not mixed with other waves of radiant energy and that they are of the same brightness. Insects are definitely sensitive to certain of the light rays of the color spectrum, although they appear to be comparatively insensitive to the red end, seldom reacting beyond the orange-red ray at 6,500 Å., although some butterflies and the Firefly *Photinus* do react up to 6,900 Å. At the other end of the spectrum they are exceedingly sensitive, reacting to ultraviolet rays as far down as 2,537 Å., which is considerably farther down than man can go. There are of

course many exceptions; some ants may see infrared and some butterflies discriminate between yellow and green better than than they do
between colors in the blue range, although most butterflies see clearly
and prefer violet, purple, and blue. Bees distinguish between the yellow-green group, the blue, and the blue-violet.

**461. Does the insect eye have any potentialities that the human
eye lacks?**   The eyes of bees and ants have been shown to have a
polarization analyzer that man can get only from his optician. It has
been suggested that the eight radially arranged retinal cells of the ommatidia give patterns of different intensities depending upon the direction from which the light is received.

462. How has polarization ability been demonstrated by insects?
Foraging bees, returning to the hive, are able to communicate to the
other members of the colony the direction and the distance of the
food supply which they have found. This is done by using the sun as
a point of reference in a dance routine which they perform on the
side of the hive.

463. What is the structure of the ocelli?   An ocellus usually has a
corneal lens and a crystalline lens. It acts primarily as a photorecep-
tive cell usually capable of little more than distinguishing between
light and dark.

464. How well do caterpillars see?   Bearing in mind that they have
only ocelli, one can appreciate that they see poorly. Most caterpillars
probably do not see more than one or two centimeters distant with
a single ocellus. However, *Lymantria* larvae, using all of their ocelli,
are able to see more than a foot away and are able to distinguish two
silhouettes, one 3.6 inches tall and one 4 inches tall, choosing the
taller of the two.

465. Are eyes different in day-flying and night-flying insects?   In
most day-flying insects the ommatidia are completely surrounded by
pigmented cells through which light cannot pass. Each ommatidium
therefore receives light only from an object directly above it. Thus
the complete image is made up of tiny bits and is called a mosaic, or
apposition image. Most nocturnal insects on the other hand have more
elongate ommatidia in which the pigmented cells are concentrated

forward near the crystalline cone. As a result the light rays can cross through adjacent ommatidia and form a superposition image. Nocturnal insects are able to adapt slightly to changes in light intensity by expanding and contracting the pigment cells.

466. Can insects move or focus their eyes? No. Insects are near-sighted; distant objects are blurred. Optimum distance of perception of stationary objects is probably but a few inches, possibly up to a yard. Moving objects can be detected more easily because the image moves across more than one ommatidium, and can therefore be detected at a greater distance. Dragonflies can see a waving net many yards distant.

467. Why do the eyes of some moths gleam at night? Some species of nocturnal moths have a layer of tracheal tubes at the back of the eye. This reflects light.

468. Why do the eyes of some insects looked mottled? Many butterflies have a central dark spot, or *pseudopupil,* sometimes surrounded by a varying number of smaller spots. The central spot marks the point where light rays are being absorbed by the rhabdome. The other spots may be due to migratory pigment cells that are producing reflections.

469. Are any insects blind? The workers of some species of ants are blind. They have vestigial eyes which, for us, are reminders of the oft-repeated adage, "Disuse leads to atrophy." This same reduction in eyes has occurred in species of several orders, notably the Orthoptera, Coleoptera, Collembola, and Thysanura, that have taken up life in dark caves. They show all degrees of reduction and degeneration even to complete absence of structures.

LIGHT PRODUCTION

470. What insects produce light? Many insects glow, although sometimes the luminosity is not of their own making but is due to the presence in their bodies of luminous bacteria. However, there are many insects that do produce light. The well-known Fireflies belonging to the family of beetles, Lampyridae, and the closely related family

Phengodidae, produce light in all of their instars, even the egg. Several species of Ground Beetles (Carabidae) and of Click Beetles (Elateridae) produce light. So also do some Midges (Chironomidae) and Springtails, as well as all of the Fungus Gnats (Mycetophilidae). The European Tiger Moth, *Arctia caja,* gives off a luminous secretion.

471. How is the light produced? It is the result of an oxidation process in which luciferin is oxidized in the presence of an enzyme luciferase.

472. Where are the light-producing organs located? In some Phengodid beetles there are eleven or twelve segmentally arranged pairs of organs located along the sides of the body and one under the prothorax, but in other beetles the organs are on the pronotum and underneath the base of the abdomen. In the Lampyrids they are principally on the under side of the sixth and seventh abdominal segments.

473. What is the color of insect-produced light? It varies from greenish-blue to golden-red and is entirely free of ultraviolet. It occupies the region of the light spectrum to which the human eye is most sensitive. Some species may produce more than one color: a Phengodid Beetle in the tropics emits red light from the head and greenish-yellow from the sides of the body. *Pyrophorus,* a Click Beetle of the tropics, commonly known as the "cucujo," produces red light in the abdomen when it is in flight but green light in the thorax when it is at rest.

474. Why is insect light considered unique? It releases practically no heat. In *Pyrophorus* the heat produced is $\frac{1}{80,000}$ of the heat that would be produced by a candle flame of the same intensity. Only recently has man been able to manufacture so cold a light, and then only at cost that makes it impractical.

475. Why do Firefly lights sometimes flash on and off? The flashing seems to be regulated by nervously controlled cells which adjust the oxygen that is supplied to the photogenic tissue; but the stimulus that innervates these cells is not known. The intermittent flashing is done only at certain periods, and some photogenic insects never flash intermittently but glow continuously.

476. Do Firefly lights glow just at night or is it that we only see them at night? Our common eastern Firefly, *Photinus marginalis,* begins flashing just at dusk and stops when the evening is fully dark, although a few individuals may keep flashing much later. Other species of the genus flash until midnight or so.

477. Is there any pattern or system to the flashing? Each species has a characteristic type of flashing as well as a characteristic color and intensity. The flashings, usually more brilliant in the male, may be single or they may be in twos or, as in one species, in series of 3, 4, or 5 flashes by the male, to be answered by 1, 2, or 3 from the female. In one species the beetles, flying close to the ground in an undulating flight, flash only as they ascend. In the tropics synchronous flashing by many individuals has been observed; but this is probably coincidental, being determined by factors of temperature, humidity, and pressure affecting all individuals simultaneously. It has even been noticed that individuals on one bank of a stream will flash all together, while those on the other bank are following in a different rhythm.

478. Is light production of any value to the insects? Most biologists think that any benefit from light production is incidental. The larvae of Fungus Gnats are carnivorous; perhaps their luminosity attracts or lures their prey. The light of luminescent Fireflies appears to attract the opposite sex; but their nonluminescent relatives seem to be just as successful in finding mates.

479. Has man ever made use of insect light? Many a child has gone to bed with a bottle of glowing Fireflies pressed to his body beneath the covers and pondered upon the potential use of so much illumination. Tropical natives frequently tie specimens of *Pyrophorus* to their ankles as they travel through the jungles at night, or carry a dozen or so of them in a cheesecloth bag to light the trail. Tropical belles fasten them to their hair as attractive ornaments. There is one report of a doctor in the tropics performing an emergency operation at night by the light of some large tropical beetles when the regular lighting failed.

VIII. INSECT BEHAVIOR AND ACTIVITIES

480. Is insect behavior instinctive?   The word *instinct* has been so widely abused as to be almost meaningless. All kinds of things like "mother love," "mother fixation," "forethought," "fear," and the like, are vaguely attributed to instinct. Much, perhaps most, insect behavior is *inherent* or *innate;* i.e., due to a definite set of hereditary characters. It is often initiated by external stimuli, the response to which may be determined by the insect's physiological condition at that particular time.

481. Is insect behavior stereotyped?   Most of it is. Each insect has a set of structures and a behavior pattern nearly identical with those of every other individual of its species. Little is left to chance, little is left to the individual's decision (of which it is incapable) on the basis of learning from past experience. In most insects a small amount of behavior is subject to some slight changes, i.e., is modifiable. But this usually concerns only minor details such as which of two almost identical leaves a caterpillar should eat first. Inherited factors caused the caterpillar to develop as a caterpillar, with a set of leaf-eating jaws and an appetite for certain leaves, and to have a behavior pattern that leads it to climb up objects (plant stems) of a certain size, shape, and odor.

482. Does this explain the insects' great success?   To a large degree it does. The insects have been able to evolve fixed behavior patterns, usually of great complexity, that make certain the survival of the species and the consequent continuation of the behavior patterns. Just as the structurally abnormal, less efficient individuals are "weeded out" by natural selection, so are the behaviorally less efficient ones eliminated.

483. Can insects evolve changed behavior?   Some can, just as they can evolve changed structures. Both are equally subject to inherited variation and to selection of the best-adapted individuals. Industrial melanism studies have shown that in a soot-darkened environment darker-colored individuals are more successful in escaping the attacks of birds. But this is only when they rest on dark backgrounds. They have evolved the habit of resting on such matching backgrounds along with the darker coloration. Light-colored individuals similarly rest on light-colored backgrounds.

484. Are any insects capable of learning? A good many can learn and "profit by experience" to a limited degree, both by habituation and by association.

485. What is habituation learning? Meal Moth larvae (*Ephestia*) can be made to crawl around and around a circular course. Removed from this they continue for some time to crawl in a circular path. *Drosophila* flies are normally repelled by the odor of peppermint; but if reared with the odor for their entire larval life they will be attracted to it. An Ichneumonid Wasp that normally oviposits only in *Ephestia* larvae, to which the characteristic odor attracts it, will show a marked preference for the larvae of the Wax Moth if it was reared in these.

486. What are some examples of learning by association? Cockroaches, which normally avoid light, can be trained to stay in the light if they receive an electric shock whenever they approach a dark area. They also learn to follow the pattern of a maze. Young ant and bee workers learn much by association in following certain pathways to sources of food. Bees and wasps can be trained rather quickly when a positive association method is employed, learning by rewards. A number of dishes are placed on variously patterned backgrounds: a square, a triangle, a circle, an *X* mark, radiating lines, etc. In one dish only is sugar water, in the others just water. After a trial-and-error period the insects come directly to the sugar water. When this is moved, say from the *X* mark to the triangle, the insects return to the *X* mark where there is only water.

487. Is such learning retained long? Sometimes it is. Bees have been known to return in the spring to the location of a fountain where they got water in the autumn, even though the fountain was no longer there. A female Hunting Wasp who prepares a nest before searching for prey makes a complicated series of location flights over and around it before departing. She may go far away and not return to the spot for some time but when she returns she goes to the exact spot with precision. Tests have been made by changing or moving prominent landmarks near the nest. A burrow in smooth sand, for example, might be inside a small triangle of pebbles. If these were moved six inches, the wasp in returning would alight inside the triangle, not where the nest was.

488. Do bees and other insects show a "homing" sense? Persistent although this idea is, it seems to be without foundation. Ants chiefly follow odor trails. Young bees must learn the landmarks about the hive and, as they grow older, in an increasing radius outward. Older bees must learn the new landmarks if the hive is moved, an important matter when hives are moved in orange groves during pollination time. Bees also orient themselves by the sun, and to some degree keep up with its daily movement by a certain time sense.

489. Do insects show a sense of time? Bees have been trained to come for food at a particular time of day. This appears to be under the control of an internal "physiological clock" since the sense of timing persists even when they are kept in controlled darkness. Lowered temperatures, which slow down the bees' internal activities, impair the time sense.

490. Is there any evidence of a time sense in bees under natural conditions? Bees show a very definite time sense in visiting particular flowers that open only at a certain time of day. There are morning-opening flowers and afternoon-opening flowers; and only certain bees will visit each. This is important in insects that are good pollinators.

491. Do any insects show a rhythmic behavior? Quite a few do, the most interesting of which show a rhythm that persists independently of external factors. One species of Firefly, although kept constantly in the dark, will still light up at the normal time of 7 P.M.; another will persist in starting its period of flashing at intervals of 24 hours, for four days after being placed in uniform darkness. Meadow Grasshoppers that normally sing in the latter part of the day, 12 hours after the last period of darkness, if kept under conditions where the light periods are reversed, will continue to sing 12 hours after the last period of darkness even though it means they sing in the morning. Crickets show a diurnal rhythm of general activity which will persist for two weeks even when kept in continuous darkness at constant temperature and humidity. Studies of such physiological clocks show that many insect activities are due to internal timing mechanisms rather than to simple external factors.

492. Do any insects learn by precept?   Among the social insects the younger workers definitely learn associatively by following the precept of older workers. Since worker ants may live for several years, there will always be a number of older workers in an established colony. There is, of course, no question of deliberate instruction; but the callow workers do follow older work starters and thus by association learn paths and food sources.

493. Do any insects communicate with each other?   Ants certainly transmit information to one another concerning the existence, if not the exact location, of foraging grounds. The remarkable work of Dr. Karl von Frisch has shown that Honeybees have an elaborate system of communication with their fellow hive members. It may be that other insects have equally exact systems of communication but that man has been lacking in the perception and the ingenuity to comprehend them. Many insects make sounds, and since those same insects have ears attuned to those sounds there is undoubtedly some kind of communication.

494. How do Honeybees inform each other of the location of a foraging ground?   They do this by a series of dances. A round dance made up of a series of figure eights attracts the attention of the other workers, the intensity of the performance being relative to the abundance of the food. A tail-wagging dance with straight runs interspersed with the figure eights indicates the direction of the food supply in relation to the sun. If the straight runs are made upward on the vertical side of the hive, the food lies in the direction of the sun; if at a 30-degree angle to the right, then the food lies 30 degrees to the right of the position of the sun. The smell and taste of the food brought back by the dancing forager automatically transmits the information about what food will be found.

495. Do any insects show territorial behavior like that of birds?
The exclusion of strangers from a colony (in which the colony odor
is the main factor) is a type of territoriality. This may extend to a
colony's foraging trails. Among Solitary Wasps the females of some
species are notoriously quarrelsome with others of their same species,
driving them away from their nests. This is especially marked among
the Bembicine Wasps that provision their nests progressively, even
though they do not tend to nest together. The same is true of the big
Carpenter Bees (*Xylocopa*). Some Dragonflies have regular "beats"
and perches, from which they dart out, often chasing other individuals
of their species; but this may be a mating rather than a territorial behavior. Many butterflies are quite pugnacious. Some of these such as
the Admirals (*Limenitis*) have regular perches which they occupy
day after day. A Red Admiral (*Vanessa atalanta*) may be seen evening after evening at the same perch, from the vicinity of which it
drives other butterflies. We have watched male Hackberry and Tawny
Emperor Butterflies (*Asterocampa*) do the same in a grove of Desert
Hackberry trees (*Celtis*), each male having an exact perching spot on
a trunk, to which it invariably returned after each aerial "combat."
Such actions are definitely territorial, and show at least the insects'
ability to learn and recognize landmarks. Unfortunately this subject
has been little investigated.

ASSEMBLAGES

496. How do insects benefit by assemblages?   Some caterpillars
(many Notodontidae) that as individuals gain protection by as-
suming warning positions or by ejecting irritating secretions, acquire
still greater protection by the mass display. Sometimes assemblages
for the purposes of hibernation (as with Ladybirds) gain warmth by
the activities of the many individuals. The majority of aggregations of
insects probably indicate gregariousness and are of no great benefit.

497. What are sleeping assemblages?   The Monarch Butterflies,
when migrating, assemble by the thousands at night, sometimes in the
same place year after year. Heliconiid Butterflies in the tropics often
return nightly to the same trees, hundreds of individuals of several
species sleeping together. One individual was recorded as sleeping

every night for more than two months within a few inches of the same spot. Bees and wasps often form sleeping groups.

498. What are mud-puddle associations?   These are not so much associations as they are a "gathering of the boys at the pub." Young bachelor males of many species of butterflies collect to sip at mud puddles with a gregariousness that lasts only until the later-emerging females arrive. The Clouded Sulphur, the Tiger Swallowtails, the White Admiral, and the Red Spotted Purple are noted for this habit, often forming groups of one hundred to two hundred individuals. The highly protected Lycid Beetles have been observed forming similar drinking assemblages.

499. What are insect processions?   The larvae of some species (*Sciara*) of Fungus Gnats (Mycetophilidae) are famous for their gregarious habits. Large numbers often travel over the ground in a file so close together that the group resembles a large worm or snake many feet long. They sometimes pile up on top of each other, the top ones going faster until they get in front and then come down and add their bodies to the bottom layer. These processions are often called army worms or snake worms. Another famous procession is that of the European Processionary Caterpillars (*Thaumotopoea*). They spend the winter in a communal web, going out in the spring in a long straight file to feed. Sometimes these files are forty feet long, and made up of as many as three hundred individuals. The line has no leader; each individual follows the trail of whoever happens to be in front.

MIGRATION

500. Do insects migrate?   If one defines migration (as in birds) as a seasonal movement for purposes of breeding, with a return flight of the same individuals, then insects do not migrate. However, many insects undertake mass movements with seasonal regularity which in the broad sense may be called migration. The Monarch Butterfly, *Danaus plexippus,* is the only one that makes a return flight; however, this is not similar to the return of birds in migration because the Monarchs that go back south in the spring are the offspring of the ones that started north in the fall. They leave the tropical or subtropical regions in the spring flying northward, the females laying eggs as they go. Their progeny, after reaching adulthood, continue the northward flight into Canada. In the fall they work southward in tremendous numbers, sometimes roosting at night by the thousands in the same place similar swarms have roosted in previous years.

Another famous migrant is *Vanessa cardui,* the Painted Lady. It is probably the most migratory of all insects. Swarms forty miles wide and containing an estimated three billion individuals have passed through Portachula Pass in Venezuela. Each spring flying masses of this species cross the Mediterranean from Africa. There is no return flight.

A Calico Moth (*Utetheisa*) and the Death's Head Sphinx, *Acherontia atropos,* as well as several other moths, migrate north to Europe from Africa each year. A famous Owlet Moth, *Agrotis ypsilon,* flies north to the cool Himalayas from India. A few species of Dragonflies sometimes take long flights that resemble migrations. And of course each continent has a species of Locust that at times builds up an enormous population and then produces long-winged forms that take flight in incredible hordes. One such was once reported over the Red Sea to be 2,000 miles in extent. *Libytheana bachmani,* a Snout Butterfly, was reported in 1921 in Texas to have formed a swarm with a 250-mile front that was eighteen days crossing one point; at one time their numbers in passing were reported to be 1,250,000 a minute.

501. What causes these migrations? No one knows, other than that they occur when an enormous population has built up. In the case of the Locusts it certainly is not hunger, because they do not feed during most of the flight, but live on the reserves stored in the body. It is only when they settle down that the Locusts ravish the land of everything edible. Nor is it necessarily for breeding purposes. The Cotton Moth, *Alabama argillacea,* that swarms north in the United States in the fall and that arrives in New York in such numbers that it even gets down into the subways, goes north far beyond the region where there is any cotton on which its larvae must feed.

Occasionally migrating species do get established in new regions but the explanation of the forces that drive the species into these tremendous movements are not understood.

502. Do migrating swarms have a leader?   Apparently not. Each individual seems to be on its own, although they all have a tendency to stay together.

503. Are there any species that make regular round trips as the birds do?   A few, but their trips are not transcontinental, being mostly in mountain regions where they move from the valleys up into the mountains, as does the Bogong Moth of Australia.

504. Are all swarms of insects migrating swarms?   No, many of them are simple dispersal flights that may last for only a few hours or for a few days, taking the insect relatively short distances. Thrips, Aphids, termites, Crickets, beetles, flies, and ants, all under certain conditions, either of overcrowding, the need for new feeding areas, or the requirements of colonizing, may swarm. Other swarms may be so-called nuptial flights, as is the case of Mayflies dancing in great clouds over a stream or a lake shore. These swarms are mostly made up of males which have emerged before the females. When a female enters the swarm she is captured by a male who carries her off. Other swarms have been discussed under the social insects.

505. Are insects dispersed by their own power?   Sometimes. But they are often carried great distances by wind or air currents. The Spruce Aphis, *Lachnis piceae,* has been found on the fresh snow of the icecap of Northeast Land, Spitsbergen, having been carried 800 miles from the Kola Peninsula of Russia. Some aphids spin spiny or waxy filaments or silken threads that bear them aloft.

INACTIVITY—AKINESIS

506. Do insects sleep?   Most insects rest, sometimes from fatigue, sometimes because of a drop in temperature or the fading of the light; and other times at regular intervals. Often, when resting, they are in a comatose condition which can be called sleep.

507. What is estivation?   It is a state of inactivity that enables an animal to live through a period of intense heat or drought. It occurs among animals living in arid or desert regions and in the tropics. The Colorado Potato Beetle estivates in the dry season in the tropics, but further north it hibernates. Certain wood-boring Buprestid Beetles of the tropics have remained in their tunnels for from 10 to 26 years without emergence; it is believed that for much of that time they were in a state of estivation.

508. Do insects hibernate? Hibernation, a state of quiescence induced by the cold, is almost the rule with insects in temperate or arctic regions. The great majority spend the winter in the egg stage. However, many bugs and Scale Insects winter as nymphs; some beetles as larvae; many butterflies and moths as pupae; some beetles and bugs as adults under bark or stones or even in the ground; and many aquatic beetles and bugs in the mud at the bottom of ponds, occasionally coming to the surface on warm winter days (Haliplids and Backswimmers are often seen swimming beneath the ice). Since insects are cold-blooded this hibernation is not comparable to that in warm-blooded animals. In all groups there are some species that depart from the general rule: some butterflies, notably the Mourning Cloak, spend the winter as adults, and Mosquitoes show widely differing habits.

509. Where do Mosquitoes spend the winter? The common species *Culex pipiens* survives the winter because the female seeks shelter in cellars, caves, sheds, or holes in tree trunks, hanging by the thousands in such sheltered spots. Other species, such as the Tree Hole Mosquitoes, live as larvae in the leaves of the Pitcher Plant or in water in tree holes, a spell of premature warm weather bringing the adults out in great numbers. Most species, however, winter over as eggs.

510. Where do Houseflies spend the winter? The adults seek shelter in buildings when the temperature drops much below 60°, coming out again on warm fall days. The majority that survive the entire winter are fertilized females, but only if they have been able to find quarters where the temperature does not go below 20°.

511. Are all the flies that winter in our attics and cellars or sheds Houseflies? A large majority may be the slightly larger Cluster Fly (*Pollenia*), which can stand temperatures down to −1°. An occasional Bluebottle or Greenbottle Fly (*Lucilia*) hibernates in the house.

WALKING

512. What is the gait of insects? When an insect walks it is always supported on a triangle made by the middle leg of one side and the fore and hind legs of the other. The three legs of the tripod are not lifted simultaneously. The foreleg acts as a tractor, the middle leg as a support or for lifting its own side of the body, and the hind leg as the propulsion and turning device. As the insect walks the three legs of one side come to lie on the same spot.

513. How do larvae crawl? Some walk on the thoracic legs as do the adults. Most Sawfly and Lepidoptera larvae have prolegs on the abdomen which move in a series of waves that run forward along the body, the anal pair of legs being carried forward first and then the others in succession. Legless maggots move by peristaltic movements or lateral twistings of the body wall, aided by friction between the body and the surface along which they are moving. Some beetle larvae (Carabidae and Staphylinidae) propel themselves by means of an eversible structure, a *pygopidium,* on the terminal segment of the abdomen. Some flies and Fleas have a similar device. Caterpillars of Geometrid Moths are called Inchworms or Measuring Worms because of the way in which they first bring the abdominal prolegs forward by looping up the abdomen and then push the thoracic legs forward by a flattening of the "loop."

514. How do insects walk on glass or on the ceiling? If a surface is sufficiently rough an insect can cling to it with its sharp tarsal claws, but if the surface is very smooth the insect depends upon adhesive organs on the *pulvilli.* The pulvilli are cushionlike structures on the ventral surface of the tarsal segments. Sometimes they exude a sticky substance; sometimes they are clothed with hollow hairs, the *tenent hairs.* There has been some controversy about whether the pulvilli cling to the surface in the manner of suckers or whether they are held by the surface tension of the fluid secretions; by cohesion or adhesion; or by a combination. Many Diptera and Hymenoptera have a special structure between the tarsal claws which is an additional aid in walking on smooth surfaces.

COURTSHIP

515. How do insects attract their mates?   They do this in a number
of ways. Fireflies flash their lights; Mayflies swarm in great dancing
masses; male Tree Crickets sing; the females of many moths secrete
a particular scent that attracts the males, sometimes from a great distance; many males are elaborately ornamented with horns and knobs
(it would be anthropomorphism to suggest that these attract the opposite sex; certainly they are a factor in recognition); and some
species have a definite pattern of courtship behavior.

516. What is meant by courtship behavior?   It is a stylized behavior displayed before mating; it is usually more strongly shown by
the male, the female playing the more passive or receptive role. It
sometimes consists of a rapid vibration of the wings, a licking of the
female, a circling of the female, or other posturing acts. The most
romantic to our way of thinking is that of the male Dance Flies
(Empididae) who wrap a delectable insect in a mass of silk as a gift
to the female. While she is busy unwrapping the gift and feasting on
it, mating takes place. Not so "romantic" is the male who presents
the wrapping with an inedible stick inside, or even just the wrapping
with nothing inside.

IX. INSECT SOCIETIES

THE SOCIAL INSECTS

517. What are the true social insects?   The true social insects comprise the termites, the ants, many bees, and some wasps.

518. What is a social insect?   In a strict sense a social insect is one that lives in an organized society, the members of which are dependent upon each other. Many insects are *gregarious,* forming associations for the purpose of feeding, sleeping, swarming, migrating, mating, estivating, or hibernating. Their "togetherness" may result in mutual benefits but it involves no interdependence. Such insects may be *sociable,* or *communal,* or *subsocial;* they are not truly social.

519. What are the characteristics of true social insects?   Social insects live in groups; they coöperate with each other to the point of a definite division of labor; they care for their young, feeding them progressively; they often practice trophallaxis; they build nests of varying degrees of complexity; and they usually stem from one matriarch. In respect to each characteristic there is a tremendous variation within each group.

520. What is trophallaxis?   Trophallaxis is the mutual exchange, between members of a society, of food or desirable substances. Adults, sexual and neuter (workers), feed each other with regurgitated substances and feed the developing larvae or nymphs. Often the wasp larvae on being fed or stimulated emit a drop of liquid greatly relished by the stimulating worker. Among termites mutual licking of each other's bodies, on which apparently desirable substances are secreted, is a prominent activity. Among ants the workers constantly lick and mouth the larvae and eggs. The mutual benefits thus exchanged form the strongest bond that holds together the members of a colony.

521. Is trophallaxis ever abused?   Wasp workers, relishing the larval secretions, may often stimulate a larva to give up a drop of its secretion without feeding it. This exploitation may result in larval malnutrition, even starvation. Such workers are actually social parasites in their own society.

522. Does trophallaxis ever take place between nonrelated species? The larvae of many myrmecophiles, especially of beetles, and the caterpillars of many Lycaenid Butterflies, secrete a greatly relished substance from special glands. They are therefore welcomed, attended, and cared for, and often fed by ants, sometimes even at the expense of the ant brood.

523. How did insect social life originate? Most insect parents never live to see their offspring. Insect societies began to evolve when the lives of the parents became long enough to overlap those of their offspring, and when modifications of behavior evolved that kept the adults and the young together and, so to speak, gave the adults an interest in caring for the young. Trophallaxis is certainly such an interest. It is absent in bees, which must have evolved other cohesive attractions. Even in a primitive society enough advantage would accrue to encourage (by natural selection) the ever greater evolution of such bonds.

524. Is there any evidence today of possible ways in which insect societies may have evolved? Many Solitary Wasps (Sphecoidea and Vespoidea) and bees (Apoidea) prepare special nests which they provision with food, and in which they lay eggs. Thus the emerging offspring is provided with food by a parent it will never see. This represents at least a first step toward a parent-offspring association.

525. What is the next important step in the evolution of an insect society? The next step is represented by Solitary Wasps that lay the egg in a cell with an inadequate supply of food, or even with none, and then return from time to time with more prey (usually flies). Here the mother feeds the young larva directly. Some species of the genus *Synagris* do this; others of the genus *Bembix* go a step further and feed the young larva regularly. Some wasps of the genus *Zethus* even chew the food into a paste before feeding it to the larva, thus establishing a more intimate contact between mother and offspring.

526. Are there many Solitary Wasps?   There are several thousand species of Solitary Wasps in the world. Most of them are hunting wasps.

527. Are there many Solitary Bees?   There are thousands of species of Solitary Bees in North America alone.

528. Are the Solitary Bees varied?   Some are only an eighth of an inch long; others are larger than the Bumblebees. The young of all species feed on stored nectar and pollen, but many species parasitize others, laying their eggs in the other bees' nests where their young feed on the hosts' stores. Most carry pollen on the extremely hairy hind legs; but some, the Leaf Cutters, have special rows of pollen-carrying bristles beneath the abdomen. The majority dig tunnels in the ground; but some make or use tunnels in wood or hollow stems, and others make mud or clay cells. The material used inside the nests are also diverse: some use shredded plant fibers, others use clay, and the Leaf Cutters cut pieces of leaves (or flower petals) with which to construct thimble-shaped containers in the nests.

529. Do any Solitary Bees have habits that indicate the beginning of a social structure?   A number of Solitary Bees are called *sociable* because of their habit of building their single-celled or many-celled nests adjoining those of other bees, sometimes in a burrow with a common entrance. In a very few species the individuals may take on special tasks, such as acting as guardians of the entrance for the whole group.

530. Are there any insects other than the truly social ones that care for their young?   A few species of bugs remain with their eggs until they hatch and until the nymphs have gone through one or two instars. The nymphs may cling to the underside of the female or be herded by her from leaf to leaf. A few beetles provide some maternal care: the Horned *Passalus* and one Rove Beetle (Staphylinidae) guard their young; Ambrosia Beetles (Ipidae) and some Engraver Beetles (Scolytidae) mingle with their larvae in the tunnels they excavate in wood, providing food for them. The female Earwig is noted for her faithfulness in brooding a batch of 40 to 90 eggs in a chamber which she has made in the ground; keeping them in a pile, frequently mouthing them to clean them of mold and, if necessary, moving them to dryer ground. After the eggs hatch she stays with them through several instars, fighting off intruders. The Embiids, too, have a parent-offspring relationship as they run back and forth together in the tunnels they excavate under bark, in the ground, and under manure. The larvae participate in lining the tunnels with silk and share in a minimum of communal living. All such associations could in time evolve into societies.

531. Is there any group of insects that has division of labor but does not form a true society?   A few Halictid Bees have most of the characteristics of social insects but are usually not classed with the true social species because their colony is not made up of individuals with common parentage. They may be on the way to evolving a truly social life not based on the conventional pattern.

CASTES

532. What are the castes in an insect society?   Basically there are two: reproductive individuals, *males* (occasionally called *kings*) and *queens;* and nonreproductive ones, *workers.* This is the primary division of labor: one caste carries on reproduction, and usually founds the colony; the other does not reproduce save in rare exceptions, and does all the work.

533. Are there ever more than these two castes?   Some authorities treat the reproductive males, the reproductive females, and the different types of neuters, the workers and soldiers, as different castes. This may obscure the fact that the fundamental difference lies between reproductive and nonreproductive individuals.

534. How is the sex of an individual determined?   The sex of an individual is determined at the time of fertilization, the union of egg and sperm. It is of special importance in ants, bees, and wasps, for in these insects fertilized eggs regularly develop into female individuals; unfertilized eggs develop, but only into males. In the termites all eggs are fertilized and the resulting individuals may be either males or females.

535. What is the difference between the termite workers and the workers of ants, bees, and wasps?   A termite worker may be a nonreproductive male or a nonreproductive female. All ant, bee, and wasp workers are nonreproductive females.

536. What determines whether an individual may develop into a worker or into a reproductive individual?   This is apparently due to different mechanisms in ants, bees, wasps, and termites; and even within the bees there are at least two different mechanisms.

537. What determines whether a female wasp larva will develop into a worker or a queen?   The chief factor is nutrition. With sufficient and adequate food the larva develops into a queen. If underfed or improperly fed, or exploited too much in trophallaxis, it develops into a worker.

538. What determines whether a female Honeybee larva will develop into a worker or a queen?   Here it is definitely the quality of the food. Every larva is fed by the workers on *royal jelly* for at least three days. If it receives this during its entire larval life it develops into a queen. But if, after the first three days, the larva is fed *bee bread,* it develops into a worker. Queen larvae are reared in large cells, worker larvae in small ones.

539. What is royal jelly?   It is a white paste secreted from special glands connected with the mouth of the worker Honeybee. It contains hormones. Royal jelly is fed to all Honeybee larvae for three days and to those who become queens for their entire larval life.

540. What is bee bread?   This is the name sometimes used for the mixture of honey and pollen that is fed to most Honeybee larvae after the third day.

541. How is caste determined in other social bees?   In Bumblebees the larvae destined to develop into queens are reared in larger cells. There appears to be no distinctive food given to them; perhaps there is special hormone feeding. In the tropical Stingless Bees (Meliponinae) at least some genetic factors appear to be involved in the production of workers.

542. How is the caste of an individual determined in ants? The determining factor seems to be something within the egg; of course, only potentially female larvae can develop into workers. But there may be an inhibiting hormone involved as well (as in termites).

543. What determines the caste of an individual in termites? Factors of sex and heredity seem to have no part. A termite nymph apparently can develop into any of the castes or subcastes; but most of them do not, ending their development as nymphlike workers. The reason seems to be that each special caste and subcaste secretes, on the surface of the body, a hormonelike substance that inhibits nymphs from developing into that particular type of individual. These substances are passed about the colony by the constant grooming and licking of each other in which termites indulge. As long as the colony's quota of soldiers is complete, for example, there will be enough soldier-inhibiting hormone reaching each developing nymph to prevent it developing into a soldier. Let the proportion of soldiers drop; the amount of soldier-inhibiting hormone then lessens; and some nymphs will develop into soldiers, filling the quota again.

544. The word *drone* has come to imply laziness. Why? Because drones appear by comparison with the bustling workers to be lazy and self-indulgent. Drones are the males of the Honeybees; their only duty is to fertilize the queens when they are aloft in the marriage flight. After performing this one task they die, their genital organs having been left in the body of the females.

545. How are drones different from workers? The drones are males, the workers are sterile females. Drones are heavier-bodied, having larger eyes, and of course lack the sting and the special pollen-carrying structures of the workers.

546. How does the Honeybee queen determine the sex of each individual as she lays her eggs? If a droplet of fluid containing sperms is added to an egg as it is laid, the egg becomes fertilized and develops into a female (usually a worker). The unfertilized egg, from which sperms are withheld, develops into a drone. Worker eggs are laid in cells slightly smaller in diameter than those in which drone eggs are laid. Apparently it is the diameter of the cell that mechanically stimulates the abdomen of the egg-laying queen to add or withhold sperms.

547. Are all queens of social insects winged?   Most ant queens are winged, as are most males. When they settle down to found or join a colony they remove their wings. In some of the specialized ants, such as the Legionary Ants, the queens are wingless from the start; and in some other ants the males are degenerate, wingless, and almost pupiform.

548. How do ant and termite queens differ from workers?   Usually the queen is much larger than the worker. Of course she has the scars on her thorax where her wings were attached. Her abdomen is usually somewhat swollen, due to the large ovaries within it. The abdomen of some queen termites may be three inches long and more than an inch in diameter, looking like a small potato. In some ants the very large young queen who goes out on her mating and colonization flight carries along a number of tiny workers clinging to her body or legs. Queens and males, especially of ants, usually have very well-developed eyes, although the workers may have reduced or vestigial ones.

549. What are some of the types or subcastes of workers?   Among both ants and termites, part of the workers of many species are *soldiers,* usually larger and with much more powerful jaws than ordinary workers. Among termites some soldiers are of a peculiar type, known as *nasuti,* with the front of the head protruding in a long, tubular snout; through this a sticky irritating liquid can be squirted at disturbers of the colony. In some ants certain workers have especially powerful jaws and function as seed-crushers for the colony. In the genus *Colobopsis,* which nests in hollow twigs, are found workers with an enormous head, flat in front, that act as living plugs for the entrance of the nest. In several groups of ants some of the workers act as living storage pots. Our North American Honey Ant (*Myrmecocystus mexicanus horti-deorum*) feeds on honeydew from Aphids and Scale Insects and the sweet exudate from Oak Galls. Certain workers that remain in the underground nest chambers are able to take in and store in their crops so much honeydew that their abdomens grow as round and large as a large pea. They are known as *repletes*. Unable to walk, they hang in scores in chambers. When stimulated they regurgitate the honeydew to the other workers. An Australian Ant has evolved the same habit, and various other species have semireplete workers.

550. Is there ever more than one queen in a colony? The queens of some wasps of the genus *Polistes* tend to be gregarious and build their colonies together. These queens are often sisters who in the early spring have returned to the site of the old nest for a few days and thus start together to build their own. An aggregation of wasps may thus appear to be a single colony with several queens when actually it is made up of several colonies. Sometimes, too, a young queen deserts her own beginning nest and moves to that of another young queen.

Ant colonies sometimes combine in the same way and so seem to have more than one queen; they also occasionally adopt young queens, so that several will be found in one colony.

The termites often have secondary reproductive individuals beside the original king and queen.

551. What colonies have kings? Only the termites have kings. Male ants, bees, and wasps die after the mating flight.

552. If a queen dies who takes over her duties? Termites have a secondary reproductive caste, called neoteinic kings and queens, which may be thought of as replacements. Sometimes when a queen dies, sterile workers lay eggs. Sometimes they do it anyway even when she is still alive. This builds up a colony of nonworking males and so may be disastrous. When a Honeybee colony loses a queen a young female larva is immediately transferred to a larger cell, is kept on the necessary diet of royal jelly, and thus becomes a queen.

553. Why are the terms *king* and *queen* misnomers? Among termites the kings and queens, and among Hymenoptera the queens, are merely sexually reproductive individuals. They do no ruling, guiding, or directing. The queen lays the eggs and thus is the mother of the rest of the colony. She is larger and lives longer; and the life of the colony revolves about her.

554. Do queens live longer than workers?   They invariably do, barring accidents. It is believed (on deductive reasoning) that some queen termites may live one hundred years or more. Queen ants have been kept alive in captivity for fifteen or more years, workers for up to five years. A Honeybee queen may live for two or three years; the average worker during the busy summer lives only six weeks.

555. What do ants feed their larvae?   In general ants feed their larvae whatever is the food of the species, although it may be chewed up and more or less predigested. Some primitive Ponerine Ants, which are carnivorous, feed them the prey scarcely dismembered.

556. What do ants eat?   Army Ants, Driver Ants, and most primitive ants feed on other insects and small invertebrates; some specialize on certain types of prey, such as other ants and termites. Other ants are more or less exclusively seed eaters; still others live mostly on honeydew secreted by Aphids, Scale Insects, Leaf Hoppers, Tree Hoppers, etc. Leaf Cutter Ants cultivate fungi which make up their entire food. Many are general feeders or scavengers on a wide variety of whatever is available, often showing a marked preference for sweets. If we are to be successful in controlling them in our houses we must know the food preference of the species.

557. What are agricultural insects?   A few species of ants and termites that supposedly cultivate plants are called agricultural insects. Ants of the tribe Attini of Central and South America (one species gets up into Texas), commonly called Leaf Cutter Ants, cut pieces out of leaves and carry them down into their nests as a medium on which to grow fungi. They particularly relish the fruiting bodies of these fungi. Cultures of the fungi are "treasured"; queens leaving the colony to start a new home carry a "starting" of the culture just as early New England brides carried a starting of yeast. Other Attines raise the fungi on feces of other insects or on stolen grain or miscellaneous plant debris. In Africa and Asia some species of termites cultivate fungi on their own excrement set apart in separate chambers.

558. What are the rings of plants that often grow around ant nests?
Contrary to popular opinion these are not gardens planted by the ants, but are growths that have sprung up from seeds that have been

dropped or discarded by them. *Pheidole* and *Pogonomyrmex* are often called Harvester Ants because of these plantations around their nests. They eat and store seeds.

559. What do termites feed their young? The chief, usually the only, food of most termites is wood and the substances contained in the wood cells. They feed the young nymphs this wood substance more or less chewed up or predigested. The nymphs begin feeding for themselves very early and then eat whatever the adults eat. Some termites of course grow fungi in their nests, as the Leaf Cutter Ants do, either feeding on it or infecting the wood with it.

560. What do wasps feed their larvae? The great majority use insects and other prey, usually well chewed to a paste. Often they add a little nectar. Some wasps subsist entirely on nectar and pollen themselves.

COLONIES

561. What is distinctive about each social insect colony? Its odor. Each colony, even of the same species, has its distinctive odor. An individual lacking this is immediately assaulted and killed or thrown out. Watch two bees or ants meeting; there is a momentary twiddling together of antennae, perhaps of palpi, with perhaps an exchange of a fraternal drop of liquid food. We do not know and cannot analyze the imperceptible differences of odor in two colonies of the same species only a few feet apart.

562. How can a beekeeper introduce a new queen into a hive? When an old queen is lost and no normal replacement created, the beekeeper procures a new queen from elsewhere. She is put into the hive in a small container with wire mesh, sealed with a plug of hard sugar. By the time this has been gnawed away the new queen will have acquired the colony odor and be acceptable.

563. How many individuals may there be in a single colony? Colonies of the Paper Wasps *Polistes,* and related tropical genera, have the fewest number of individuals, sometimes only 50 or so. Bumblebees may have 300–400 in a colony; the Bald-faced Hornet

Vespula maculata, 5,000; Honeybees, 35,000–50,000. Some African and Australian termites have several million. But the Mound Building Ants, often with 1,500 nests in a communal group, will have hundreds of millions of individuals.

564. Do colonies of social insects live over the winter?   In temperate regions the Bumblebee colony dies off in the fall with the exception of the young fertilized queens who hibernate in the ground. Paper Wasps also die off in the fall, only the young queens surviving. The colonies of most other social insects are more or less permanent.

565. How are new colonies started?   In Honeybees an old queen, accompanied by a large number of workers (sometimes as many as 35,000), leaves the old nest to her as yet untransformed successor, and seeks a new one. The workers have previously gorged themselves on honey and are in a state of seeming frenzy as they swarm out with the queen. In the Stingless Bees it is the young queens who participate in the colonizing swarm.

In the Paper Wasps and Bumblebees the queen starts the new colony alone in the spring, all other members of the society having died off in the autumn. The queens feed their first young on nectar and pollen and chewed-up insects.

The ant queen, too, usually starts the colony alone. After her mating flight she drops to the ground, finds a site, and removes her wings. When her first larvae hatch she feeds them with salivary secretions containing substances derived from her degenerating wing muscles.

A male and female termite drop from the dispersal flight, shed their wings, find a suitable site, start tunneling out their nest, and then (and not until then) mate. The colony builds up very slowly in numbers, the king and queen feeding the few larvae in a leisurely manner with secretions from their mouth.

566. Are all swarms of social insects mating swarms?   Only the ants, among the social Hymenoptera, mate during swarming flight. Their flights may consist of hundreds or thousands of males and females. Termites have similar flights during which males and females pair off and begin new colonies, although they defer mating for some time. The Honeybee swarm is a colonizing one, the queen in it being the hive's old queen.

567. Do insects of more than one species normally form colonies together? Usually not, because most species zealously guard the integrity of the species. Occasionally however a colony of ants that is composed of two different species may be found living amicably together. They may have reached this state of semi-intermingling because the two queens who started the colonies happened to start them in close proximity. At other times a mixed colony may arise because one of the species is parasitic on the other, or is enslaved by the other.

568. What are inquilines? They are guests within the nest of another species. Thousands of species live in this way. Those that live in ant nests are called *mymecophiles;* those in termite nests, *termitophiles.* Some are welcome; some are tolerated; and some are actively persecuted, but, like the agile little myrmecophilous Crickets, survive.

569. What kinds of animals live as myrmecophiles or termitophiles? Roundworms, Crustacea, Mites, and many thousands of insects live in this way. Of the insects a few are Apterygota, many are Crickets and Roaches, a few are the larvae of Lepidoptera and flies, but the vast majority are beetles.

570. Are any ants habitual guests in colonies of other ants? Species of small ants live in other ant colonies, maintaining their own separate brood chambers, which they defend vigorously, but remaining free to clamber about on the backs of the host species, grooming them and being fed by them in return. They are welcome guests. The classic example is that of a species of *Leptothorax* that lives in a *Myrmica* nest.

571. What are thief ants? Some species of ants, usually small and agile, build their nests close to other ant colonies. They quite regularly enter their neighbors' galleries in search of refuse, food, or even the ant brood, snatching this loot sometimes from the very jaws of the larger hosts. They are apparently protected against reprisals by their bad odor. These little thief ants occasionally raid man's kitchens where they become a nuisance. Such a species in the tiny *Solenopsis fugax.*

572. What are ant slaves? Many ants, such as those of the genus *Harpagoxenus,* the famous Amazons of the genus *Polyergus,* and even a few species of *Formica,* make regular raids on the nests of other ants, putting to flight or killing the workers and seizing the larvae and pupae which they carry back to their own colonies. In due time the captives mature and become active, productive members of the colony, having equal status with the regular members of the colony. In the case of the amazons the slaves do all the work; the sickle-shaped mandibles of the captors are so long and sharp that they cannot care for the brood. They even seem psychologically unable to feed themselves, starving to death if no slave is around to feed them.

573. What is a social parasite? A social parasite is a species of social insect that has become parasitic upon another social species. The young queen of such a social parasite manages to gain entrance into a colony of a species normally parasitized by her species. After a time, when she has acquired the characteristic colony odor, she is tolerated and fed by the workers. Then, when she lays her eggs, these and the larvae that hatch from them will be cared for by the workers as well as those of their own species. In some species the intruding queen kills the host queen, in at least one species by biting off her head. Since the intruder is then the only fertile female, her offspring supplant the original workers as the latter die off. The colony then is entirely composed of the socially parasitic, intruder species. The widely distributed North American *Formica exsectoides,* our woodland Mound Builder, gets its start by parasitizing its congener *Formica fusca.*

574. Are any other social insects social parasites? In every group, one or more species similarly parasitizes colonies of its relatives. Among the Bumblebees, species of *Psithyrus* parasitize their cousins of the genus *Bombus.* Among the Hornets, one species each of *Vespula* and *Dolichovespula* parasitize colonies of very closely related species. In the Paper Wasps *Polistes,* there are socially parasitic species in Europe, and one suspect North American species. Among the Stingless Bees there are no parasitic species, but one species is a bold robber, raiding the nests of other species in swarms, and stealing the honey.

NESTS

575. Which of the social species use wax in their nests? The social bees do. Wild Honeybees build nests in hollow trees using wax and propolis in the construction of the combs. The Bumblebees usually build in the ground, the Stingless Bees of the tropics in hollow trees.

576. What is propolis? It is a substance made up of resins collected by bees and used to seal and weatherproof their nests.

577. What social insects build their nests of paper? The paper-making Wasps belong to the family Vespidae. The members of the genus *Polistes* build open-celled paper combs beneath eaves and sheds. Their tropical relatives make nests that are sometimes three feet or more in length, hanging them in shrubbery and in trees. Other Hornets and Yellow Jackets (*Vespa, Vespula, Dolichovespula*) build tiers of combs which are sheathed with a tough paper covering, with only a small entrance at the bottom or at the side. A few build these nests in the ground. Many tropical termites and ants make nests of tough, durable paper that are penetrated with chambers and passages.

578. What is the paper in these nests? Paper-making insects chew up weathered and rotting wood, dead stems, bark, or man-made paper and cardboard, mix it with salivary secretions to make a pulpy mass, and then shape it as they wish. It dries into a tough gray or brown paper, or *carton*.

579. Do all ants and termites nest in the ground? The majority of ants and termites nest in the ground but many species of each group build their nests elsewhere. Many are arboreal, living in hollow stems. Many termites build large carton nests on tree trunks; these are always, however, connected to the ground by an enclosed tunnel. Many of both groups, especially the termites, live in tunnels in wood, ranging from living tree trunks to dead logs and man's wooden structures. The Oriental Tree Ants sew together green leaves into tight nests as large as a football. Many ants nest in abandoned galls, nuts or acorns.

580. What are the towering "ant nests" of the Old World tropics?
These structures, which may be nine or ten feet high and as hard as concrete, are the nests of various termites ("white ants"), never of true ants. They are especially prominent features of the landscape of many dry regions of Africa and Australia.

581. What ants make no nests?   The Legionary Ants of the New World and the Driver Ants of Africa, collectively called Army Ants, make no fixed nests. For a considerable period (about seventeen days in one species) the entire colony keeps on the move all day, killing all possible animals in their path and carrying the developing larvae along. Then comes a "statary" phase. During this period the larvae pupate and transform to adults, chiefly workers; and the queen lays enormous numbers of eggs. Then the colony begins moving again in another nomadic phase. During the halts perhaps 50,000 to 100,-000 workers cling to each other to form a great mass, with tunnels and internal chambers, in which are the queen and the brood and nurse workers. Literally this great cluster of living individuals is the nest.

582. What is the queen of the Legionary Ants like?   She is wingless from birth, unlike most other ant and termite queens. She is much larger than the workers and, especially during the statary period, has an enormously swollen abdomen. Over a period of five to several days she can produce more than 25,000 eggs. On the other hand the Legionary males are winged.

583. How do Army Ants capture their prey?   The large soldiers, which have enormous hooked jaws, swarm over even quite large prey, overpowering them by sheer numbers. The legs of large insects are soon severed and the game then cut up and carried to the main colony by the large and small workers.

584. How do Army Ants form new colonies?   At intervals a brood of young wingless queens and winged males is produced. After mating a young queen wanders off accompanied by a group of workers, and in time builds up a new, large colony.

585. Are Army Ants ever dangerous to man? The New World Legionary Ants seldom attack larger vertebrate animals, although what a swarm might do to a completely helpless person would not be pleasant to contemplate. The African Driver Ants, however, may kill penned or tethered domestic animals if a village lies in their path.

X. AQUATIC INSECTS

586. Is the aquatic way of life a primitive characteristic of insects?
No. It is true that the Arthropod ancestors from which all insects
evolved were aquatic, but the insects themselves all became established first on land and there developed their characteristic tracheal
respiration, an air-breathing system. Since all of the aquatic insects
today have a tracheal system, they must have evolved from terrestrial
insect ancestors. Various groups then pushed into the as yet largely
unexploited fresh waters for at least part of their existence, and became readapted to the aquatic life.

587. Are there many groups of aquatic insects?   Thirteen orders
contain aquatic families. Four of these—the Mayflies, Stoneflies,
Dragonflies and Damselflies, and the Caddisflies—are called the true
aquatic orders because, with very few exceptions, all of their members
lay their eggs in the water and spend their entire larval life there. The
adults of these four orders are airborne and breathe as normal insects.
Individual species and families of Springtails, Mole Crickets, Dobsonflies and Alder Flies (Megaloptera), Spongilla Flies (Neuroptera),
beetles, bugs, flies, wasps, and moths are aquatic for part or all of
their lives.

588. Are any insects aquatic when adults?   Sixteen families of
bugs, ten families of beetles, and one genus of moths live in or on the
water as adults. One genus of wasps that is parasitic on Caddisflies
lives under water in the adult stage, but since it lives in a silken air-
filled case it is not truly aquatic.

589. Do any aquatic insects breed in temporary bodies of water?
Quite a few Mosquitoes are noted for breeding in pools and water
holes that may contain water for only a week or so, which is long
enough for their development. The worst malaria carrier of Africa,
Anopheles gambiae, has been found breeding in water-filled foot-
prints and the ruts of roads. Many others breed in old tin cans and
almost anything that will hold water. The infamous carrier of yellow

fever, *Aedes aegypti,* has a special predilection for man-made containers and has been found breeding in the water in a flower vase in a yellow-fever patient's room. We have found it breeding by the million in rain barrels in Puerto Rico. The North American *Culex pipiens,* an abundant and widely distributed pest Mosquito, is often called the Rain Barrel Mosquito because of its preference for artificial containers.

Strong flying Dragonflies frequently breed in temporary water reservoirs.

590. Do any Mosquitoes breed in water in tree holes? Quite a few do, including several Mosquitoes that breed nowhere else. Among these is the genus *Toxorhynchites,* Mosquitoes more than half an inch long as larvae; they are predaceous on the other Mosquito larvae in tree holes but as adults live strictly on plant juices. The adults have bright metallic blue and green colors. Also found in tree holes are the larvae of Helodid Beetles, and Rat-tailed Maggots, the larvae of the Drone Fly.

591. Do any insects breed in the water reservoirs of plants? The water reservoirs of Pitcher Plants and of various epiphytic plants of the Pineapple family (Bromeliaceae) that are abundant in the tropics, are home to a varied fauna that includes several Mosquitoes and even, in Costa Rica, one Damselfly. The Mosquitoes include the members of the genus *Wyeomyia,* and in the Neotropical region the members of the genus *Haemagogus* that are carriers of a very dangerous yellow fever. The evolutionary history of such insects may give us pause: their original Arthropod ancestors were marine; then they evolved as land insects; then they returned to the fresh waters; finally they have moved high up in the forest canopy where the epiphytic plants grow.

592. What insects live in Sponges? The Spongilla Flies of the family Sisyridae (Neuroptera) lay their eggs under a silken web close to the water's edge. The larvae crawl down into the water, find a Sponge, insert their long slender mouthparts into the openings in the body of the Sponge, and feed upon its tissues. Since the Sponge is an animal this is true parasitism.

593. Do insects live in deep water? The deep water of lakes has very few insects. Some Chironomid Midge larvae may live in the bottom ooze and a few Mosquitoes are occasionally found; but for the most part there is little insect life in deep water.

594. In what type of water are insects found most abundantly? In ponds, especially those rich in vegetation, insects are found in abundance. In shallow streams, even where the water flows very rapidly, there are many characteristic species; but in the large rivers there are relatively fewer.

595. What insects live at the surface of the water? Whirligig Beetles (Gyrinidae) gyrate in numbers in the surface film. They occasionally dive beneath, taking a bubble of air down with them, but most of their adult life is at the surface. Water Striders (Gerridae and Veliidae) run lightly over the surface film, never breaking through it. Marsh Treaders (Hydrometridae) do not venture far but creep over the surface near vegetation. Springtails of several species are found, sometimes in enormous numbers, on the surface of quiet pools or backwaters, an occasional individual leaving the mass to dart beneath.

A few small beetles of several small families live submerged in the water but often break the surface film with their sharp tarsal claws and crawl along underneath it, suspended upside down.

596. What insects live submerged in the water but must obtain air at the surface? The aquatic bugs and beetles (except for the larvae of one family and a scattering of others) and many of the dipterous larvae.

597. Which insects do not have to come to the surface for air? The larvae of the four true aquatic orders, as well as the larvae of the Dobsonflies and the Alder Flies (Megaloptera), the Spongilla Flies Neuroptera), a few flies (Blackflies and Midges,), the Lepidoptera, the larvae of the beetles of the family Donaciidae, and a few rare bugs.

598. What are the chief problems in becoming adapted to aquatic life? The first big problem is respiration, then food-getting, locomotion, anchorage, oviposition and emergence.

Above: A Silverfish, *Lepisma saccharina,* may slip inconspicuously beneath a pile of linen or behind the bookshelves. *Below:* The large Cockroach, *Periplaneta americana,* is often an intruder in our buildings.

Above: The translucent green wings of a Meadow Grasshopper, *Scudderia* sp., give it a cryptic, leaf-like appearance. *Below:* Camel, or Cave, Crickets, *Ceuthophilus* sp., are common scavengers in dark, damp places.

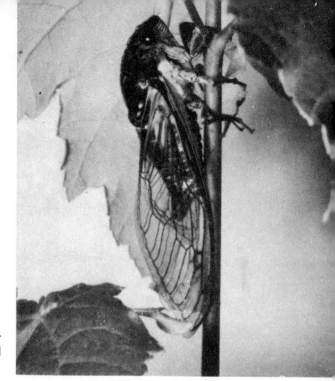

"Happy are the Cicadas' lives, for they all have voiceless wives."

The European Mantis, *Mantis religiosa*, is common in the northeastern states.

Above: Lace Bugs, *Co-rythuca* sp., live in mixed groups of adults and nymphs beneath the leaves of many trees. *Left:* The Milk-weed Bug, *Oncopeltis fasciatus,* has bright colors that warn of its inedibility.

Above: The male Dobsonfly, *Corydalus cornutus,* has enormous jaws, the female much shorter ones. *Below:* Ants, *Prenolepis imparis,* attending aphids for the sweet honeydew which they exude.

An adult Antlion, *Hesperoleon* sp., has large eyes but small, weak mouth-parts; but the larva, almost blind, has enormous, powerful jaws.

Above: The long, slender beak of the Acorn Weevil, *Curculio* sp., has a set of tiny, boring mouthparts at the tip. *Below:* The "eyes" of the Eyed Elater, *Alaus oculatus,* are merely pigment spots on the thorax; the head and real eyes are almost hidden beneath this.

The enormous jaws of this Stag Beetle, *Pesudolucanus capreolus*, are purely defensive (or courtship) weapons.

This is the defense attitude of a Pinacaté Beetle, *Eleodes* sp., of the western plains and deserts.

A group of small, white Yucca Moths, *Tegeticula yuccasella,* inside a Yucca flower.

The enormous, plumy antennae of a male Polyphemus Moth, *Telea polyphemus,* are an aid in finding a mate.

Above: A Viceroy Butterfly, *Limenitis archippus,* with its long proboscis coiled beneath its face. *Below:* The Green Marvel, *Agriopodes fallax,* is a perfect match in both color and pattern for the lichens on which it may rest.

Above: The enormous, green caterpillars of the Tomato Hornworm, *Phlegethontius quinquemaculatus* (a Sphinx Moth), may be destructive to tomato and tobacco leaves. *Below:* A hairy *Apatelodes* caterpillar looks like a miniature Skye Terrier. Its feet are coral pink.

Above: The eyes of the viciously biting Deer Flies, *Chrysops* sp., are brilliantly patterned with iridescent gold, orange and black. *Below:* A House, or Rain Barrel Mosquito, *Culex pipiens,* one of the commonest species about our houses.

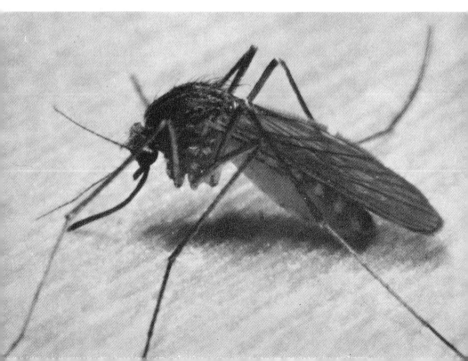

Above: A Tachinid Fly, *Archytas apicifera*, a member of a group highly beneficial to man. *Below:* A black and yellow Syrphid Fly, *Syrphus* sp., which as a larva fed on aphids.

Above: A parasitized caterpillar of the Tomato Hornworm bearing the cocoons of the Braconid wasp larvae that have been growing to maturity within it. *Below:* A Pigeon Tremex, *Tremex columba,* female, one of our largest wood-boring sawflies. *Opposite page:* A large Ichneumon Wasp. *Heteropelma fulvicorne,* laying eggs on caterpillars of the Red Humped Apple Worm, *Schizura concinna.*

Above: A small nest of the Paper Wasp, *Polistes annularis*, with **eggs** in some cells, larvae in others and pupae in the capped ones. *Below:* A worker Bumblebee, *Bombus impatiens*, gathering nectar and pollen.

RESPIRATION

599. How do aquatic insects obtain their oxygen? Obviously the ones who stay on the surface have no problem. The groups that come to the surface to get air have open spiracles and so respire just as terrestrial insects do. Since diffusion of oxygen through gas is about one million times as fast as through tissues, this is much the simplest way for them to use it. Some of them have a tube which they project through the surface film; others have devices for carrying a supply of air down with them. The insects that stay submerged have to get their oxygen by diffusion from the water or from aquatic plants.

600. How does the temperature of the water affect aquatic respiration? A vital factor is the ability of water to dissolve far more oxygen and other gases as it grows colder. Insects living in warmer waters therefore have greater respiratory problems than those in cold water. Fortunately most insects have a rather low oxygen consumption.

601. What insects have a tube with which they pierce the surface film? Many Cranefly larvae (Tipulidae) and other flies that live in shallow water or near the surface do this. The Rat-tailed Maggots (Syrphidae) have a long telescopic tube at the rear of the abdomen which they extend through the surface film as they lie in mud or moist decaying matter. A rosette of hairs that expands on the surface of the water protects the spiracle which lies at the tip of the tube. Water Scorpions (*Nepa* and *Ranatra*) have at the end of the abdomen two long filaments which fit together to form a tube. They cling to submerged vegetation, with this forerunner of the snorkel penetrating the surface film; and then make occasional, lengthy forays beneath, using the air with which they have filled their tracheae. Mosquito larvae have a tube, varying in length in different species, which they project through the film. The pair of spiracles at its tip is protected by a rosette of hairs that spreads out on the surface. Their pupae also break through the surface film, using a pair of spiracle-bearing thoracic appendages for the purpose. When disturbed the Mosquito larvae and pupae "wriggle" off beneath the surface, sometimes staying submerged for ten minutes or longer.

602. What insects carry a supply of air down with them? The aquatic bugs and beetles do this. Most bugs break the surface film with the tip of the abdomen; but the Water Boatmen (Corixidae) break it with their head. The Giant Water Bugs (Belostomatidae) do it with special straplike flaps at the ends of the spiracles. Air is drawn in through spiracles which are at the tip of the abdomen, or is drawn and channeled, sometimes along troughs made of hydrofuge hairs, to the space under the wings; and, in all except the Giant Water Bugs, to the ventral surface of the body as well, where it is carried as a shining, silvery coating.

Most of the beetles break the surface film with the tip of the abdomen; but the Water Scavengers (Hydrophilidae) break it with the unwettable clubs of their antennae, which are held so as to permit the formation of a funnel of air that connects with the air under the elytra, and to a coating of air that is held on the under surface of the body. In the other beetles the air is channeled to fill the spaces beneath the elytra; and in the Haliplidae to the space under the expanded hind coxae where it protrudes in a sizable bubble.

603. How long can aquatic bugs and beetles stay submerged? The time depends on the temperature, the oxygen concentration of the water, and their activity while submerged. Backswimmers (Notonectidae) often stay down thirty minutes or so, although they have been known to stay down as long as an hour. The amount of air a Dytiscid Beetle takes down is only sufficient for twenty minutes, yet it can stay down for thirty-six hours. This is possible because as the insect uses the oxygen in the bubble the carbon dioxide that is given off diffuses out into the water. The oxygen pressure is therefore reduced in the bubble and more diffuses in from the water. The bubble is therefore serving as a sort of gill.

604. What is plastron respiration? It is respiration through a coating of air that does not have to be replenished. The beetles and bugs that carry a silvery film of air down from the surface have a type of respiration that is very similar to plastron respiration, but the oxygen that diffuses in to the bubble never quite equals the amount being used by the insect, so the supply has to be replenished. The Naucorid Bug *Aphelocheirus* is a good example of an insect having true plastron respiration. The body is coated with a thin layer of air held in place by a dense pile, 2,000,000 hairs per square millimeter, each hair bent at right angles at the tip. This bug never has to come to the surface, the original gaseous layer being formed from the gases absorbed by the young nymph through its body wall. A few beetles have a plastron which is held, not by hairs, but by fine granular particles.

605. How do the insects that remain submerged get their oxygen? They are able to get it by diffusion, because of the pressure differential between the oxygen in the water and that in their tracheal system. They get it by diffusion through the body wall, through tracheal gills, or through blood gills. A few insects get it from aquatic plants.

606. What are tracheal gills? They are thin-walled cutaneous structures that contain many air-filled tracheae. The oxygen diffuses into them directly from the water.

607. What insects have tracheal gills on the outside of the body? The Damselflies (Zygoptera) have three elongated postabdominal gill plates. Stoneflies have tufts of tracheal gill filaments attached either at the base of the legs, under the head, or at the rear of the abdomen. Mayflies have 2–7 pairs of gill plates located on the sides of the abdominal segments; the middle pairs are kept constantly in motion to keep water currents flowing over them. Caddisflies have caudal filaments. *Corydalis* and *Sialis* (Megaloptera) have paired lateral filaments. Mosquitoes have anal gills but these seem to be concerned more with the diffusion of ions than of gases. The lepidopterous larvae have filamentous gills in some species; *Nymphula* has as many as four hundred. Larvae of the Gyrinid Beetles, a few Hydrophilidae, Dryopidae, and Psephenidae have fringed gills or gill tufts.

608. Which larvae have internal tracheal gills? The Dragonfly larvae have rows of tracheal gills in the lining of the rectum. So do the Damselflies; and since the latter have been found to survive removal of their three caudal gills, it may be that they use the caudal gills more for steering purposes, depending primarily upon these rectal gills for respiration. Some Caddisfly larvae also have rectal gills.

609. What insects have blood gills?　Blood gills, which are thin-walled cutaneous expansions that contain blood, take oxygen out of the water the way the tracheal gills do; but since the blood of the insects having blood gills contains hemoglobin they are capable of carrying more oxygen. Blood gills, rare among insects, are found only in the blood worms of the family Chironomidae (Nonbiting Midges), a few Caddisflies, a few Pyralid Moth larvae, and a few exotic beetles.

610. How do insects get oxygen from submerged plants?　Some get it from the intercellular spaces of the plant tissue, either by chewing on the tissue or by piercing it with special structures. Others get the oxygen from the bubbles of gas, largely oxygen, produced by the plant in photosynthesis. The larvae of certain Chrysomelid Beetles (*Donacia*) and the weevil *Lissorhaptus* have sharp movable spines with which they pierce the plant tissue. Larvae and pupae of a few Mosquitoes (*Mansonia*) perforate the plant tissue with the sharp end of the breathing tube with which other Mosquito larvae pierce the surface film. Many Diptera have a postabdominal siphon which they insert in the bubbles on the plant leaves without penetrating the tissue.

Some insects live entirely within the tissues of aquatic plants: a few Chironomid Midges mine in the leaves, and a few beetle and moth larvae bore in the stems. Numbers of moth larvae, especially of the genus *Nymphula,* build a case of pieces of green leaves and thus, living inside of this, have the benefit of the oxygen being given off in the photosynthesis of their own case.

FOOD GETTING

611. What do aquatic insects eat?　Some species eat plant tissues directly; some eat insects that fall onto the surface; and some are actively predaceous. Others have learned to feed on plankton, the microscopic plants and animals; and others are general scavengers and sewage feeders. A few species, mostly Mosquitoes, live at least partly on solutes in the water.

612. What aquatic insects feed on the insects that fall on the surface?　The surface-living Water Striders (Gerridae and Veliidae), and to some extent the Whirligig Beetles (Gyrinidae), snap up insects that fall onto the surface.

613. What aquatic insects are plankton feeders? The Water Boatmen (Corixidae) are especially well adapted for this. The front tarsi are formed into heavily spined scoops which winnow from the water algae, protozoa, and other tiny organisms, as well as Mosquito larvae and other small insects. Their mouth has a special masticating structure which is unusual in bugs whose mouthparts are normally adapted solely for piercing and sucking.

Blackfly larvae (*Simulium*), which live attached by suction disks to the surface of stones in fast-flowing water, reach out with large fanlike structures of hairs on the head, to gather and strain from the water organic matter and plankton. Many Chironomid larvae feed on plankton, some of them spinning nets for catching it, as well as on the ooze and detritus on the bottom, and so do a few Mayflies. Caddisflies of the families Hydropsychidae, Philopotamidae, and Psychomyiidae weave strong silken nets which filter out plankton and even small insects in running water. The nets of the first-named family are stretched across the larva's place of concealment and may be camouflaged with bits of wood or leaves; those of the other two families are finger-shaped or trumpet-shaped and so fastened as to be distended by the current in the water.

Insects that thus strain food out of the water are called *filter feeders,* as are the Sponges, Clams, Barnacles, and even the largest of all living animals, the great Whalebone Whales.

614. What are the chief plant eaters among the aquatic insects? The majority of the Mayflies, Stoneflies, and Caddisflies are herbivorous. So also are the Lepidoptera, some of the Hydrophilid Beetles, the Water Pennies (larvae of the Psephenid Beetles), an aquatic Weevil and the larvae of a few Craneflies (Tipulidae), Chironomid Midges, the Net-winged Midges, and a few other flies. These are the primary consumers, which transform basic plant material into animal matter, and are thus the essential first link in the animal food chain.

615. What are the chief predators among the aquatic insects? The larvae of the Odonata, the bugs (except for the Corixidae), most of the beetles (except for the Hydrophilidae and Psephenidae), the larvae of the Megaloptera, a few flies, two groups of Mosquitoes, and most of the Chironomid Midges and the Punkies (Biting Midges, Heleidae) are the chief predators.

616. What insects feed on sewage?   The larvae of some flies and Chironomid Midges live in sewage, feeding on it. So also do some Spongilla Flies, most of which, however, live and feed on Sponges. Some species of Moth-winged Flies (Psychodidae) live in drains. The larvae withstand rather high temperatures and a considerable concentration of soap. The adults may emerge in great numbers from the drains. The other members of the Psychodidae are not truly aquatic although they do live in manure, sewage, or exuding sap on trees.

617. How are the Odonata specialized for preying on animals? The Odonata nymphs are successful predators because of the stealthy way they lurk in vegetation or lie concealed in silt or weeds; the jet propulsion which enables them to dart out with great speed; and the alacrity with which the large, hinged lower lip shoots forward. This, the labium, usually folded under the head, can reach forward some distance, grasping the prey with the claws and spines on its scoop-shaped tip.

618. How are aquatic bugs adapted for predation?   Many, especially the Naucoridae and Giant Water Bugs (Belostomatidae), have raptorial front legs that are very efficient. The femur of these is wide and flat, sometimes with a grooved anterior edge; the sharp-edged tibia snaps back on the femur, like the blade of a clasp knife. *Ranatra* (Nepidae) and the Marsh Treaders (Hydrometridae), which have weaker raptorial forelegs, are concealed by their elongate reedlike form and thus undoubtedly are undetected by many unwary victims. All predaceous bugs have a piercing beak with which they can sting, sometimes sharply, and with which they suck the juices of their prey. The Marsh Treaders are particularly skillful at spearing Mosquitoes and other insects at the surface film.

619. How are aquatic beetles adapted for predation?   The beetles' main skill probably lies, in most families, in their streamlined bodies that enable them to dart swiftly at their prey, which they grasp and hold with their jaws. The larvae of the Dytiscidae, called water tigers, Gyrinidae, and Haliplidae have enormous, sickle-shaped, hollow mandibles through which the juices of the victims can drain down into the mouth.

OVIPOSITION

620. Where do aquatic insects lay their eggs? Most of those species that live in the water as adults lay their eggs quite easily either in plant tissues or on plant, rock, and other surfaces. Those whose adults are not aquatic either lay them on dry land, on branches or structures overhanging the water, or on the surface of the water; or else they drop them into the water, place them in submerged plant tissue, or make a dash beneath the surface to lay them in some underwater place.

621. Do any aquatic insects lay eggs on other animals? The females of three genera of Giant Water Bugs (Belostomatidae) hold the male firmly while they cement the eggs to his back. Unable to spread his wings and fly, he remains in the water until the eggs hatch. One Water Boatman (Corixidae) attaches her eggs to a Crayfish.

622. What aquatic insects lay their eggs on land? Some Mosquitoes of the genus *Aedes* lay their eggs in dry places; the eggs do not hatch until the rains or melting snows wet them, sometimes having to wait two years. Some Tabanid Flies, as well as the Dobsonflies and Alder Flies (Megaloptera), lay theirs on branches or under bridges overhanging the water. Net-winged Midges (Blephariceridae) of some species lay their eggs at the edges of fast-flowing streams where the hatching larvae can easily crawl into the water; and a few Chironomids lay gelatinous masses of eggs just above the water line.

623. What insects lay their eggs on the surface of the water? *Anopheles* Mosquitoes lay their eggs singly on the surface of the water, but species of *Culex* lay them in masses in the form of little concave rafts.

624. What insects just drop their eggs as they fly over the water? Many Mayflies and Stoneflies do this. They can sometimes be seen flying with two cylindrical packets of eggs protruding from the abdomen. Short-lived species of Mayflies drop their eggs in a mass; longer-lived species drop them singly by alighting on the surface of the water, permitting the eggs to be washed off. Mayfly eggs have skeins of fine yellow threads that expand on being wetted; these anchor the egg by becoming entangled in vegetation or by means of adhesive buttonlike disks at the end of some of the filaments.

625. How do Dragonflies oviposit?   Those having an ovipositor lay their eggs in mats of submerged vegetation, on plants, or in woody stems emergent from or near the water. Or they may lay them in floating nuts, or other floating plant material; or in sand or gravel where the water is shallow enough for them to reach down with their long slender abdomens. The Gomphidae or Libellulidae female, who does not have an ovipositor, dips the tip of the abdomen into the water again and again, sometimes accompanied by the male who flies with her tandem style. He may drop to the water with her or remain beating time overhead, rejoining her as she rises.

626. Do any airborne insects go beneath the water to oviposit? A few species of Mayflies wrap their wings about their bodies and creep beneath the water enclosed in a film of air. The female Black-flies (*Simulium*) dart in and out of the swift-moving water, fastening an egg at a time to submerged rocks or plants. Some Damselflies fold their wings and back down into the water to oviposit in sand or gravel, sometimes remaining half an hour. A few parasitic Ichneumonid Wasps that go beneath to oviposit on Caddisflies are encased in an air bubble held by their dense pubescence. The Pyralid Moths dart down rapidly, using their hind legs as oars; some of the females of the genus *Acentropus* that are short-winged or wingless never leave the water.

LOCOMOTION

627. Do the insects on the surface have special adaptations for locomotion?   The Gerridae and Hydrometridae have conspicuously long slender legs that spread out spiderlike as they move. The legs as well as the body are covered with a velvety pile and in some species have tarsal glands that secrete a fatty substance to increase the hydrofuge properties of the cuticle and hairs. In the Gerridae the claws are well back from the tips of the tarsi, and thus do not pierce the surface film. The Broad-shouldered Water Strider *Rhagovelia* has a fanlike tuft of hairs on the middle tarsus which spreads out to make a paddling structure.

The Gyrinid hind legs (and sometimes the middle ones) are remarkable structures, flattened and paddlelike with all segments, including the tarsal ones, hinged fanlike at the side; their antennae are short and clubbed; and their eyes are divided into two distinct parts, one on the upper part of the body that remains dry and one on the lower part that lies below the surface film.

628. What special adaptations do submerged bugs and beetles have for locomotion?   A general streamlining of the body identifies most aquatic bugs and beetles. Some are keeled and boat-shaped, and many have smooth, slippery cuticles. The majority have one or more pairs of the legs streamlined, flattened, and fringed with long hairs to form swimming or paddling organs. Many beetles have the coxa greatly expanded and closely adherent to the body; others have this segment attached to the trochanter and femur at one side so that the three almost pivot upon each other. In the aquatic bugs and many aquatic beetles the antennae can fold back into grooves in the side of the head. A few families of aquatic beetles that cannot swim have sharp tarsal claws for clinging to stones in swift water and may, as do the Dryopidae and the Elmidae (Riffle Beetles), pull their heads in under the prothorax and thus present a smooth surface under which the water currents cannot get.

629. How do submerged larvae move about?   Most of them swim with lateral undulations of the abdomen, sometimes aided by abdominal tails or bristles that probably act as rudders. Two Midges, *Corethra* and *Mochlonyx,* have modified hydrostatic organs that give them buoyancy. The most highly specialized device is that of the Odonata, especially the Dragonflies; they suck water in through the anal opening so that in passing over the rectal gills the respiratory exchange of gases can take place; they then eject this water with an almost explosive force which shoots the body forward. (This jet propulsion technique can be observed if a bit of carbon or powdered coloring matter is added to the water of a container in which they are swimming.)

ANCHORAGE

630. Why is anchorage a problem?   It is a problem because of the great buoyancy given insects by their air-filled tracheae. The bubble or plastron of air which adults take beneath the surface adds to this. Furthermore the wake of moving organisms in quiet waters, and the current itself in swift-moving waters, tend to sweep delicate insects along.

631. What are some devices for anchorage?   Most bug and beetle adults have to cling with a tarsal claw to submerged vegetation or else they will rise to the surface. Caddisfly larvae build cases of sand, gravel, or wood, some of which have considerable weight in themselves, and many others of which are cemented to rocks.

632. What aquatic insects have sucking or adhesive devices for anchorage?   Blackfly (*Simulium*) larvae and pupae have adhesive disks at the rear end of the body which fasten them to rock surfaces and permit them to stand upright in the fast current and thus reach out for passing food. The larvae of Net-winged Midges (Blephariceridae) and the Deuterophlebiidae crawl over rocks in very fast water or in waterfalls, being held fast by means of six ventral suckers, one on each of the five abdominal segments and one on the fused head and thorax. These larvae, because of the lateral expansions of each segment, appear to be deeply incised and loosely segmented. The larvae of a few Psychodid Moths live just above the water line but in the splash of waterfalls; they, too, have ventral suckers. The Water Pennies (larvae of the Psephenidae) have broad, flat lateral expansions on each segment also; but they are semifused, thus giving the body an oval, flattened, almost scalelike form that clings to the surface, not by means of suckers, but by the suction of its whole form. Some Mayflies that live in very fast water have the abdominal segments expanded laterally with the lateral gills broad and platelike; this helps to hold the abdomen to the surface of rocks. In the genus *Rithrogena* the gills of some species are expanded, flattened, and overlapping on the ventral side, forming a disk which provides suction.

EMERGENCE

633. Do insects have difficulty emerging from the water as adults?
The Mayflies, Stoneflies, Dragonflies, and Damselflies, having incomplete metamorphosis, have only to crawl up on emergent plant stems, on bridges or pilings, or even on shrubbery and buildings on the shore to undergo their last molt and emerge as adults. Their cast skins can be seen in great numbers at times. Those insects having complete metamorphosis which also pupate in the water, such as Caddisflies, moths, flies. Mosquitoes, and Midges, have more difficulty. The Caddisflies pupate within their cases or in cocoons. The mature pupa has to cut its way out of the case and then swim to the surface; there it either crawls up on some object before emergence, or molts as it reaches the surface, in which case the adult must take wing at once. The Lepidoptera pupate in silken cases or feltlike cocoons in which a slit is usually made by the larva. The adult upon emergence swims to the surface. Mosquitoes and Midges either actively swim near the surface as pupae, or come to the surface just before emergence; then upon molting the emergent adults take flight at once. The Blackfly bursts from its pupal shell and rises to the surface in a bubble of air.

634. Where do the Neuroptera and Megaloptera pupate? The Spongilla Flies (Neuroptera) pupate in silken cocoons hidden in crevices sometimes as much as fifty feet from the water. The Dobsonflies and Alder Flies make earthen cells in the ground or in rotting logs; these too may be some distance from the water, often as much as thirty feet.

635. Where do aquatic beetles pupate? Most of them pupate on the shore in mud, silt, or damp vegetation. Gyrinid larvae carry sand or mud or other adherent matter up the bank and then build the case around themselves. One of the few aquatic pupae known among beetles is that of the Water Pennies (Psephenidae); it is oval and flattened like the larva, with tufts of gills on the abdomen, and clings to the rocks. Some Chrysomelids pupate in plant tissues or in gas-filled cocoons attached to plants.

636. Do the adults that live in the water ever fly? All of the adult bugs will fly if the water in which they live dries up. The Giant Water Bugs and the Water Boatmen, however, fly quite often, sometimes being attracted in to lights at night in great numbers. Many of the beetles, especially the Dytiscidae, fly occasionally. The Hydrophilidae often make mass dispersal flights; the Gyrinidae occasionally take short flights. Others fly some; but in the case of most families little is known about their ability or inclination to do so

XI. INSECTS AND PLANTS

637. How are insects associated with plants? Insects, like all animals, are dependent upon plants directly or indirectly for food. In addition a great many insects are dependent upon plants for shelter and for the material with which they build their nests.

638. Are plants reciprocally dependent upon insects? A great many are directly dependent upon insects. Many others receive indirect benefits from insects. The majority of plants, however, could probably exist without insects and perhaps would be better off without them.

639. Do particular insects specialize upon visiting or feeding upon particular plants? The great majority of plant-eating insects are rather narrow specialists. Not only do they feed upon certain plants only (often upon only one species of plant), but they often feed upon only a certain part of the plant; furthermore they may do this only when in the larval or adult stage.

640. Do both larval and adult instars usually feed upon the same plant? Often they do, but more often they do not. A caterpillar may eat the leaves of Oak, but after it has transformed to an adult butterfly it will visit only flowers of other plants, sometimes of only a very few kinds.

INSECTS AND FLOWERS

641. Why do insects visit flowers? Most insects that visit flowers do so because the flowers are a source of food to them. Sometimes they themselves feed upon the flower; sometimes they lay their eggs upon it and their larvae feed upon it. A good many insects visit flowers as a place to rest, or in which to lie in wait for their prey—other flower visitors.

642. What do flower feeders eat? The chief sources of insect food in a flower are the pollen and the nectar. A great many insects feed on these, often upon nothing else. Some eat other parts of the flower, such as the petals and sepals. The larvae of many insects eat the seeds and fruits that develop from the flower parts.

643. What is pollen?   Pollen grains are tiny cells, produced by most flowers in enormous quantities, that represent the male element in the reproduction of the plant. They are found on floral parts called *stamens* in chambers known as *anthers*. In most flowering plants the pollen must be transferred to a receptive structure, the *stigma,* on an organ called the *pistil,* usually of another flower. This transfer is known as pollination.

644. How is pollination accomplished?   A great many plants are wind-pollinated; a great many others are dependent upon insects or such birds as Hummingbirds. Some plants have special means of pollinating their own flowers.

645. Are the insect-pollinated plants dependent upon insects? The vast majority of them are, and could hardly continue to exist without insects. Some, like the Violets, can pollinate their own flowers if, after a time, they have not been pollinated by an insect.

646. What is nectar?   Nectar is a sweet liquid secreted by special parts of the flower. It is mostly contained in nectaries, small reservoirs deep in the base of the flower, from which it can be sucked out. Sometimes the petals, too, are wet with a sugary solution.

647. What insects feed upon pollen?   Since pollen is a solid food, it is eaten only by insects that have chewing mouthparts. Many beetles, such as the Tumbling Flower Beetles (Mordellidae), Checkered Beetles (Cleridae), many Long Horned Beetles (Cerambycidae), many Scarabaeid Flower Beetles and Chafers, and various insects of other groups feed on pollen as adults. The bees, and some wasps, collect pollen to take back to their nests, where it serves as food for their larvae.

648. Does it harm the plants to have so much pollen eaten?   The amount of pollen eaten by insects is a very small price to pay for the benefits of pollination. Wind-pollinated plants must produce much greater amounts of pollen, most of which fails to reach another flower of the same species, and thus is wasted.

649. What are the chief nectar-feeding insects? The bees are easily the primary group, seconded by the butterflies and most of the moths. Several families of flies, notably the Flower Flies (Syrphidae), Bee Flies (Bombyliidae), and Thick Headed Flies (Conopidae) are consistent flower visitors; and many members of other families and orders feed at least occasionally on nectar.

650. Are all flower-visiting insects important as pollinators? No, many transfer very little or no pollen from flower to flower. Primarily it is the hairy or densely scaly insects that carry pollen grains in such a way that they can be brushed off against the pistil of another flower. Insects with smooth slippery bodies, like the ants and many wasps, may visit many flowers without transferring pollen. The hairs of bees are plumose or finely feathered, and make ideal pollen carriers; so do the scales of moths and butterflies.

651. Do valuable pollinators have other characteristics? The habit of sucking nectar leads the insect deep into close contact with the flower. Mere pollen eaters usually stay more on the surface. Tubular, sucking mouthparts, therefore, mark most of the important pollinators. In addition the insect should be a consistent and repeated flower visitor, going from one flower to another of the same species with little delay.

652. Why are ants and hornets harmful to flowers? These insects in particular (and various others including many beetles) often bite holes into the base of the flower to get to the nectary. They thus avoid the usual route which leads past the pollen masses. They also are taking nectar which might have gone to valuable pollinators.

653. Are any flowers specialized to exclude ants and such insects? Many plants have hairy, sticky stems which probably act as a barrier to many ants and other insects that are useless as pollinators.

654. Are Flower Beetles valuable pollinators? The Scarabaeid Flower Beetles are densely hairy and often so covered with pollen

that they look bright yellow from it. In flying from flower to flower
they do a great deal of pollination.

**655. Is the pollination of flowers by insects merely incidental to
their visits?**   Apparently it is. There is one case, however, where the
act of pollination seems to be almost deliberate. The Yucca Moths
(*Tegeticula*) feed on the nectar of the Yucca Flowers, the female lays
her eggs in the Yucca ovary, and the larvae feed only on Yucca seeds;
thus the species is dependent upon the continued existence of the
Yucca. As the female feeds she gathers a great ball of pollen upon the
special, unique, long tentacles of her first maxillae. She carries this to
another flower, pushing it down upon the end of the stigma. Then,
moving down to the base of the flower, she lays one or two eggs.
Since the Yucca ovary produces many seeds, the one or two larvae
cannot consume them all. The Yucca flower is pollinated in no other
way, and thus the plant and the insect have become mutually dependent. This behavior on the part of the insect does not seem to be
merely incidental.

656. What attracts certain insects to some plants and not to others?
How certain insects became attracted to certain plants in the first
place is impossible to say. We do know that many flower visitors can
be conditioned into changing their tastes. Certainly color, odor, and
sugar content of the nectar are important. The aroma of one species
of flower may attract one insect and repel another. The sugar content of nectar is especially important to bees; they will ignore orange
nectar when its sugar is reduced to as little as 16 percent, as it may be
on a humid day, but will rush to it on a dry day when the sugar content is up to 25 percent.

**657. Does an insect ever carry pollen of one species of flower to a
different species?**   Of course it does. But as a rule when an insect
is feeding on one species it tends to continue to go to that same
species. Often when the source of supply is failing it may be forced
to go to another. When that happens the pollen is wasted as far as the
plants are concerned. The Honeybee is particularly valuable as a pol-
linator because it tends to be consistent in the flowers it visits.

658. When insects are visiting flowers do they cover a wide area?
Most of them tend to visit flowers in a very small area and often may
be seen returning to the same bush or plant again and again.

659. How are the bees especially adapted for flower visiting?
The bees have evolved a more interdependent relationship with flowering plants than any other insects. They have a sucking proboscis and
a capacious crop for carrying nectar. They also have special pollen-
gathering and carrying structures, the pollen brushes, pollen baskets,
and pollen combs, as well as plumose hairs.

660. What are pollen brushes?   These are brushes of stiff hairs
found on most bees. They usually are on the hind leg, sometimes along
most of the leg but sometimes only on the tibia and metatarsus. In one
family, the Megachilidae, they are on the ventral surface of the abdomen. They are used for scraping off and also for carrying the pollen
caught on the body hairs.

661. What are pollen baskets?   Pollen baskets, known as *cor-
biculae,* are found on the queens and workers of Bumblebees and on
the workers of Honeybees. Each consists of a fringe of long curved
hairs surrounding the bare outer surface of the hind tibiae. These
baskets can be so loaded with pollen that a bee may have trouble
flying because of the weight of the enormous golden ball on each hind
leg.

662. What is a pollen comb?   In the worker Honeybees the pollen
brushes on the inner surface of the metatarsus of the leg that bears the
pollen basket are arranged in rows. These make up a special pollen
comb that is used in scraping the pollen from the body hairs and
transporting it to the pollen basket.

**663. Have flowers become adapted to facilitate pollination by in-
sects?**   The flowers of wind-pollinated plants, such as grasses, are
modified in ways that have nothing to do with insects. Those of the
insect-pollinated plants have evolved a great many features that directly concern the attraction of insects and ensure, as nearly as possible, successful pollination by insects. Some people go so far as to

say that "insects have made flowers." By this they mean that the evolution of the flower has been based upon changes that were necessary to keep up with the changes in insects. The reverse might also be said. Insects and flowers have certainly evolved together, of that there is no question, each group continually affecting the evolution of the other; many flower characteristics can be pointed out that indicate an adaptation that facilitates pollination.

664. What are the chief floral characteristics that facilitate insect pollination? Size, shape, pattern, color, scent, and nectar (nearly everything about the flowers with which we are most familiar) are features that attract insects and act as aids to recognition. In addition, flowers have many features that make cross-pollination more certain.

665. How is the color of the flower of importance in pollination? Obviously the bright color of the flower is important in drawing insects in the first place. Furthermore it serves in making such an impression on insects that they continue to visit the same kind of flower. In the case of bees, which distinguish between the yellow-green group of colors, the blue, and the blue-violet, bright colors are especially important; whereas with many Lepidoptera the more delicate colors are attractive. Carrion feeders are attracted to livid purples and browns not unlike the rotting, putrescent foods they prefer.

666. Do flowers have unsual patterns of color that attract insects? Many have contrasting lines of color, called honey guides, that lead down the throat of the flower in the direction of the nectaries. Since many insects are attracted to vertical lines they are drawn to the center of the flower. One very unusual pattern is that of the Fly (and Wasp) Orchids of Europe. Here the lip of the flower is curiously swollen and patterned so that it duplicates the appearance of the abdomen of certain species of wasps found in the region. The male wasps are attracted to the semblance of the female and attempt to mate with it. In the process they pollinate the flower.

667. What color are night-blooming flowers? Flowers that open at dusk and at night are usually white or pale yellow. This enables night-flying insects to find them more easily.

668. Do the scents of flowers play an important part in attracting insects? They may be of great importance, especially in flowers blooming at night when visibility is poor. Many scents have been shown to attract specific insects strongly and to keep them visiting flowers of the same species.

669. Do insects go to flowers with unpleasant odors? Many flowers smell like carrion, excrement, and other substances very unpleasant to humans. They are far from unpleasant to animals that feed on such substances or lay their eggs on them. Some of the Trilliums (such as the Purple Trillium), Skunk Cabbage, and many members of the large African genus *Stapelia* of fleshy, cactuslike plants have putrescent-smelling flowers. These attract, not the usual flower visitor, but the various carrion-feeding beetles and other insects. One Australian Orchid smells like the female of a certain wasp and thus attracts males of the species.

670. How does flower shape facilitate pollination? Shallow, wide-open flowers may miss many chances of pollination because the visiting insect fails to contact the anthers or pistil. The long, tubular shape of many flowers (such as those of Trumpet Vine, Honeysuckle, Nicotiana, and Petunia) forces insects to push bodily down inside the flowers if they are to reach the nectar. In doing this they must rub against the anthers which bear the pollen, or the stigma which receives it. Very small insects such as ants may manage to slip past these organs without touching them. The large Sphinx Moths, which have a proboscis up to several inches long, usually hover in front of such flowers, uncoiling and inserting the proboscis without alighting. But they often pick up pollen on the proboscis and (like Hummingbirds) on the front of the head.

671. What is the longest insect proboscis known? A Sphinx Moth in Madagascar has an eleven-inch proboscis, the longest known. Before it was known to exist the great naturalist Alfred Russel Wallace predicted that such a moth would be found, since a Madagascan Orchid has a corolla eleven inches deep. Twelve years later the moth was discovered, its proboscis, as Wallace had specified, long enough to reach the orchid nectaries.

672. Has it been demonstrated that an insect with a long proboscis is essential for the pollination of certain flowers? Yes. White Clover has a short corolla and can be pollinated by Honeybees. Red Clover, however, has a long-tubed corolla, too long for the Honeybee proboscis but not too long for that of the Bumblebee. This was overlooked when Red Clover was introduced to New Zealand many years ago. Honeybees were abundant but the Red Clover failed to set much seed. It was not until Bumblebees were also introduced that pollination was obtained and a good crop of Red Clover seed produced.

673. Are flowers in clusters more easily pollinated? They often are, although here the biological value of pollination may not be as great as though the flowers were on separate plants. Many flowers, such as Daisies, Asters, and Chrysanthemums, that may look like single flowers are really clusters of dozens or hundreds of flowers. An insect walking or crawling over such a cluster must accomplish a great deal of pollen transfer. Some very small insects such as Thrips regularly live in such multiple flowers.

674. Does pollen itself tend to adhere to insects? Much pollen is more or less sticky and thus tends to fasten itself to an insect until rubbed off.

675. What are pollinia? Pollinia are special structures, bearing masses of pollen, that become fastened to an insect. Those of many Orchids have special adhesive disks that fasten to the proboscis, face, or eye of an insect. Those of the Milkweeds have a snap spring, like a mousetrap, that catches on to an insect's feet or to spines or bristles. We have seen large, dark-brown insects so covered with pollinia that they looked yellow.

676. What are some other floral devices that promote pollination? There are so many of these that volumes have been written about them. The chief types are mechanisms that admit only certain insects and exclude others; timing devices that ensure synchronization of the mature floral parts with the insects; and traps that literally force the insect to pollinate the flower, and sometimes imprison it until the flower has been pollinated.

677. How can a flower admit only certain insects? Many Snap-dragons and Orchids, for example, have petals so fused around the floral parts that only very strong, large insects, such as bees, can force their way in. This excludes many insects that would not be efficient pollinators. One Convolvulus-type flower in the Indo-Australian region normally remains closed, opening only when fanned with a certain rhythm and force. These are provided by the wing beats of a Sphinx Moth which hovers in front of the flower until it opens. The Sphinx Moth inserts its proboscis, but all other insects are excluded.

678. Why is the proper timing of flower and insect important? By having flowers mature and open at exactly the time that the best pollinators are flying, many plants have evolved very efficient pollination. Some desert flowers, for example, open only in the early morning and are then visited by certain species of bees that fly only at that time. Other flowers open only in the afternoon and are visited then only by other bees.

679. How do flowers entrap insects and thus ensure pollination? Petals and other flower parts may be so arranged that a visiting insect can enter the flower by only one route. As it does so it will trip a trigger mechanism that will slap a load of pollen onto it from the anthers. In Orchids such as the Lady's Slippers an entering bee enters a chamber by a narrow slit that shuts behind it. The only way out forces it to crawl over and through the anthers and pistil. In some tropical Orchids the insect lands on a hinged lip which snaps over and propels the insect into the center of the flower.

680. How can a flower hold an insect prisoner until pollination is ensured? The Jack-in-the-Pulpit has circular clusters of tiny flowers upon a central, purple spadix. The upper flowers are abortive and hairlike, and so arranged that an insect can pass in but cannot come back out; the next are the staminate flowers; and below are the pistillate. The pistillate flowers mature first, so if the insect has brought pollen from another plant these flowers can be pollinated. By the time the uppermost hairlike flowers have withered, permitting the insect to depart, the staminate flowers are ready to give up their pollen. Many *Aristolochia* flowers have inward-directed hairs that keep an insect from emerging until the pollen is ripe, in much the same way.

GALLS

681. What is a gall?   A gall is an abnormal proliferation of plant cells resulting from some outside stimulus. The stimulus may be a mechanical irritation or injury, a fungus growth, or the activity of a Nematode Worm, a Mite, or an insect. Some masses of "scar" tissue or calloused areas are really galls.

682. How can an insect cause the formation of a gall?   It was once believed that the plant produced the excess tissue in order to heal the wound made by the insect either in feeding upon the plant or ovipositing in it. It is now believed that it is not the mechanical injury of the tissue that stimulates the plant but the chemical secretion released by the growing larvae after hatching from the egg. The one exception seems to be the galls that are induced by Sawflies. They are the result of the secretion injected into the plant tissue at the time of oviposition.

683. What is the nature of the larval secretions that initiate gall growth?   They may be hormones similar to the auxins that regulate plant growth by their concentrations.

684. What plants are most frequently attacked by gall-making insects?   More than one-half of the plant families are attacked. Oaks, however, are hosts to galls caused by the greatest number of species. Willows, Roses, legumes, and composites are also very commonly attacked.

685. Where on the plant are galls formed?   On nearly all parts of various plants: root, stem, bark, bud, flower, leaf, and petiole. The formation occurs only in meristematic tissue, which is tissue that is in the growth stage.

686. Are there many gall insects?   There are a great many, more than 1,500 species in North America alone. Since there are probably several times as many parasites and other insects that invade galls, this is a major way of insect life.

687. To what groups do the chief gall insects belong? The largest group are Diptera, the majority being Gall Midges (Cecidomyiidae). Second in numbers are Hymenoptera, especially the Gall Wasps (Cynipidae), 86 percent of whose galls are on Oak. There are smaller numbers of Coleoptera, chiefly Weevils (Curculionidae), Metallic Wood Borers (Buprestidae), and Long Horns (Cerambycidae); of Homoptera, chiefly Aphids (Aphididae); of Lepidoptera, in a number of families of the "micro" moths; and of Thysanoptera (Thrips).

688. What benefits does the gall insect receive from the gall? The tissues of galls are especially nutritious, being very rich in proteins. And, of course, the insect inside the gall is well sheltered from the weather and protected against desiccation.

689. Is the gall insect protected against predatory and parasitic enemies? To a certain degree it is, but parasitic insects seem to have little trouble in attacking the gall insects. Birds not infrequently tear open galls to get at the insects within.

690. Does man make any use of galls? Most Oak galls are extremely rich in tannic acid, widely used in tanning and in making certain insecticides, inks, and medicines. Galls have also been used in supplying materials for dyes.

691. What are some of the inks and dyes made from galls? Turkey red, a scarlet dye much used in Asia Minor for fabrics and rugs, is obtained from the "mad apple" gall. A very durable ink used for legal papers and the bank notes of many nations is made from the Aleppo Gall of the Near East; in some countries the law still requires that this ink be used in many legal documents. Synthesized chemicals have largely replaced the galls in the manufacture of most inks and dyes.

692. Are galls ever used for food by humans? Despite their high nutritional value most galls are unsuitable for food because of high content of tannic acid or other substances. In the Near East a Gall Wasp gall on Sage has been eaten, prepared with honey and sugar. In the Midwestern United States a Cynipid gall has been used as an emergency food for livestock.

693. Are all galls caused by insects? A great many galls are caused by Mites, and a great many more by fungi. The latter lack the central cavities of animal-caused galls, unless some animal has invaded the gall.

694. Are galls specific in size and shape? The galls are, in fact, more easily identified than the gall insects themselves. A given species of insect will always cause a gall of a distinctive size, shape, and color on a particular part of a particular plant.

695. What are the two main types of insect galls? These are known as *closed* and *open*. The cavity in a closed gall, in which the insect feeds, is entirely shut away from the outer world. That of an open gall has a connection, sometimes very small, with the outer world, through which the fully developed insect can make its escape.

696. Do different types of insects make the two different types of galls? Insects with chewing mouthparts usually live in closed galls; they can bite their way out or, as larvae, prepare an exit for the adult. These are chiefly wasps, moths, and flies. Insects with sucking mouthparts are found in open galls from which they can emerge with no trouble. These are chiefly Aphids and Mites.

697. Do galls differ greatly in size? Among insect galls the largest may be two inches in diameter, the smallest less than one-sixteenth of an inch. The so-called "spot galls" on leaves are little more than small, thickened areas.

698. Do galls differ greatly in shape? Some kind of gall may be almost any shape. The Oak Apple and Bullet Galls are perfect spheres. Many galls are ovoid, sometimes bearing characteristic spines. Others are elongate, spindle-shaped, or bottle-shaped. Many are irregular, looking like rounded masses kneaded together. Blister and spot galls are thin disks.

699. What are Bunch Galls? These are a characteristic type of stem gall. The elongation of the stem ceases, but the whorls of leaves develop, clumped together about the gall. A common one on Goldenrod stems in eastern North America is caused by a Gall Fly, *Rhopalomyia solidaginis*.

700. What are Pine Cone Galls?　These are not found on Pine trees, but on Willows, at the tips of twigs. They look like small cones, an inch or so long, and are caused by various species of Gall Flies.

701. What are Mossy Galls?　These are rounded, soft, mossy-looking masses, found on twigs of such plants as Oak and Rose. They are caused by various Gall Wasps.

702. What are Oak Apple Galls?　These are large, globular galls found on leaves. There are two chief ones in eastern North America: one has the interior largely filled with a spongy mass; the other has a central cell with many fine fibers radiating out to the outer shell. They are caused by Gall Wasps.

703. What are Bullet Galls?　These are smaller, spherical galls of many different Gall Wasps, found chiefly on Oak twigs and leaves, often in clusters. Different ones range in size from an eighth of an inch to an inch in diameter.

704. What causes Witch Hazel Cone Galls?　These abundant small, sharp, conical galls on the leaves of Witch Hazel are caused by an Aphid, *Hormaphis hamamelidis*. Each has an opening on the lower surface of the leaf.

705. Are any common galls caused by moths?　The Elliptical Goldenrod Gall on the stems of a number of species is spindle-shaped and about an inch long. It is caused by a "micro" moth *Gnorimoschema gallaesolidaginis*. The caterpillar prepares a round exit hole at one end before it pupates, closing it with a neatly beveled stopper that the moth can punch out from inside.

706. Are there similar Goldenrod stem galls with which this might be confused?　A Trypetid Fly with pictured wings causes an almost globular stem gall much like that of the moth. The exit hole is on the side, and is not plugged with a stopper; furthermore the gall contains no silk. Another fly of the same genus (*Eurosta*) causes similar globular galls on the Goldenrod roots.

707. Is the insect that one finds inside the gall the one that made the gall?　Not necessarily, because in the gall is often found a very busy community made up of a variety of insects, some of which are mere transient opportunists. One may thus find, living within the gall, the insect that made it; but there is an even greater likelihood that one will find one or more Chalcid Wasp larvae that have lived upon and destroyed the original inhabitant; or one may find parasites upon these parasites. With these, or instead of these, one may find various guests that are living as invaders or *inquilines,* utilizing the food supply. The inquilines, too, may have their parasites and their hyperparasites. And always there is the possibility that hovering around the whole there may be a predator or two, attracted to this teeming world of insect life. One study of the Pine Cone Willow gall reported 31 different species of insects living within it in addition to the gall maker: 10 inquilines, 16 parasites, 5 transients.

708. Does a gall-making insect always cause the same type of gall? Usually, although there are a few exceptions. In the case of insects having alternation of generations, as in many Aphids and Cynipid Wasps, the two different generations may each produce a different kind of gall.

709. Can one species of plant have more than one type of gall on it? Yes; a single Oak may have dozens of different galls on it. Even though it is the plant tissue that makes the gall, it is the species of insect that determines the type of gall.

710. Are any gall insects of special value to man? The Chalcid Wasp, *Blastophaga psenes,* makes the culture of the Smyrna Fig possible. The Smyrna Fig flowers are exclusively female and do not set good fruit unless pollinated. The Wild Caprifig, which is not desirable as fruit, has pollen-bearing flowers. The two kinds of figs must be planted together if good Smyrna fruit is to be obtained. The female Fig Wasp lays its eggs in the Caprifig flowers; the larvae develop into males and females within tiny galls formed by the flower. The wingless male emerges from its gall and crawls over the other galls until he finds one containing a female, whom he then fertilizes through a tiny puncture in the gall. The female emerges from the gall and leaves the flower, picking up pollen as she goes. If she finds a Smyrna flower she will enter it but will not oviposit; however, the pollen will be dusted off onto the Smyrna pistillate flower. Smyrna Figs cannot be grown, then, unless there is also present the Wild Caprifig and its gall-making wasp.

711. Are any gallmakers harmful? Most gallmakers do little harm, aside from spoiling the appearance of plants at times. However, there are a few that are considered rather serious pests. Among these are the Clover Leaf Midge, the Chrysanthemum Midge, the Wheat Joint Worm, and most notorious of all, the Grape Phylloxera.

712. Why is the Grape Phylloxera notorious? In 1860, or thereabouts, the Aphid *Phylloxera vitifoliae* was introduced into France. Almost immediately it became a serious pest upon the famous Grapes of the wine-growing districts. In twenty-five years it had destroyed more than two and a half million acres of vines and was threatening to wipe out Grape culture in France. These little yellowish Aphids pepper the Grape leaf with tiny galls, the size of half a pea, causing the leaves to yellow and wither; but they also cause root galls which open the way to a rot that quickly saps the strength of the vine. Insecticides proved of little value.

713. How can one species of Aphid cause galls on both the leaves and the roots? The generation that develops in the leaf galls alternates with a generation in the root galls. The offspring of each generation migrates to the other part of the plant.

714. How was the Phylloxera finally controlled? Fortunately the root systems of native American grapes are highly resistant to the Phylloxera. So American rootstocks were cultivated in great numbers and planted in France, and the stems of the European wine Grape varieties grafted on to them. Many millions of French grapevines are now growing on American root systems.

715. Doesn't this affect the quality of the European Grapes? The quality of the fruit is determined by the characteristics of the stem and leaf system, not of the roots. The Grapes therefore have the distinctive features, which largely influence the characteristics of the wine, that they had when grown on their own rootstocks. Some people think that the quality of vintages has changed, but most agree that it has not.

LEAF ROLLERS AND FOLDERS

716. What is a leaf roller?   It is an insect which, usually as a larva, rolls a leaf, thus making a shelter in which it rests and from which it feeds.

717. How is this rolling done?   By spinning silk across the upper side of the leaf from edge to edge; this may be done crosswise or lengthwise. When the silk dries it shrinks and pulls the edges together. A repetition of this process will eventually produce a tight roll. A few Lepidoptera cut a small flap and roll that into a cone.

718. Do any adults roll leaves for their larvae?   In a subfamily of Weevils, the Attelabini, the adult female makes a thimble-shaped roll of a spirally wound strip of leaf and lays an egg in it. The larva feeds on the leaf from inside the roll.

719. Do any adults roll leaves for their own use?   An unusual nocturnal Grasshopper, *Camptonotus carolinensis,* which feeds on Aphids, rolls up a leaf in which it lives.

720. What larval insects are leaf rollers?   Only those insects that spin silk can roll leaves. It is done by the larvae of seventeen different families of Lepidoptera, principally the "micro" moths, and a few web-spinning Sawflies.

721. Do any other insects use leaf rolls made by others?   Many insects utilize these shelters, sometimes for protection or for pupation, and sometimes so as to feed upon the debris left there. Mites, Spiders, and Scavenging Beetles will be found in abundance in abandoned leaf rolls, especially in damp weather, the spiders often adding their own silk to the untidy contents of the roll.

722. Do leaf rollers pupate in their rolls?   The great majority do, although a few depart to pupate elsewhere.

723. Do any butterfly caterpillars roll leaves? Quite a few do, notably those of some of the Swallowtails, which make a loose roll in which to rest in concealment. The very young caterpillars of the Viceroy make a tight, silk-lined roll of the basal part of a leaf, fastening it to the twig with silk. In this they spend the winter. For this reason it is called a *hibernaculum.*

724. What are leaf folders and leaf tyers? Some "micro" moths and a few Midges (Cecidomyiidae) fold over the edge of the leaf and then fasten it down with silk. Many young Skipper larvae cut a square flap at the edge of a leaf which they then fold and tie down. Others tie together two or more leaves, sometimes tying in flowers and fruit and thus making a sizable protective nest or web. The leaf webbers, Web Worms, and Ugly Nest Caterpillars make great untidy bundles in trees and shrubs. Occasional Sawflies do the same, especially in Plum, Cherry, and Pine.

725. How do the Green Tree Ants of the Orient make their webbed nests? There are, in Africa and Asia, several species of Tree Ants (*Oecophylla*) that web leaves with silk. The larvae produce the silk; the workers do not. So the workers pick up the larvae, squeeze them, and then use them as shuttles to carry the thread back and forth as they sew the leaves together.

726. Are the leaf folds and webs occupied by more than one insect? They differ. The Hydrangea leaf tyer sews two terminal leaves together and occupies the nest alone. But if a batch of these larvae have emerged together from their eggs they may tie two leaves together, all eating together, skeletonizing the leaf together, and then as they grow older, drawing in more leaves, rolling and tying, rolling and tying.

727. Do leaf tyers always feed inside their nest? Usually, but not always. The caterpillar of the big Silver Spotted Skipper, *Epargyreus clarus,* uses its nest, made of the leaflets of Locust trees, only as a shelter in which to rest, and as a sort of loose, simple cocoon in which to pupate.

LEAF CUTTERS

728. Which insects cut out pieces of leaves?   The best known are the Leaf-Cutter Ants and Leaf-Cutter Bees. These insects make very different uses of their leaves, however.

729. What do the Leaf-Cutter Ants do with the pieces of leaf? These ants, chiefly of the genus *Atta,* inhabit the Neotropical regions. Their enormous ground nests may cover an acre or more and go deep underground. In the subterranean chambers they grow fungi on the pieces of leaf brought in.

730. How do Leaf-Cutter Bees use pieces of leaf?   The females of these bees (Megachilidae) use the pieces to make thimble-shaped chambers along a tunnel in the ground or in a hollow plant stem. In each chamber a supply of honey and pollen is accumulated and an egg laid. The bee larva then has a snug nest in which to develop and a goodly supply of food.

LEAF MINERS

731. What is a leaf miner?   Any insect which, as a larva, lives and feeds between the two layers of a leaf for some period of its life is a miner. They form no taxonomic group, for the habit has been adopted by representatives of four different orders.

732. Do many insects mine in leaves?   In North America about 400 Lepidoptera of 20 different families, over 200 species of Diptera (mostly Agromyzidae and Anthomyidae), about 50 species of Coleoptera (Buprestidae, Chrysomelidae, and Curculionidae), and possibly 15 species of Hymenoptera (Tenthredinidae) live in mines for at least part of their lives.

733. What effect does leaf mining have on the plant?   Foliage is disfigured; when the plant is used for decorative purposes (Nasturtiums, Delphiniums, Chrysanthemums, etc.) or when it is edible (Spinach, Beets, etc.) this is of considerable economic importance. Soft leaves of herbaceous plants wilt. Leaves of woody plants usually remain turgid but suffer from reduction of chlorophyll tissue, with a resulting handicap for the plant. We have seen small trees killed by a heavy infestation of a moth leaf miner.

734. Do leaf miners attack any particular group of plants?   Nearly all plant families are attacked, including aquatic plants, milky-juice plants, and even Poison Ivy. Oak is attacked by more than fifty species. Even grasses and the needles of Pine and Spruce are mined.

735. How have larvae become adapted for leaf mining?   Many are extremely small; the Nepticulid Moths, almost all miners (some in bark), may have a wing expanse of no more than 3 millimeters. The larvae of specialized groups are very flat and have a reduction of legs, antennae, eyes, and in some instances mouthparts. Sometimes the head is wedge-shaped to facilitate pushing between the upper and lower epidermal layers of the leaf.

736. On what do the larvae feed?   They feed on the internal cells of the leaf which form the spongy mesophyll. These cells are very thin-walled and have a high liquid and carbohydrate content. Some species emerge from the leaf when they get older, and live as skeletonizers in a rolled-up leaf.

737. Are the larval mouthparts adapted for such special feeding?   The mandibles (which the larvae of Diptera lack entirely) are often flattened and protrude forward. They act like scissors, shearing the delicate cells rather than chewing them.

738. Do leaf miners ever move on to other leaves?   Very rarely. In most cases the larvae are so small, even when full grown, that only a small part of one leaf furnishes enough food for its entire development. Sometimes wilting of the leaf forces removal to another.

739. Where do leaf miners pupate?   Not infrequently the pupa is formed in the mine; sometimes an emergence hole is prepared beforehand. Usually, however, the mature larva leaves the mine and pupates nearby or in the ground. Some leaf-mining moth larvae spin a cocoon on the leaf over the mine.

740. How do leaf miners dispose of their excrement? Sometimes this is pushed out of the mine. More often the moth larvae leave it in the mine, but usually in a distinct pattern (which helps identify different groups). The solid wastes, in small pellets, may be strung out in a line, pushed to the edges, or gathered in masses.

741. Do the mines of different species or groups have characteristic shapes? They almost always do. *Blotch* mines are broad and rounded; *digitate* mines have slender, fingerlike extensions; *trumpet* mines are long and slender and enlarge rather abruptly; *serpentine* mines are slender and wind and twist. Knowing the species of plant, the shape of mine, and the method of excrement disposal should enable one to identify a mine easily.

742. Does a leaf miner cut through the veins? Some are impeded in their progress by the tough veins, and confine their activities to the tissue between veins; others cut across the smaller ones, though seldom through the midrib.

743. Do any insects mine in other parts of plants? A good many species, of the same groups as leaf miners, mine in the soft epidermis or bark of stems. Others mine beneath the epidermis of fruit.

BORERS

744. Are borers in plant tissues of much economic significance? Yes, they are many in number and the damage they do is great. Since they work beneath the surface the damage is often not detected for some time; and for the same reason control is difficult, because they cannot be easily reached.

745. In what parts of plants do insects bore? They bore in buds, in leaves, in fruits, seeds, and nuts, in herbaceous stems, in woody stems, sometimes in or beneath the bark, or even in the hard wood. Of course leaf miners are borers in a modest way.

746. What insects are borers? The chief borers are to be found among the Isoptera, Coleoptera, Diptera, Lepidoptera, and Hymenoptera. Usually they bore only in the larval stage; but in the social groups such as the termites and ants, the entire colony, adults and larvae, lives in the tunnels, the boring being done chiefly or entirely by adults. One Australian Cricket and one American Roach have taken up wood boring.

747. Are wood-boring larvae adapted in any special way? They are cylindrical, often legless, or with reduced legs, and often have the head either flattened or partly telescoped into the thorax. The whole thorax may be enlarged, sometimes flattened. Needless to say they usually have very strong mandibles (dipterous larvae being exceptions).

748. Do wood borers bore in solid wood? In this respect wood borers are of two general types: those that bore deep into the hard wood and those that make shallow burrows, remaining mostly in the softer layers under the bark.

749. Are they both harmful? The shallow borers do greater harm to the living tree because they cut into the growing tissue. The deep borers make the wood much less valuable for use as lumber.

750. Do many borers attack dead wood? A great many do, many of them exclusively. Some start in living trees but may remain and continue working in the wood even after it has been cut and sawed into lumber. Some of these have been known to emerge from finished furniture years after the wood was cut. Others which never attack living or fresh wood enter the wood only after it has been used in buildings or furniture.

751. Why do wood borers live so long? They develop slowly because their food has so little nourishment. Many spend several years in the larval stage.

752. How can logs be stored so that borers will not get into them? The best way usually is to submerge them in a lake or pond. Logs will last many years under water and in the meantime are safe from most borers.

753. Can wood be treated to keep out borers? Treatment with creosote by painting or impregnation is fairly effective. It is often impractical or impossible to treat the interiors of large pieces of lumber.

754. What insects invade and damage wooden houses? The chief ones are various termites. The Death Watch and Powder Post Beetles (Anobiidae and Lyctidae) are destructive to houses and furniture, making tiny but extensive holes. Carpenter Ants (*Camponotus*) sometimes are destructive to houses.

755. Do borers actually eat wood? Most of them do, but they do not digest the wood themselves. A few species of Cerambycid Beetle larvae seem to have an enzyme, cellulase, that digests cellulose, but most wood-eating insects are dependent upon symbiotic organisms in their digestive tracts, or else actually utilize only the contents of the wood cells or the fungi that may be breaking down the wood. The termites have an immense number of protozoa in their intestines, sometimes of many kinds, that are capable of digesting wood.

756. Do any of the borers enter plant tissue just for shelter and not for food? A great many do. Carpenter Ants excavate wholly for nesting purposes. The large Carpenter Bees make deep holes half an inch or more in diameter in hard wood for their nests; and many of the Solitary Bees and Wasps bore tunnels in hard wood or clean out pith cavities in stems in which, after provisioning, they lay one or more eggs.

757. Are there many borers in the stems of plants? Many insects bore in the stems of herbaceous plants and grasses, especially in hollow or pithy stems. Some of the worst agricultural pests do this. The larvae of the European Corn Borer Moth and the Hessian Fly, to cite only two of many, so weaken the stem that it breaks prematurely.

758. Do any insects bore in roots? Quite a number do, although not as many as live above ground. The chief root borers are beetle larvae. The very large Prioninae, a group of Long-horned Beetles, bore in woody roots, especially of stumps.

759. Do many insects bore in fruits? There are probably very few plants in the fruit of which some species of insect does not bore.

This includes fruits other than edible ones. A Cotton boll is a fruit; the larvae of the Cotton Boll Weevil do millions of dollars' damage boring in them; so do the Pink Boll Worms, larvae of a tropical moth; and the Cotton Boll Worms, the larvae of an Owlet Moth, *Heliothis obsoleta,* which also attacks the fruits of Tomato and Corn, and are then known as Tomato Fruit Worms and Corn Worms.

760. What are the worms found boring in apples? The majority are the larvae of the Codling Moth, *Laspeyresia pomonella.* Originally imported from Europe, this moth has spread over all apple-growing regions of North America and cost untold millions of dollars in damage and in the cost of spraying (sometimes as many as seven times a year) for its control.

761. Are there many seed borers? Many of the larvae found boring in fruits are really eating seeds, but a great many bore in individual seeds. Many of these are Weevils, many other are the larvae of moths, flies, Chalcid Wasps, and other groups. They are collectively enormously destructive both to seeds used as food by man and domestic animals and to those of other useful plants. Some examples are the Wheat Midge, *Contarmia tritici,* and the Clover Seed Midge, *Dasyneura leguminicola,* both the larvae of small flies; the Pea and Bean Weevils, *Bruchus pisorum* and *B. obtectus;* and the Apple Seed Chalcid, *Torymus druparum,* and Clover Seed Chalcid, *Bruchophagus gibbus.*

PLANT DISEASES

762. How are insects responsible for plant diseases? In injuring plant tissue, either by feeding upon it, ovipositing in it, or boring in it, they open the way for the entrance of disease-causing organisms. Sometimes insects are guilty of carrying the disease organism from one plant to another either on or in their bodies. This they may actually inject into the plant tissue or merely leave on the surface or in previously made lesions. In many cases, however, they actually harbor the organism within their bodies, protecting it from adverse conditions or serving as an essential host to some part of the organism's life cycle.

763. What type of plant diseases attack plants because of injury by insects? Molds and rots often become established in the injury. The blight that affects Potatoes after Flea Beetle injury, or the Chestnut blight that follows the attack of Bark-boring Beetles, are examples of these.

764. What type of plant diseases do insects transport on their bodies? Bacteria as well as fungus spores are easily transported on the body and legs of insects. Some fungus spores build up an electrical charge opposite to that of the insect body, which enables them to adhere to it. The Dutch Elm disease spores are thus carried from infected Elms to healthy ones by Bark-boring Beetles. Bacteria and fungus spores may also be carried on the insect mouthparts; the bacterial Black Rot of Cabbage and the fungus Brown Rot of many orchard fruits are carried in this way.

765. Do insects transmit any virus diseases of plants? They transmit many virus diseases, inoculating the healthy plants as they feed upon them. In fact, the first virus ever to be described, long before its true nature was understood, was that of the Tobacco Mosaic transmitted by the Green Peach Aphid. A very serious virus disease of the Potato is transmitted by a small Psyllid.

766. What plant diseases actually pass through part of their development within the insect body? Among the best known are the Cucumber Wilt caused by the Striped Cucumber Beetles and the bacterial Corn Wilt carried by the Corn Flea Beetle. Many of the virus diseases are dependent upon a period of development within Psyllids and Leaf Hoppers.

INSECTIVOROUS PLANTS

767. Are there many plants that catch and eat insects? There are some 450 known higher plants (excluding fungi) that regularly catch and kill insects. While it has not been shown in all cases that they actually use the insects for nourishment, this is most probable.

768. What are the chief insectivorous plants? The chief New World groups are the Pitcher Plants (*Sarracenia*), Sundews (*Dro-*

sera), Venus Fly Trap (*Dionaea*), Butterworts (*Pinguicula*), and Bladderworts (*Utricularia*). In Asia the large genus *Nepenthes* has many species with hanging pitcherlike receptacles. Each of these groups has its own method of trapping insects.

769. How do the Pitcher Plants entrap insects?   The leaves form long pitchers which fill with water. Downward-slanting hairs encourage an insect to crawl into the pitcher but prevent its crawling out again. It falls into the water, drowns, and is at least partly digested and used by the plant.

770. How do the Sundews catch insects?   Many short, stiff, hollow hairs arise from the Sundew leaf. Each of these secretes a drop of glistening, extremely sticky liquid at its tip. An insect, touching one of these drops, sticks fast, and by struggling thoroughly entangles itself. The leaf then closes slowly around the insect and digests its tissues.

771. How does the Venus Fly Trap catch insects?   The oval, terminal part of the leaf is hinged along the middle. Protruding from one surface are a number of spines. When an insect touches off a trigger mechanism the leaf quickly folds shut around it, the spines keeping it from escaping, like the bars of a cage. After it is digested the leaf unfolds and awaits another victim.

772. What are Butterworts?   These are small plants that grow in moist spots. Each has a flat rosette of leaves which are covered above with a sticky secretion that both attracts and holds insects. The edges of the leaf roll inward, surrounding the captive.

773. Where do Bladderworts grow?   These plants grow in shallow water, often in bogs. On the leaves are small bladders. Triggered by contact with a small aquatic animal the bladder expands, sucking the animal in and then snapping shut around it.

774. Do any insects feed on or make use of these insect-catching plants?   Quite a few insects have evolved means of exploiting the plants while avoiding their dangers. The larvae of one Mosquito, *Wyeomyia smithii,* and of one Sarcophagid fly, live only in the water in Pitcher Plant leaves, feeding on the decaying insect substances. One Owlet Moth of the genus *Exyra* manages to enter the pitchers to lay her eggs and then get out again; her larvae eat the pitchers themselves. Another Owlet Moth does the same in the Asiatic *Nepenthes*.

775. Do any other types of plants attack insects?   A great many fungi regularly infect insects. A common type develops inside the bodies of many flies, including the Housefly. Eventually the fly dies, and dense masses of the sporangia of the fungus grow out from its body. We have seen a heavy infestation of Snipe Flies by such a fungus, the bodies of the flies being plastered onto the under surfaces of leaves by the scores of thousands. Many other insects, including Grasshoppers, Crickets, and Aphids, are similarly attacked.

776. Does man make use of such fungi?   Their use as a method of controlling harmful insects has been attempted but with success in only a few instances. In China, caterpillars mummified by a fungus attack are considered a special delicacy and sold in markets in bundles.

777. What are flowering caterpillars and flowering Cicadas? These are the bodies of caterpillars (and pupae) and of Cicada nymphs living in the soil that are attacked by a fungus of the genus *Cordyceps*. The fungus, when mature, sends up a bright red or orange fruiting body that may grow two or three inches above the surface.

778. Are insects subject to infection by bacteria?   A great many are, the bacteria often causing fatal diseases. Milky Disease of Japanese Beetles, caused by spore-forming bacteria, and Foul Brood of Honeybees are two outstanding ones; the former, beneficial to man, and the latter, costly to man. Insects also suffer virus, protozoan, and worm infections.

779. Has man made use of these bacterial diseases?   Only a limited use has been made, since it is difficult to get an infection spread throughout a large insect population. But in a few instances bacterial control of insects is proving its worth.

XII. INSECTS AND OTHER ANIMALS

INSECTS AS PREDATORS

780. What distinguishes a predator? Typical predators kill their prey quickly and violently. A special type of predator, very abundant among insects, behaves more like a parasite in feeding gently and slowly on its prey, which may remain alive for several days or weeks. Such "gentle" predators are called *parasitoids*. True parasites do not kill their hosts. We here use the term *predator* for the conventional "violent" ones.

781. Why are predaceous insects important to man? The great majority feed on other insects, many of which are harmful to man. A few, however, kill species beneficial to man.

782. What particular insects are predaceous? There are tens of thousands of species. The chief groups are the Dragonflies, the Mantids, several families of bugs, most Neuroptera, a great many beetles, many flies, many Hunting Wasps, and a scattering of members of other orders.

783. Are Dragonflies and Damselflies beneficial to man? On the whole they probably are, since many of them kill a great many Mosquitoes and Blackflies, both as nymphs and as adults. They also, of course, kill many insects that are important as fish food; but they themselves are in turn eaten by fishes, so that this is not a total loss. A few of the big Dragonflies, particularly *Coryphaeschna ingens,* are a minor pest because they sometimes feed on Honeybees.

784. Are Preying Mantids beneficial? On the whole they probably are, although the majority are of no great importance one way or the other. This is contrary to the popular opinion that Mantids are voracious feeders on harmful insects exclusively, and that they are therefore protected by law. Neither is true.

785. What bugs are beneficial as predators? The Flower Bugs (Anthocoridae) live primarily in flowers and shrubbery where they feed busily on Thrips, Mites, and the young of several groups of insects. The Ambush Bugs (Phymatidae), which have the forelegs remarkably developed for grasping, catch fairly large insects such as Cabbage Butterflies and bees and wasps, even though they themselves are only one-half inch long. Unfortunately some of the insects that they kill may be valuable, and many are of no direct importance to man. The Damsel Bugs (Nabidae) are very largely beneficial. A few Leaf Bugs (Miridae), a few Leaf-footed Bugs (Coreidae), and a few Stink Bugs (Pentatomidae) prey considerably upon harmful insects, although many other members of these families are pests on food plants. The Assassin Bugs (Reduviidae) sometimes attack man and Honeybees, but they do kill many harmful Leaf Hoppers and caterpillars.

786. What beetles are beneficial as predators? In the Coleoptera man has many good allies. The Ladybird Beetles (Coccinellidae), the Ground Beetles (Carabidae), and the Tiger Beetles (Cicindelidae) are the most conspicuous. But the larvae of many Rove Beetles (Staphylinidae) consume large numbers of Aphids; the larvae of the Checkered Beetles (Cleridae) and of the Fireflies (Lampyridae) do the same. The larvae of some Blister and Oil Beetles (Meloidae) eat the eggs of Grasshoppers.

787. Are all species of Ladybirds valuable for the control of insects? There are nearly 4,000 species of Ladybirds in the world and about 370 in North America. A few species, but only a very few, are pests, so one can say that in general Ladybirds should be protected as well as encouraged, because in both larval and adult life they rank among our most beneficial insects. The reddish-orange ones, of which we have about 40 species, feed primarily on Aphids; the blackish species prefer Scale Insects, Mealy Bugs, and White Flies. When food is scarce they will nibble on plant material, however. Many species will eat, not just certain species of insects, but only certain stages of these species, so that not all Ladybirds can be used to control any particular pest.

788. How much do Ladybirds actually eat? A larva has been known to eat from 200 to 300 Aphids before pupating. A newly emerged female may require 200–500 medium-sized Aphids to get sufficient nourishment to produce her eggs, and will continue to eat at the same high rate for some time.

789. Are the big Carabid Beetles valuable predators? The majority are, feeding largely on such pests as Wireworms, Cutworms, and other ground-dwelling insects. A few are plant eaters. The European *Calosoma sycophanta* was introduced into New England to control the Gypsy and Brown-tail Moths. The beetle became well established for a time but was not successful in controlling these two pests. It is a useful insect to have around, however, because like most big Carabids it is a valuable predator. Our native *Calosoma scrutator* is nearly as large and is common.

790. How are Tiger Beetles beneficial? They are active predators, running swiftly over the ground seeking out their prey. They have long, toothed mandibles which are extremely efficient in grasping and killing many harmful caterpillars. Their larvae, too, feed on insects, reaching out from their tunnels in the ground.

791. What are Aphis Lions and Ant Lions? Aphis Lions are the larvae of the gauzy, lovely, but strong-smelling Green-eyed Lacewings (Chrysopidae). They have long, sharp, pointed mandibles that are grooved along the inner surface so that when fitted to the maxillae they form closed tubes through which the juices of their victims are sucked. They scurry over plant foliage seeking and consuming large numbers of Aphids. One larva in captivity ate 202 Aphids. The larvae of the Brown Lacewings (Hemerobiidae) are equally beneficial.

Ant Lions are the larvae of the Myrmeleontidae. They feed on insects but, since they live at the bottom of their conical pits and do not go actively in search of prey, are not of such great economic importance.

792. What flies are predaceous? Not many adult flies are. The Robber Flies (Asilidae) are an outstanding family of predatory flies. Although they seem to us to be clumsy, they are very successful in catching the prey on the wing or in dropping on it from the air. A few species have the harmful habit of specializing on bees, particularly Honeybees. The members of some genera resemble hairy Bumblebees, which may help them in sneaking up on unwary prey (since Bumblebees are not predatory) and may protect them from the attack of larger predators.

793. Are any fly larvae predaceous?   The larvae of several families of flies are predaceous, especially of the Soldier Flies (Stratiomyiidae) and the Hover or Flower Flies (Syrphidae). The latter, although eyeless, legless, and jawless (they have mouth hooks), creep around on vegetation catching many Aphids and small insects, and are extremely beneficial. They may live in a mass of Aphids, often nearly concealed by the Aphid secretions, but inconspicuously decimating the colony, often bringing it under control.

794. Are wasps of value as predators?   It is hard to convince the general public, especially the gardener whose flowerheads have been riddled with the chewing of the big *Vespa crabro,* that wasps are beneficial. But the Paper Wasps, *Vespula* and *Dolichovespula,* as well as *Vespa crabro,* the Potter Wasps, *Eumenes* and *Odynerus,* and most of the other Hunting Wasps, are actively predaceous upon insects of nearly all groups, carrying them in a paralyzed state to their nests as food for their young. They are extremely beneficial to man since most of their victims are injurious species.

795. Has man utilized any of these predatory insects in his attempt to control insect pests?   It was 160 years ago that Erasmus Darwin first suggested using Syrphid Flies to control Aphids. Sixteen years later Ladybird Beetles were used to control Aphids that were ruining the Hop vines. Since that time the search has gone on with increasing zeal; there have been many failures but there have also been successes. Two of the outstanding successes have been the control of the Sugarcane Leafhopper in the Hawaiian Islands by a bug of the family Miricidae, that was found to devour the pest's eggs; and the control of the Cottony Cushion Scale in California by the introduction of the Australian Ladybird, the Vedalia, *Rhodolia cardinalis.* The Scale itself had been accidentally introduced into California in 1868 from either Australia or New Zealand. By 1890 it had killed hundreds of thousands of trees and was threatening the entire Orange industry of the state. Entomologists, sent to Australia by the government, brought back 140 of the little beetles and turned them loose on a few screened trees. Within a year and a half their progeny had brought the infestation of Cottony Cushion Scale under control. In recent years at least ten different Scale Insects and a Mealybug that had built up into serious pests in various parts of the world have been similarly brought under control by introduced predators.

796. Are any predaceous insects in this country sold for insect-control purposes? Ladybird Beetles are used extensively in insect control and are sold for that purpose. They are collected at their winter hibernation quarters in the mountains of California in large quantities and shipped out as far away as Texas. Some of the collectors sell as many as ten gallons a year. Farmers would probably do better to depend upon their own local Ladybird Beetles, and should protect them more carefully from poison sprays.

797. Are Spiders of value in control of pest insects? Spiders have not been introduced as predators for any specific pest insects; but time and time again they have been observed to be present in great abundance following a pest outbreak, with a subsequent reduction in the number of insects. Natural increases in the numbers of a large ornamental Jumping Spider in Fiji follow periodic outbreaks of a moth infestation of the Coconut Palms, bringing the moths under control. Similar natural controls have been noted for many outbreaks in the United States, including those of the Gypsy Moth, Cotton Worm, and Pea Aphis.

INSECTS AS PARASITOIDS

798. What insects live as parasitoids? The largest group of parasitoids comprises the great majority of the members of several superfamilies of wasps, chiefly the Ichneumonidea and Chalcidoidea. These contain many tens of thousands of species. Next are the Tachinid Flies, a very large world-wide family containing several thousand species. There are also a few small groups of beetles such as the Oil and Blister Beetles (Meloidae); a few small families of flies such as the Bee Flies (Bombyliidae), Thick-headed Flies (Conopidae), and Dexiid Flies; the small order Strepsiptera, the Twisted Wing Insects; and a scattering of small groups in various other orders.

799. How do parasitoids develop?   The female deposits her eggs near, on, or in larvae of the host (or prey) insect. By one means or another the parasitoid larva gets inside the body of the host and begins feeding on it. At first it does little damage, feeding on nonvital parts. The host may continue feeding and growing for some days or weeks; if a larva it may even pupate. Eventually, however, the parasitoid larva feeds on the host's vital organs and thus kills it. Typically the parasitoid larva leaves the host before the latter's death, pupates, and transforms to an adult.

800. Do all parasitoids attack larvae only?   By no means. A great many are egg parasites, the parasitoid larva developing fully inside a single egg of the host. Others may develop in the host's egg mass or oötheca. Many others develop only in a pupa of the host.

801. Are egg parasites very small?   Those that feed within a single egg are extremely small, some of them the smallest of insects. The Mymaridae, or Fairyflies, and Trichogrammatidae range in size from about one-hundredth to one-twentieth of an inch in length. Like most egg parasites they belong to the Chalcidoid Wasps.

802. Are egg parasites valuable to man?   Many of the most beneficial of all insects are the egg parasites which, by killing the host in the egg stage, prevent its doing any damage as a larva. *Trichogramma minutum* parasitizes the eggs of more than a hundred different insects of six orders.

803. How do the egg parasites get into the host's egg?   The female parasitoid, who has a piercing ovipositor, lays her egg inside that of the host. Some of the female Fairyflies go beneath the surface of the water to parasitize the eggs of aquatic insects such as Damselflies and Backswimmers. Many egg parasites attack the eggs of even such extremely small insects as Scale Insects and Aphids.

804. What groups parasitize the larvae of other insects?   Members of practically every group of the parasitoids specialize on larval (or nymphal) hosts. This is, in fact, the commonest parasitoid habit.

805. How do the parasitoid larvae get into the host larvae?   Different ones do this in different ways. In the wasps with piercing ovipositors, the female inserts the egg into the host. In others, especially many Tachinid Flies, the female fastens the egg to the body of the host, and the parasitoid larva emerges from it on the inner surface ready to burrow into the host. In still others the eggs are laid in the vicinity of the host, perhaps in leaves that it may eat. When this happens the parasitoid egg hatches inside the host's digestive tract and the larva burrows through the walls of this into the body cavity.

806. Do parasitoids ever lay more than one egg in a single host? As a rule they lay only one, or at most a very small number.

807. Can a parasitoid female recognize a host that has already been parasitized? In some cases this has been shown to be the case. She then usually refrains from parasitizing it again.

808. Does more than one species of parasitoid ever attack the same species of host? This is very frequent; some insects are attacked by many species of parasitoids belonging to all the major groups.

809. Does more than one species of parasitoid ever attack the same host individual? This, too, often happens. A single larva may be the host to two or three different parasitoid species. When the parasitoids are direct feeders on the host the larvae that grow the fastest, or that had a head start, usually end by devouring their competitors.

810. Do any parasitoids regularly attack other parasitoids? An enormous number of them do, being, therefore, "parasitic" on other parasitoids rather than on the original host. Nor does the matter end there, for there are parasitoids that attack parasitoids that attack parasitoids that attack the basic host.

811. Do the parasitoid insects attack only other insects? No, many use as hosts other land invertebrates, such as Spiders. Centipedes, and Isopod Crustacea.

812. Do any parasitoid insects specialize on the pupae of their hosts? Quite a number do. Females have been observed standing by a larva until it pupated and then ovipositing in the pupa. Of course adult parasitoids which emerge from a pupa usually developed in the host larva. We have obtained as many as two hundred minute Chalcid Wasps from a single pupa of an Anglewing Butterfly (*Polygonia*), probably a case of polyembryonic development.

813. What is polyembryony? This is the phenomenon of the development of a number of distinct individuals from a single egg. It is a regular feature in many parasitoids of small size that attack relatively large hosts. The large number of individuals thus produced is of course additionally advantageous. It is the same thing as the occurrence of "identical" twins in humans and some other animals, and of the four identical offspring of the Nine-banded Armadillo.

814. Are parasitoids specific as to their hosts, or do they attack many different species? Some appear to be specific, attacking only one species of host. (Many of the recorded cases of this may be due to our ignorance, the parasitoid having been reared from a known host once or twice). Some others are quite generalized, attacking members of several orders and many families. The majority are somewhere in between, tending to specialize on a relatively small number of host species that are related to each other. And most parasitoids are quite specific in attacking only the eggs, larvae, or pupae of the host.

815. Is host specificity desirable from the viewpoint of the usefulness of parasitoids to man? It is highly desirable that a parasitoid should concentrate on one, or a small number of host species. A parasitoid that attacks, for example, the Gypsy Moth will be a more efficient control of this pest if it attacks chiefly Gypsy Moths and does not expend much of its energy attacking many noninjurious species. On the other hand it is also desirable that when the pest is rare the parasite should be able to maintain a good population by attacking other insects, and thus be ready to forestall a sudden increase in the numbers of the pest.

816. Does man make wide use of parasitoid insects for the control of injurious species? Great use is made of many species, and new ones are constantly being tried. Some are native species; many more are introduced ones that are known to be valuable on an introduced pest in the land of its origin. Among the most widely used are the Chalcidoid Wasps *Trichogramma evanescens* and *T. minutum,* which parasitize the eggs of many serious pests such as the Codling Moth, Tent Caterpillar, Oriental Fruit Moth, Cotton Moth, and Browntail Moth. A South American Chalcidoid Wasp, *Leptomastix dactylopii,* gives excellent control of Mealybugs in California. Two other Chalcidoids from Australia, *Coccophagus gurneyi* and *Tetracnemis pretiosus,* do the same, especially controlling citrophilous Mealybugs. A Tachinid Fly, *Ceromasia sphenophori,* imported into Hawaii, controls the Cane Borer Weevil.

817. Are any of the parasitoids available commercially? The *Trichogramma* mentioned above is produced commercially and can be bought and liberated where control is needed. It is especially valuable in greenhouses.

818. How are such parasitoids used in general? Large numbers (many millions) of the wasps are reared in laboratories on convenient host insects. The *Trichogramma,* for example, are reared in the eggs of the Angoumois Grain Moth, itself a world-wide pest of stored foods. Then, when an outbreak of a pest, for which the parasitoid is suitable, shows signs of erupting, great numbers of the parasitoid are released where and when they may bring the pest under control.

819. What are the Twisted-wing Flies? The members of the Order Strepsiptera are true parasites, living mostly upon wasps, bees, and some Homoptera. The larvae, after emerging from the mother's body, run about on flowers until they can attach themselves to the body of the host insect. They then transform into another type of larva, a legless grub that lives within the body of the host on blood and fat body. They pupate with one end projecting out between two abdominal segments. The female adult never leaves the pupal shell. In addition to being examples of the phenomena of ovoviparity, hypermetamorphosis, and parasitism, these insects are responsible for *stylopism,* which is the castration of the host, with subsequent abnormalities of development. The name comes from the genus *Stylops* of Twisted-wing Flies.

HUNTING WASPS

820. Why are Hunting or Solitary Wasps not normal predators?
These wasps have an unusual method of preying on Spiders and on
other insects that represents a special type of predation with features
that approach parasitism, and yet in some ways has led to the evolution of insect social life.

821. What do the Hunting Wasps do? A female, after mating,
hunts for Spiders or particular insects suitable for prey. Catching
one, she stings it in such a way that it is not killed but merely
paralyzed. She then stores it away, usually in a specially prepared
nest. On or within it she lays an egg. She then seals up the nest and
leaves.

822. Does the Hunting Wasp ever eat the prey herself? Nearly
always she does not. She may chew (malaxate) it and drink some of
the expressed juices. But almost invariably she leaves it in the nest.

823. Does the larva then eat the prey? The larva that hatches
from the egg eats the prey in a very definite sequence, eating first
only the nonvital organs and tissues. In this way the prey remains
alive for several days. It is this slow and selective eating, as well as
the paralysis, without killing, of the prey, that sets this apart from the
quick killing and eating of normal predators.

824. Of what advantage is it that the prey is not killed at once?
If this were not done it would soon putrefy, well before that larva
could eat it all. Keeping the prey alive, but paralyzed, ensures the
larva having enough food, as does also the eating of it delicately so
that it remains alive until the last possible minute.

825. How does the female wasp paralyze but not kill the prey?
She was not taught this, nor does she know this. She has developed a
fixed, but complicated, pattern of behavior which is characteristic for
her species, just as she developed specific characteristic structures,
color, form, wing venation, and other habits of her species. She
stings the prey in the large nerve ganglion in the ventral part of the

thorax. This blocks the motor nerve connections of the prey which, thereafter, can move little or not at all.

826. Is the behavior of such a wasp stereotyped? It is almost completely so and can be varied by any individual only to a very slight degree.

827. Do all females of the same species hunt the same kind of prey? They do, often within very narrow limits. One species will hunt only small Orb-Web Spiders; another, only big Tarantulas; another, only Weevils; another, only Long-horned Grasshoppers; another, only moth caterpillars, and so on. The wasps of one group will hunt only by burrowing in loose, rich soil (hunting Scarabaeid Beetle grubs); of another group only in trees (hunting Cicadas). They pay little attention to prey of another kind. An *Ammophila* who preys on caterpillars ignores a Meadow Grasshopper, for instance.

828. Do all wasps of the same species prepare similar nests? Within certain limits they do. Some nest in burrows which they dig in sandy soil; others excavate in firm soil; others excavate the soft pithy centers of twigs; others use holes in twigs or wood already made by some other insect. These hole users sometimes adopt unusual cavities: we know one who stocked her nest in the drainage holes of our wooden station-wagon body; and another who was recorded plugging the mouthpiece of a tin trumpet hung on a farmhouse porch. The Scoliid that burrows in search of grubs in a compost heap may merely leave the grub, paralyzed and bearing her egg, where she found it. The Tarantula-hunting Pompilid of the deserts may merely stuff her giant prey back into its own burrow. The *Larra* that hunts Mole Crickets also uses the prey's burrow.

829. Do any Hunting Wasps construct nests? The Mud Daubers construct a nest of softened mud that hardens to form a firm structure. These are built in sheltered spots such as under eaves, sheds, or bridges. One, *Scelephron caementarium,* makes rectangular nests. Others of the genus *Trypoxylon* make long, tubular "organ-pipe" nests. All provision the nests with paralyzed Spiders. The Potter Wasps (*Eumenes*) make almost spherical, juglike nests which they fasten to twigs; they use paralyzed caterpillars. A number of other genera make oval cells hidden away in crevices, using clay, leaves, plant fibers, etc.

830. Do any wasps eat nectar and pollen?   Most of the adults do. In a few groups such as the solitary *Pseudomasaris,* and the social *Brachygastra* and other Honey Wasps of the tropics, nectar and pollen are also used to feed the young and are stored in paper nests.

831. Do Solitary Wasps prepare the nest first or hunt and secure the prey first?   Different species differ in this respect. Some prepare the nest, seal it temporarily, and then go hunting. Others, including those that make no nest at all, first catch the prey.

832. How does a Solitary Wasp find her nest?   She locates it by "memorizing" landmarks. On leaving a prepared nest the wasp usually makes a complicated pattern of flights over it, with ever-widening curves that serve to fix its location in her mind. Experiments, made by moving prominent landmarks, have shown that the returning wasp depends on sight and her (unconscious) memory.

833. How do the wasps bring the paralyzed prey to the nest? The species that use small prey usually fly, carrying the prey in the legs. Many species pack a number of prey individuals in each nest, necessitating a number of journeys in and out. Those that use relatively large, heavy prey may have to climb up on a bush so as to take off from a high start. Still others, such as *Ammophila* which uses caterpillars, straddle the prey and drag it along the ground, sometimes for a hundred yards or more—an incredibly long, toilsome, and complicated journey.

834. How do wasps prepare the nests?   Burrowing species use the legs, chiefly the forelegs, as shovels. They are extremely active, literally making the sand and dirt fly in clouds. They also use the mandibles for picking up larger objects such as pebbles. Those that fashion nests of clay use the mandibles chiefly. Some carry loose earth in "baskets" formed by the long, fringed labial palpi.

835. Do any of the wasps use tools?   The *Ammophila* caterpillar hunters use a small pebble as a tool when closing their burrows in the soil. With this held in the mandibles they tamp the earth down hard.

836. How do the wasps hide their nests?   Some do not, but the majority of the ground-nesting species camouflage the nest entrance quite elaborately. Loose dirt is carried away and dumped elsewhere. Bits of gravel, twigs, dried leaves, and debris are placed about so that there is no trace of the excavation. It is difficult to escape the feeling when watching this that the wasp has a certain consciousness of what it is doing and is not merely following a stereotyped pattern.

837. Does the male ever help the female in nest building and provisioning?   This is known in a few Solitary Wasps to a slight degree. In the Mud-Dauber genus *Trypoxylon* the male guards the incompletely provisioned nest while the female is absent. The co-operation in colony starting of both male and female is a constant feature in termites but is unknown in social Hymenoptera. The Mud-Daubers do not form societies, but at least *Trypoxylon* shows that in the order there is some potentiality for "togetherness."

838. Are the Hunting Wasps parasitized by other insects?   A great many flies (Tachinidae) and other wasps of various families parasitize the stored prey of Hunting Wasps. A parasite (or inquiline) female lays her egg in the nest (or on the prey) of a Hunting Wasp; her larva, hatching early, eats the egg or young larva of the "rightful owner" and the stored food as well. The Cuckoo Wasps (Chrysididae) and Velvet Ants (Mutillidae) nearly all do this; and among the various groups of the Hunting Wasps are occasional species or genera that thus act as parasites instead of making and provisioning their own nests. This curious combination of parasitoid predatism and inquilinism also occurs among the social ants, wasps, and bees.

INSECT DEFENSES

839. How do insects protect themselves from their enemies?   Insects have numerous devices for this. Their protection may lie in their agility in escaping the danger; or it may lie in feigning death, dropping to the ground out of sight, adopting threatening attitudes, or in attacking the enemy with a sting, poisonous secretions, or gas. Sometimes their protection lies in their inherent bad taste or in unpalatable structures such as hairs, bristles, or spines. Sometimes they gain their protection by protective form or color which enables them to escape detection or pursuit.

840. What insects are specialized for escape? Many have great agility in making a quick take-off. Dragonflies can get into the air with great speed and then dodge pursuit. Tiger Beetles run rapidly, get into the air quickly, and as quickly realight on the ground but a short distance away. Many insects, such as Grasshoppers, Flea Beetles, and Fleas, have strong femoral muscles that enable them to leap. Others have even more specialized devices for leaping, such as the curious mechanism on the lower surface of the abdomen of Springtails. This structure, evolved from what were originally the paired appendages, includes a long spring bent forward and caught in a catch, after the fashion of a mousetrap. When suddenly released it hurls the insect far and away. Click Beetles (Elateridae), when picked up, click in a sufficiently startling manner to cause the bird or reptile which may have pounced upon them to drop them in surprise. If the beetle falls on its back it is able to give another loud click which results in its being catapulted into the air. This is made possible by the loose cross joint between the large prothorax and the rest of the body, which permits the insect to arch itself. As it does this a sharp spine on the prothorax glides along a groove on the lower side of the mesothorax, passes over a ridge, drops into a hollow, and forms a snap mechanism that throws the beetle.

841. What insects feign death? Some Giant Water Bugs (Belostomatidae) when removed from the water remain in a catatonic state for nearly fifteen minutes. Many Carrion Beetles (Silphidae), Fungus Gnats (Mycetophilidae), Weevils, and various small beetles feign death. When a small beetle pulls its head in, bends back its antennae so that they lie close to the body, and folds its legs under, it looks like a small immobile seed.

842. What insects drop to the ground when startled? Many do this, especially many caterpillars that pay out a silken thread as they fall, later crawling back up on the thread, eating it as they go. Sod Moths (Crambidae) dive to the grass where they cannot be seen in the tangle of stems.

843. What insects adopt threatening attitudes? Some Rove Beetles (Staphylinidae) run over the ground with the rear of the abdomen raised when they are startled. The Pinacaté Beetles of the genus *Eleodes* (Tenebrionidae), common in the southwest United States, are a ludicrous sight as they run with the entire body held nearly straight in the air. They often stand in this posture, with the head nearly touching the ground, for all the world like an ostrich with his head "in the sand." Stag Beetles assume a threatening position with

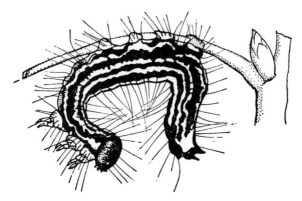

Figure 12. A *Datana* caterpillar, one of the Prominents, in a "threatening" posture.

their enormous jaws (which are sometimes as long as the rest of the beetle) held high and far apart. Many Sphingid larvae raise the enlarged thorax into the air, and many Notodontid larvae raise both the front and the rear ends of the body menacingly, some discharging burning secretions at the same time. Puss Moth caterpillars (Notodontidae) throw both ends up but in addition pull the head in under the thorax, causing that to swell greatly, and meanwhile lash the two long whiplike tails which are the especially modified rear prolegs.

844. What is reflex bleeding? Certain insects in times of stress feign death and at the same time eject fluid from the femoro-tibial articulations. A few Oriental Grasshoppers eject it from pronotal pores, the femoro-coxal articulations, and the tips of the tarsi as well. Beetles of several families and a few Lepidoptera secrete a liquid other than blood, but its origin and nature is undetermined.

845. What insects have stinging spines? Many caterpillars have stinging spines or hairs which seem to protect them from most birds. These hairs are very brittle and when broken, as they are at the slightest touch, release the poison with which they are filled. Some of the Flannel Moths (Megalopygidae) are equipped with stinging spines of great virulence, and many of their relatives, the Slug Caterpillars (Eucleidae), have barbed stings that can produce a severe rash. One group of Emperor Moth caterpillars and the caterpillars of the beautiful Morphoes have extremely irritating hairs.

846. What insects discharge a poison gas? The Bombardier Beetles of the genus *Brachinus* and some of their relatives, when startled, eject a gas which not only irritates the eyes but provides a partial smoke screen behind which the beetle can make its escape. A sac at the rear of the abdomen contains the fluid, which volatizes explosively when ejected into the air, thus making a series of pops to add to the general confusion.

847. What are osmeteria? They are saclike glands which, on eversion, protrude a fingerlike projection and discharge a volatile secretion. A forked one shoots out conspicuously from between the head and prothorax of the caterpillar of Swallowtail Butterflies. Others may be seen at the rear end of the Puss Moth caterpillar (*Cerura*) and on certain other caterpillars and some Sawfly larvae.

848. What insects emit bad odors? There are far too many to be enumerated here. Stink Bugs (Pentatomidae), Lacewings (Chrysopidae), Carrion Beetles (Silphidae), and Rove Beetles (Staphylinidae) are only a few. Some aquatic beetles exude fluids with disagreeable odors.

849. What insects emit caustic secretions? The Blister and Oil Beetles (Meloidae) are perhaps the most widely known of these. The secretions of the former are blistering to the skin; those of the latter, though not so strong, are burning and bad tasting. Many Notodontid caterpillars squirt burning secretions, and so do some Sawfly larvae.

850. What insects conceal themselves in their own secretions? Larvae of Spittle Bugs (Cercopidae) secrete liquid from the anus that becomes mixed with a mucilaginous substance from glands in the abdomen; the whole is then blown up into a meringuelike mass resembling spittle, in which the larva sits, protected from enemies and desiccation.

Aphids of some species discharge a waxy substance from the cornicles at the rear of the abdomen. This forms a flocculent substance that covers them, but it does not keep away the ants who are seeking Aphid honeydew nor the predaceous Syrphid larvae.

Scale Insects and Mealybugs (Coccidae) of many kinds secrete a protective substance, sometimes a white, flocculent, waxy substance; sometimes a "felted" mat; or a wax cyst; or a wax scale. These scales differ greatly in color, shape, and texture; they not only protect the insect but often the eggs and larvae as well.

COLORS

851. Are the colors of insects important to them? They are of great and consistent importance to most insects, usually making an enormous difference in the survival of the species. However, they play little or no part in the lives of insects that live in dark environments, such as underground or in caves, boring in wood or mining in leaves.

852. Are colors important to nocturnal insects? They are important during the daytime, unless the insect spends all daylight hours in concealment. But many night-flying insects spend the day in the open, exposed to attack.

853. In what way are colors important to insects? Their chief importance is in their protective value; they aid the insect in escaping notice, or in somehow avoiding the attack of an insectivorous animal. Color and pattern are also important in courtship and mating, aiding males and females of the same species to recognize each other.

854. What are the chief enemies against which coloration is of value? In general they are those which find and seize their prey by sight. This rules out the many insectivorous animals that hunt by scent or taste, chiefly other insects. It also largely rules out many Spiders, Frogs and Toads, Salamanders, and Bats.

855. Why is color of little importance as a protection against Spiders?   The Spiders that weave sticky webs catch and seize small prey that fall against or vibrate their web, regardless of color.

856. Why is color of little protection against Frogs and Toads? These animals, and many predaceous insects such as Mantids, seize practically any moving object. It is the motion and the suitable size of the prey that attract them. Such animals may, however, be foiled by certain types of protective form and color, such as "targets"; and some of them may be deterred by "warning, or aposematic" appearance.

857. Does the color of insects protect them from Bats?   Insect-eating Bats hunt almost entirely by sound. The Bat continually makes very high-pitched, supersonic noises and then, by hearing the echoes of these reflected back to its ears, locates and seizes a flying insect without having to see it at all.

858. What is the most common type of protective coloration and form?   It is known as *crypsis,* from the Greek *kryptos*—hidden. There are many types of crypsis but all tend to prevent the potential attacker being stimulated to seize the insect.

859. Does crypsis prevent a bird from seeing an insect which it otherwise might peck at?   It does not. The whole point of crypsis is that the insect *is* seen by the potential attacker, the bird for example. It is in plain sight. But what the bird sees does not stimulate it to peck.

860. Does a bird think that a cryptically colored insect is something else?   The bird does not *think*. It does not see a spot on the bark of a tree and think to itself, "Maybe that's a moth—I guess I'll try a peck at it." The bird has inherited a certain amount of its feeding behavior pattern; it has probably learned more by precept, watching its parents, and being fed certain objects by them; and it may have learned even more by itself—by chance trial and error. It will peck at only certain things that are within the range of its inherited or acquired behavior pattern. Other things, even though plainly seen, simply do not exist as far as pecking is concerned.

861. What is general crypsis? The insect (or other cryptic animal) does not resemble anything in particular. It merely has a form and color that blend in with the general tone and pattern of its environment. Green among foliage, brown among dead foliage, very bright tones on light sand, very dark tones on dark soil or rock— many thousands of animals thus gain protection by merely being inconspicuous in a general way.

862. What is countershading? Most objects are lit from above; the light therefore makes them look lighter on the top and darker (shadowed) beneath. If an animal is colored darker above (dorsally) and lighter beneath (ventrally), its coloration counteracts the effect of the top-lighting. The dark cancels out the light, and the light cancels out the dark. A large proportion of our most familiar birds and mammals are thus countershaded.

863. Are many insects countershaded? Not nearly as many insects as larger animals, to which the three-dimensional effect of a shadowed lower surface is most important. It is most noticeable in some of the large, fleshy caterpillars of Emperor and Sphinx Moths. In such caterpillars, which feed and rest back down, below a twig or leaf, it is the ventral surface of the caterpillar that is darker.

864. Are many insects protected by transparency? A great many insects that have transparent wings undoubtedly benefit from this type of crypsis. This is especially noticeable in many tropical butterflies belonging to groups most of whose members have normally colored wings. The Ithomiid and Pierid Butterflies of the New World tropics have quite a few members that have transparent wings. They are hard to see, or to follow, in the shaded tropical forests. Some combine transparency with disruption in a most baffling way. Others have transparent areas in wings otherwise colored like leaves.

865. What is disruption? This is a type of crypsis that breaks up the apparent outline of an animal by large, bold patches of contrasting color. A green caterpillar with a normal caterpillar shape might invite an attack. But if it is green at the ends, with a big, irregular dark splotch in the center, it looks like two or three irregular things and so escapes notice. Puss Moth caterpillars are fine examples of this.

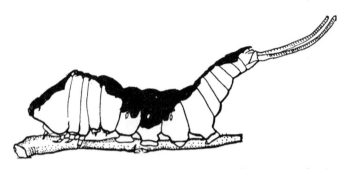

Figure 13. The Puss Moth Caterpillar is a good example of ruptive coloration.

866. What is specific crypsis?   Instead of merely not looking like itself, which is general crypsis, the insect resembles some specific object that is of no interest to an insect eater.

867. What are some objects that specifically cryptic insects resemble?   Nearly everything possible that is not tried as food by insect-eating birds. Leaves, both green and dead, twigs, bark, bark with lichens on it, lichens, thorns, buds, seeds, flowers, bird droppings, insect galls, and many, many more small, inedible objects.

868. What are some insects that resemble green leaves?   The most striking are the large, green Leaf Insects (*Phyllium*) of Asia, relatives of the Walking Sticks. The wings, held flat, are green with the vein pattern simulating the veins of a leaf; and even the legs bear flat, leaflike expansions. A great many Long Horned Grasshoppers have the fore wings green, leaf-shaped, and leaf-patterned. Our American Katydids are excellent leaf resemblers; many tropical ones are even better, with simulated holes, dead spots and other leaf imperfections. Many of our North American Fulgorids (Homoptera), such as the broad-winged *Acanalonia,* not only look like small leaves but rest along the stems of plants with similar leaves.

869. What insects resemble dead leaves? The number of these is legion. The caterpillars of some Prominent Moths, such as *Notodonta stragula,* look so much like dead, twisted, and shriveled leaves that one must see them move (which they do only very slowly) to realize what they are. The Asiatic Leaf Butterflies (*Kallima*) and the American Leaf Butterflies (*Anaea*) have the under surface of the wings dead-leaf brown, and patterned like the midrib and veins of a leaf. The wings are so shaped that when held together above the back they form the outline of a leaf, with a tail on the hindwing looking like a short leaf stem. The butterflies rest lengthwise on twigs with the wings at just the angle a leaf makes.

870. What are the most twiglike insects? Certainly the best are the Walking Sticks (Phasmida) in which every part of the insect is very long, slender, and brown or gray. Many have irregular projections like peeling bark, or are covered with spines that look like thorns. Hundreds of species of Geometrid Moth caterpillars, the "inchworms," are not only long, slender, brown, and twiglike, but even rest with the long body protruding stiffly from a small branch at just the right angle for a short, dead twig. To enable itself to hold this position without tiring, the caterpillar spins a fine silk thread that suspends its head from the branch.

871. Do many insects resemble bark? Tens of thousands do, and rest during the daytime on bark with colors and patterns that match. They may rest sideways or at just the right angle to line up the pattern of their body with the pattern of the bark. Among the best bark-resembling insects are some Mantids with very flat bodies, Stink Bugs (Pentatomidae), adult Geometridae and Owlet Moths, and the caterpillars of many groups of moths.

872. How do insects resemble bark with lichens on it? Among the bark-resembling moths are some with a bold patch of grayish green across each fore wing. When the wings are folded flat over the back these patches come together and form the image of a small patch of lichens, complete even to the details of the wavy edges of the lichen. This cuts across the outline of the whole moth, and so is a combination of lichen-crypsis and disruption. Some of the Owlet Moths like the North American Green Marvel, *Agriopodes fallax,* with the front wings held together over the back, resemble a patch of lichens, perfect to the finest detail of color and pattern.

873. What are some insects that resemble thorns? The best are many of the Tree Hoppers (Membracidae) which have the whole front part of the thorax produced forward and up at an angle to form a long point. Resting along a twig, as they do, these insects can hardly be distinguished from stout, triangular thorns. Another excellent example is to be found in the chrysalids of various butterflies, especially of the Orange Tips (Pieridae) which are fastened along twigs and have a long, projecting horn on the head.

874. What are some insects that resemble bird droppings? Moths of several families, the young caterpillars of some butterflies, and many Weevils not only resemble bird droppings but rest on the top surfaces of leaves where bird droppings are often seen. The typical color is, of course, white with dark-brown, gray, or dirty-green markings. Some of the best examples are two "micro" moths of the genus *Stenoma;* several Owlet Moths of the genus *Tarachidia;* a European Hook-Tip Moth, *Cilix glaucata;* the young caterpillars of several of the Swallowtail Butterflies (*Papilio*) and the Viceroy and Emperors (*Limenitis*); and the Plum Curculio, *Conotrachelus nenuphar.* Even an expert on insects (or bird droppings) must poke one of these insects to see what it is!

875. Are there any types of protective form and coloration other than cryptic? There are a good many, some of which rely upon just the opposite of crypsis, that is, upon actually drawing the attention of a potential attacker. Such, for example, are what is called *target presentation* and various types of *flash coloration*.

876. What is target presentation? Here the insect may be mostly dull-colored and cryptic. On some part, such as the rear part of the hind wings, however, it has some very attention-compelling markings such as eyelike spots or patches of very bright color. If a bird does peck at the insect it will almost certainly grab at one of the most obvious targets. When it does so, all it gets is a piece of wing, which the insect can do very well without. And there is a moment of delay, enough for a fast-moving insect to make its escape. Many insects have long, brightly colored, or very noticeable tails on the hind wings which they can do without.

877. What is flash coloration? This is a combination of an attention-compelling target with an extreme crypsis. The Owlet Moths of the widespread genus *Catocala* have bold orange, red, blue, or white-and-black patterns on the hind wings. Their front wings resemble bark. The moths rest on bark with the hind wings hidden beneath the front ones, thus escaping the notice of most birds. If one is disturbed by a bird it flies away, very fast and erratically, suddenly showing the blaze of color of the hind wings. The "surprise" of the sudden flash of color will probably delay the bird just enough to let the moth escape. If the bird chases the moth its attention will certainly be fixed on the bright, flash color. The moth dodges behind a tree trunk and lights on it with the dull, barklike front wings completely hiding the bright hind ones. The bird, baffled by the complete disappearance of the flash colors, will overlook the dull patch on the bark.

878. Do such surprise effects really have value? They do in many cases, as experiment has shown. Often an insect will have most realistic looking "eyespots," or distinctive patterns on the hind wing. Our North American Io Moth is a good example. So too are some Preying

Figure 14. The Spicebush Swallowtail caterpillar, *Papilio troilus*, has large eyespots on the thorax.

Mantids, Sphinx Moths, and many other large insects. The surprise or shock of suddenly seeing the display where there was nothing in particular a second before will make a bird hesitate; and that hesitation may be enough to break up the pattern of what the bird was doing (pecking at something) so that it will leave the insect alone. In many such "startling" displays the insect need not even fly away; the bird never finishes its attack.

879. Are birds frightened by displays of eyelike markings? They are certainly prevented from pressing an attack home, but to say that they are frightened, or that they think that the eyespots are the eyes of some big animal, is quite untrue. Birds and lizards are creatures of routine behavior; they do not think.

880. What is meant by protected species? Insects that have stings, or poisonous or bad-tasting secretions, or that are bad-tasting in themselves, are said to be protected.

881. Do protected species advertise the fact? Thousands of species do. Many Stink Bugs, Plant Bugs, Assassin Bugs, Carrion Beetles, Lacewings, butterflies and moths of many families, and bees and wasps, have a genuine protection. The great majority have bold, bright patterns and colors which make them extremely conspicuous. These act as warnings to birds and other insect eaters which therefore leave them alone.

882. Has the value of warning colors been actually tested? Quite extensive tests have been made, using warningly colored insects of many kinds, to see if insect-eating animals can learn to recognize them and to leave them alone. Such animals as birds, Monkeys, and lizards have been thus tested. The tests show that the warning appearance does indeed have great protective value.

883. Is the Monarch Butterfly distasteful and warningly colored? Many tests have shown that it is. After only one or two trials, Florida Jays refused to eat or even peck at Monarchs.

884. Why is the Monarch distasteful? As a larva the Monarch eats milkweed, a group of plants distasteful and poisonous to most animals. It thrives on the diet but acquires from it some characteristic that is distasteful to birds.

885. Is the Monarch distasteful to man? It seems not to be.

886. Are all brightly colored insects protected and warningly colored? By no means. Many appear to manage to elude predators by agile and swift escapes. Many others, however, are Batesian mimics of protected species.

887. What is Batesian mimicry? This is the resemblance of a perfectly edible insect to a warningly colored one that is protected by a sting, bad taste, or poisonous secretions. Birds and other animals learn to leave the protected species alone and then shun the mimics also.

888. Why is this called Batesian mimicry? The idea was noticed and first worked out by an English naturalist in Brazil, Henry Bates.

889. Are there any mimics of the Monarch? There are several, but the best known is the North American Viceroy, *Limenitis archippus*. The relatives of the Viceroy are black-and-blue or black, blue, and white butterflies, such as the White Admiral, *L. arthemis,* and the Red Spotted Purple, *L. arthemis astyanax.* But the Viceroy is golden brown with black lines and white spots, a very fine mimic of the Monarch. It is perfectly good bird food, but escapes being attacked because of its close resemblance to the Monarch.

890. Are bees and wasps mimicked by other insects? The Bee Flies (Bombyliidae), Flower Flies (Syrphidae), Robber Flies (Asilidae) and Thick Headed Flies (Conopidae), the Wasp Moths (Sesiidae), Day Flying Moths (Ctenuchidae), and several other families very definitely mimic not only many bees and wasps but also some very highly protected beetles of the family Lycidae. These mimics have evolved colors, patterns, and even behavior very similar to those of the models. Some are heavy bodied, hairy, and black and yellow, or black and red, like various Bumblebees. Others are slender bodied, smooth, and black and yellow, black and red, iridescent blue, or many other combinations that match specific wasps. The highly protected Lycid Beetles are mostly black and orange, and so are their mimics.

891. What is Müllerian mimicry? It is another major type of mimicry, the details of which were worked out by the distinguished German entomologist Fritz Müller. It concerns the mimicry of each other by warningly colored and genuinely protected insects. By mimicking each other, instead of all looking different, they gain an additional advantage; for this means that a bird, instead of having to learn a great many different warning patterns, need only learn a few. In the process of learning these it will kill fewer individuals of each species.

This type of mimicry does much to explain the remarkable similarity to each other of many groups of protected insects. Wasps of several unrelated families, for example, will all have a remarkably similar appearance, perhaps having chunky abdomens with black and yellow bands. Other wasps of the same group of families may have slender, blue-black abdomens with a patch of orange at the base. Each distinctive pattern is easily learned. Once a bird has learned to leave such a wasp alone, all wasps with the same appearance benefit.

892. What insects other than bees and wasps show Müllerian mimicry?   Some of the best-known groups are Lycid Beetles and Fireflies (Lycidae, Lampyridae); Heliconiid, Ithomiid, Danaid, and Acraeid Butterflies; and Ctenuchid (Syntomid) and Zygaenid Moths. The majority of these are tropical, but at least a few occur nearly everywhere in the Temperate zones.

893. What other kinds of disguises do some insects have?   A fairly common one is known as *masking*. This consists of the insect's decking itself with bits of objects that hide it or at least disguise its appearance. Some caterpillars of Geometrid Moths fasten to themselves bits of the flowers in which they feed, or scraps of leaves. The larvae of some of the Tortoise Beetles (Cassinae) have special spines and forked structures on the abdomen that hold a mass of the larva's own excrement above it. And Aphis Lions, the larvae of the Green Lacewings (Chrysopidae), cover themselves with a shapeless mass of the remains of the Aphids and similar insects upon which they prey. Such masking is very similar to the construction of the individual cases in which the larvae of many other insects live.

XIII. INSECTS AND MAN

BENEFICIAL INSECTS

894. How are insects beneficial to man?   Insects are of benefit to man in far more ways than most people realize. They are of great value to him in the pollination of many essential plants (Chapter XI), in the production of certain useful products, in the control of noxious weeds and harmful insects, in their service in aerating and loosening the soil, and in their work as scavengers. They are of inestimable importance in annually turning countless thousands of tons of plant material into a form that can be more quickly and economically used by plants, man, and other animals. Insects also serve as food both for many animals of value to man, and occasionally for man himself.

Insects have been extremely valuable to man in his studies of genetics, evolution, the distribution of plants and animals, sociology, and pollution. And we cannot deny that in their ability to draw a gleaming trout to the surface of a stream and in their flashing of many-hued wings in the light of a wooded path, they have added to man's enjoyment.

895. What are some of the insect products that man uses?   Many products such as honey and beeswax, dyes, shellac, silk, tannin, and medicinal substances have been of importance in man's economy. Some of them have been supplanted in recent years by new substances and by synthetics, but others are still widely used and provide many millions of dollars' worth of goods and business each year.

HONEY AND BEESWAX

896. Is much honey produced commercially in the United States?
About 200,000,000 pounds of honey are produced each year in the United States for commercial purposes. About 500,000 people keep hives and there are an estimated 5,600,000 colonies of bees.

897. From what is honey made?   The Honeybee gathers nectar from flowers. When this is mixed with the saliva, enzymes change the nectar sugars into dextrose and levulose. The mixture is passed through the bodies of the younger workers in the hive one or more times and then stored in unsealed cells until it has evaporated to the right consistency.

898. From what plants do bees gather the best honey-making nectar? About three-fourths of the commercial honey crop comes from Alfalfa, Buckwheat, Clover, Cotton, and Orange. The bees depend upon Apple and other orchard fruits, Dandelion, Mustard, and Goldenrod for much of the nectar they need in the maintenance of the hive, but store little of this in the comb cells.

899. Does man use much beeswax? Man uses about 8,000,000 pounds of beeswax a year in the United States alone. It is used in lubricants, salves, and ointments, sealing wax, furniture polish and some varnishes, insulation, and candles. It is still used to some extent in phonograph records but not as much as formerly. It is superior to most waxes because of its high melting point, about 140° F.

900. How does the bee make wax? The bee secretes it as little white flakes from glands on the under side of the abdomen. Since these glands degenerate after the bee has begun foraging in the field it is only the young workers who supply it. It is a mixture of fatty acids, alcohol, hydrocarbons, and other substances.

901. What color is beeswax? When first secreted it is white but later turns yellowish. In the brood combs it turns to a rich chocolate brown and to black.

902. Are Honeybees ever deliberately used as pollinators? Many thousands of hives are regularly moved to regions where a crop in need of pollination is blossoming. This not only ensures pollination and good fruit production, but benefits the beekeeper. Such organized use of bees is especially prevalent in citrus fruit–growing regions.

SILK

903. What is the silk that is used commercially? Most commercial silk comes from the cocoons of the "Silkworm," *Bombyx mori*. This species is raised for that purpose and has become so dependent upon cultivation that it no longer lives as a wild species.

904. What larvae other than the "Silkworm" produce silk? All Lepidoptera caterpillars spin some silk. The larvae of many Caddis-flies, some beetles, some Neuroptera, and various other insects also produce silk.

905. Do any adult insects secrete silk? Only a few. Adult Psocids cover their eggs with silk; the Embioptera line their tunnels with it; one Cricket (Gryllacrididae) sews leaves together; one Hymenopteran, *Psenolus,* covers its brood; and the Dance Flies (Empididae) use it in courtship.

906. Can any silk other than that produced by the "Silkworm" be used commercially? The caterpillars of all Emperor Moths (Saturniidae) produce silk in quantity. A few have been, and still are, cultivated in some places for the commercial use of their silk. *Antheraea cernyi,* the Chinese Oak Silkworm, produces Shantung silk. Another species, *A. paphia,* widely distributed in the Orient, produces Tussah silk. In Assam, *A. assama* is the source of Muga silk. In Assam and Bengal, *Philosamia ricini* is cultivated although its silk, the Eri silk, is very difficult to reel. A few other species have been used but to a much less degree.

907. Is sericulture still an important business? Even with the use of synthetic fibers the annual world production of silk is worth about $425,000,000.

908. Can silk be produced commercially in the United States? *Bombyx mori* can be raised in the United States if the Mulberry leaves on which it feeds can be provided. However, its culture requires too much manual labor and is too expensive to be practical. *Philosamia cynthia,* introduced into Europe and North America from India and China, as well as our native *Telea polyphemus,* yield a good-quality silk which can be used commercially but, again, their culture would be too expensive.

909. What is the color of silk? The silk produced by *Bombyx mori* is white or yellow. Shantung silk is buff colored; Tussah silk is brownish; and Eri silk is white or brick red. Other silks may be colorless, yellow, golden, or green. Some are even fluorescent.

910. Is silk a solid or a liquid?   It is a liquid when extruded but almost immediately hardens, probably because of the mechanical pressures to which it is subjected by the spinnerets. The thread has a central crystalline fiber which is surrounded by an outer coat of silk gelatin. This outer coat is soluble in water and is removed in the commercial processing.

911. What organs produce the silk?   Silk is produced by glands which have originated differently in different insects. In the Lepidoptera (and therefore in the Silkworm) and in Psocids, Trichoptera, and some Hymenoptera they are modified salivary glands opening through the middle of the lower lip. In some Coleoptera and Neuroptera it is the Malpighian tubules attached to the digestive tract that secrete the silk. In the Embioptera and one Dance Fly (Empididae) the silk glands are in the tarsi of the first pair of legs.

912. Of what use is silk to the insect?   Most caterpillars secrete silk almost continually; their lives seem to be intimately connected with it. They fasten a silken thread to serve as a foothold on a slippery stem or leaf; they mark the path of their wanderings with silk which then serves as a guide for their return, as well as a guide to others of their own kind who are seeking companionship; they may pay out a silken thread when they fall or jump from a leaf to avoid an enemy, and then climb back up on it, eating it as they go. Burrowing larvae and leaf miners line their tunnels with silk; Clothes Moths and other Webbing Moths make webs, and many species construct cases or shelters. The butterflies that do not make a cocoon swing their pupae or lash them in place with a girdle of silk. And of course many larvae make cocoons in which to pupate, sometimes winding a silken thread (as with the Silkworm), sometimes secreting a silken parchment, and sometimes mixing the silk with other secretions or with stones, sticks, leaves, and debris.

SPIDER SILK

913. Is Spider silk similar to insect silk?   Spider silk is an albuminoid protein believed by most people to be quite similar to insect silk. It is secreted, however, in special glands within the abdomen. These glands differ in type, size, and number, their presence distinguishing the Spiders from their close Arachnid relatives.

914. Is Spider silk strong?   The Spider thread may be a very slender thread indeed, sometimes only one millionth of an inch in diameter, or it may be ten to twenty times as thick; but it has great elasticity, being capable of stretching one-fifth of its length without breaking. Its tensile strength is thus greater than steel and is said to be second only to that of fused quartz fibers. The strength of the threads varies in different species; it is also dependent upon the manner in which it is spun, being stronger if drawn out very rapidly.

915. For what does the Spider use its silk?   Spiders use silk even more than insects do. A Spider scarcely moves without leaving its silken trail, or dragline, behind. It uses silk in constructing its retreat such as a web or chamber, or for its burrow lining or trap door. With silk it makes egg sacs and nurseries for its young, mating structures such as sperm webs, courtship and mating bowers, mating chambers, and even, in one group of species, a bridal veil. And with silk it builds traps and devices for snaring its prey, and then bands for binding and holding the victims.

916.   What is the dragline?   Every Spider, except for the members of one family, plays out a dragline wherever it goes. This is anchored at intervals by means of attachment disks. The dragline is made up of at least two closely adherent threads, sometimes of four or more, and may be spun out very rapidly if the Spider wishes to drop hastily from its web or off a precipice to escape danger. It is the thread that makes the framework of the webs and the retreats. The Spiders that hunt by throwing out a line, weighted with a silken drop, as an angler casts his line or a gaucho his bola (they are called Bola Spiders), spin a dragline for the purpose; and the spiderlings that drift through the air in great dispersal flights are wafted, each on its own dragline.

917. What is ballooning?   Spiders do not have wings but by a technique known as ballooning are able to float through the air on a silken dragline of their own spinning. This is done mostly by the spiderlings recently emerged from their egg sac, but may be practiced occasionally by adults of most groups. Each climbs to some point where it may be caught up in a breeze, then, wafted in the air current, it spins a dragline. Sometimes Spiders travel great distances on the air currents, having been found landing in numbers on ships 200 miles at sea. Aerial surveys have found them at altitudes of 10,000 feet. Ballooning may explain why so many species of Spiders are cosmopolitan in distribution.

918. What is gossamer?   Sheets or strands of silk are often found floating in the air or caught in vegetation. This is gossamer, or the discarded draglines of innumerable Spiders or spiderlings who have either flown or attempted to fly on their silken draglines. There are places in California where trees and shrubs will be shrouded with these silken clouds at certain times of the year.

919. Is Spider silk used commercially?   The use of Spider silk is steadily decreasing but at one time it was used extensively as cross hairs or sighting marks in a wide variety of optical instruments. The fiber was fine, it was strong, and it could withstand extremes of temperature. Silver-coated platinum wires and etching on glass have now almost entirely supplanted it for such uses.

920. Has Spider silk ever been used in textiles?   Many attempts have been made to use Spider silk in textiles, especially by the French people. The chief difficulty lay in the habits of the Spiders themselves, who are solitary, predaceous, often cannibalistic, and have to be fed living invertebrates. Only the egg-sac silk was usable; and the production of 663,522 Spiders was necessary in order to obtain one pound of silk. Furthermore, the fiber is very much finer than that of the Silkworm and much shorter. An American zoologist once tried to obtain silk by reeling it directly from the animal, and although amazed at the ease with which it could be done, found he needed 415 Spiders to get silk enough for one square yard of material, half the amount obtainable from an equal number of Silkworms.

921. Do primitive peoples use Spider silk?   Many natives in various South Pacific regions fashion ingenious fishing devices from this silk, or use it in making bags, caps, and headdresses for various purposes. The great aerial webs of *Nephila,* strong enough for ensnaring a bird, are the most widely used.

OTHER PRODUCTS

922. What dyes are obtained from insects? Certain red dyes known as cochineal dyes are obtained from Scale Insects (Coccidae). One, a crimson dye, comes from the dried ground bodies of *Dactylopius coccus* that feeds on the *Opuntia* Cacti in the southwest and Mexico. Other Scale Insects have been cultivated extensively in Peru, Honduras, Algeria, and Spain for these dyes. It is said that 70,000 insects are needed to make one pound of dye. Cochineal dyes have been used in the past for coloring cosmetics, beverages, and medicines. Tannin is widely used in making inks, and also in tanning hides. Although not produced by an insect, it does come from galls that owe their existence to insects.

923. What is lac? It is a mixture of resins, sugar, and wax that is secreted by Coccids of several genera. One species, *Laccifer* (or *Tacchardia*) *lacca,* is cultivated in the Philippines and parts of southern Asia. The bodies of these scales form layers ¼ to ½ inch thick on the twigs of Banyan and Fig trees. They are melted and flaked before being shipped to this country as stick lac, which is then processed in the making of shellac. Despite the increased use of synthetics, shellac is still responsible for a $20,000,000-a-year business in this country. Forty million pounds of stick lac are gathered yearly.

924. What medicinals are obtained from insects? Cantharidin, a powerful irritant, is obtained especially from the "Spanish Fly," *Lytta vesicatoria,* a Meloid beetle of Europe. It was formerly used widely for producing local skin stimuli and blisters (like a powerful mustard plaster), in genito-urinary disorders, and in veterinary medicine. Tannic acid from insect-induced galls is used in a variety of medicines. Bee venom has been used in arthritis.

925. What is manna? It is the sweet honeydew secreted by the Aphid, *Trabutina mannipara,* which feeds on the Tamarisk of Palestine, solidifying on the leaves of the tree and on the ground beneath. It is 55 percent sucrose, 2.5 percent invert sugar, and 19.3 percent dextrin.

926. What are ground pearls? They are the wax cysts made by female Scale Insects of the genus *Margarodes*. The natives in some tropical countries use them in necklaces because of their pretty bronze metallic colors.

927. Were insects ever used in surgery? For a time the maggots of various Blow Flies (Calliphoridae) were used to clean infected wounds. Study of this led to the discovery that by secreting allantoin the maggots promoted healing. Now allantoin obtained from other sources is widely used.

INSECTS AND WEEDS

928. Do many insects benefit man as weed controllers? Undoubtedly great numbers do, more than are appreciated.

929. Has man used insects in weed control? A few species have been used successfully, usually by introducing them to another region. The *Chrysolina* Beetle (Chrysomelidae), introduced from Australia by the U.S. Department of Agriculture, has helped reclaim hundreds of thousands of acres of grazing land in the West that was overrun by the Klamath Weed, a St.-John's-wort. The South American moth, *Cactoblastis cactorum,* introduced into Australia from South America, has given excellent control of Prickly Pear Cacti. These plants, introduced into Australia in 1840, had ruined millions of acres of fine grazing land.

930. Do insects introduced as weed killers always prove successful? A great many do not. The European Cinnabar Moth, *Tyria jacobeae,* was taken to Australia to control Ragwort, an introduced European weed. For a while it did good work, but then parasitoid insects and other predators controlled the moth.

931. Is it always safe to introduce insects for weed control? It is not only unsafe but potentially dangerous. There is a good chance that the introduced species may develop unexpected habits and prove to be a pest. Only highly competent entomologists should contemplate any such attempt.

932. Are all weed-eating insects beneficial? A great many insects that feed on weeds are also serious pests on crops. They may maintain themselves on the weeds for many years; and then when a crop is planted nearby shift to it and do great damage. Or they may work on weeds early in the season and then move over onto the crops.

933. How did the Colorado Potato Beetle gets its start? Originally this beetle fed on various Solanums, weed plants in the Rocky Mountain and western Plains regions. When Potato culture spread westward the beetle adopted the new plant, a member of the same family as its original food. The beetle spread eastward to the Atlantic, westward to the Pacific, crossed to Europe, and has become a serious pest everywhere.

INSECTS AND THE SOIL

934. Are insects important in loosening and aerating the soil? Even where we have Earthworms we need the help that is given us by the ants in this respect. Ants have been shown to move 16 tons of soil a year on an acre of ground. In North Africa a colony moved more than a ton of earth in 15 square yards in 100 days. In parts of the world where Earthworms are scarce or entirely lacking this work of the ants is essential.

935. How else do insects improve the soil? Any insect that feeds on decaying plant material, or on dead animal matter, thus returning it to the soil in a form of organic matter that can be reused in a shorter time and by a greater variety of plants, is improving the soil. The excreta of insects provide a rich fertilizer. Furthermore, any insect that scavenges on dead animal remains or on dung, much of which may carry disease organisms, is providing valuable sanitation services. By working on the substance they break it up, increasing exposure to air and water and thus increasing the rate of decay; or they remove it entirely by eating it or burying it, before flies can transmit the organisms to living animals. Among the groups of insects that are particularly valuable in this way are some of the Roaches, the Earwigs, the larvae of many flies, the Darkling Beetles (Tenebrionidae), and the great families of Scarab Beetles and Carrion Beetles (Silphidae).

Two burying beetles of the last named family can completely bury a small animal, such as a mole, in two hours.

INSECTS AS FOOD

936. What animals feed chiefly on insects? Many birds, Moles, Anteaters, and Armadillos feed almost entirely upon them; and frogs, some lizards, and some snakes consume large numbers of them. Fresh-water fish of many species feed on aquatic insects. Even man has occasionally eaten insects.

937. What insects are eaten by man? Primitive man and primitive peoples today eat insects occasionally and consider them great delicacies. It has been suggested that their high salt value gives them both appeal and value. In times of scarcity it would appear to be sound practical economy to utilize this source of food far more than man has, especially when the insects swarm in great numbers and are easy to catch. In some places Locusts, Cicadas, and Crickets are eaten quite regularly; occasionally termites and ants (especially the big Sauba Ants and the repletes of the Honey Ants), a Stink Bug or two, and a few species of Stonefly larvae. Big beetles are relished the world over, as the Goliath Beetle of Africa and the Giant Water Beetles (Dytiscidae) and the big Long Horns (*Prionus*). Clusters like those of the Snipefly *Atherix* that overhang the water, and the windrows of Brinefly puparia that can be collected by the hundreds of bushels are often eaten. Aquatic water bugs, *Corixa femorata,* of Mexico are cultivated especially for food, all the stages including the eggs being eaten.

In the delicatessens of our own town one can buy chocolate-covered bees and ants from Switzerland, tinned Grasshoppers from Japan, and fried Agave Worms from Mexico. The latter are the plump caterpillars (and pupae) of the Giant Skippers (Megathymidae) that feed on the leaves of the Maguey plant.

HARMFUL INSECTS

938. How are insects harmful to man? A few are annoying; a few sting or bite or irritate the skin; several transmit disease; many are pests in man's household and in stored foods and grains; and thousands of them damage man's crops, causing billions of dollars' damage a year and destroying nearly as much of our forests as are destroyed by fire.

939. What is the sting of an insect? The sting is the ovipositor of the female. By inserting it into the flesh and injecting the secretions of certain poison glands, the insect is performing an act of defense against its enemies, or one of offense in the capture of its prey.

940. What insects attack man with their sting? All stinging insects belong to the order Hymenoptera. The chief ones that annoy man are the Honeybees, Bumblebees, Wasps, Velvet Ants (Mutillidae), and some of the ants.

941. Is it true that a bee can sting but once? The sting of the worker Honeybee is so barbed that it cannot be readily pulled from the puncture; as a result the entire sting as well as the tip of the abdomen and the poison glands are left behind in the wound. The muscles of the abdomen may continue to pump poisons into the wound, so it should be gently squeezed out as soon as possible. A female wasp has an unbarbed sting which she can use repeatedly.

942. Are there any stingless bees and wasps? Of course all males are stingless. There is a large group of social bees (Meliponidae) in the tropical regions that either lack stings or have these structures vestigial, and so cannot sting.

943. What insects have the worst stings? The females of a family of wasps (Mutillidae), known as the Velvet Ants because they are wingless and look like hairy or velvety ants, have the most powerful stings of all insects. In some species their sting is nearly as long as the abdomen, and the poison is powerful.

944. What are "biting" insects? They are the ones that inflict a wound by means of their long, slender, needlelike mouthparts. Their injury is *not* a bite, but a stab. Female Mosquitoes, a few "biting" flies and Midges, a few bugs, and the Fleas and Lice are the main offenders.

945. Why do not male Mosquitoes attack man? Their mouth-parts are not developed for sucking blood. They live on plant juices, nectar, and other liquids.

946. What flies other than Mosquitoes attack man? The most annoying are Blackflies (*Simulium*), No-see-ums or Punkies (*Culicoides*), Deer Flies (*Chrysops*), and the Stable Fly (*Stomoxys calcitrans*).

The Blackflies are small, clear-winged, humpbacked, blackish Gnats that hover about the face or tenaciously work their way in between buttons, under the waist band, or up the trouser legs. Their stabs are not painful but cause bleeding and severe itching, and the presence of the flies in ears, nostrils, eyes, and hair can be almost unbearable. They breed in swift-flowing water. The Punkies, so tiny that they can pass through most screening, stab man during the early morning or in the evening; the stab is painful. They breed in decaying vegetation and silt, in brackish water or along the edges of pools, and in tree holes. The Deer Flies (also called Horseflies) fly around one's head, evading all attempts to ward them off. The females inflict a painful stab which draws considerable blood. They breed in damp vegetation and mud. The Stable Flies, unlike the three preceding species, often come into the house, especially before a storm, hence have been called the "Biting Houseflies." They attack man about the legs and ankles with a painful stab but one that has no lasting effect. They breed in fermenting vegetation especially when animal manure is mixed with it.

One little group of flies that is local in distribution but has bothered us to utter distraction is the genus of Eye Gnats, *Hippelates* (Chloropidae). They breed in decaying moist vegetation. We have met them in lava beds, surrounded by hundreds of miles of desert, where they were breeding in tiny pockets of the lava and swarming in such numbers that we were temporarily blinded. They sometimes carry a "pink eye" infection.

947. What flies are particularly annoying to domestic animals? Horn Flies (*Haematobia*), Stable Flies (*Stomoxys*), Horseflies (*Tabanus*), Deer Flies (*Chrysops*), and Blackflies (*Simulium*) all annoy domestic animals. All have piercing mouthparts that suck blood, causing some pain as well as annoyance. The eggs and larvae develop in damp places, especially in manure and decaying organic matter (except for the Blackflies which come from fast-flowing water). In addition the families of the Pupipara are all parasitic on animals and therefore annoying.

948. What are the Pupipara? The Pupipara is a group of the order Diptera that includes four families, all of which are parasitic on animals and have suffered partial or total degeneration of wings as a result of their parasitism. The Louse Flies (Hippoboscidae) cling to the fur and feathers of their hosts with strong bristly legs. As a rule each species has become specialized for life on a single species or group of species of hosts; there is one on game birds (Beware, oh hunter, if you carry your bag of Grouse home on your back! Watch out for the flat flies that crawl up the back of your neck!); one on Whippoorwills and Nighthawks; one on Horses; one on Camels (and a nuisance to the rider). The best known is probably the Sheep "Tick" or "Ked," which often causes skin irritations on Sheep that reduce wool production.

The other three families are the Bat Ticks (Nycteribidae), the Bat Lice (Streblidae), and the Bee Lice (Braulidae) that cling to the Honeybee, taking food directly from their mouths.

949. What flies actually live in the flesh of domestic animals? The Screwworm (*Callitroga*) can wipe out entire herds of Cattle, Hogs, Sheep, and Goats. The eggs are laid in open wounds in shinglelike masses of 200–400, a single female laying as many as 3,000. The larvae bore into the living flesh, forming little pockets; they eventually drop to the ground to pupate. Heel Flies or Ox Warbles (*Hypoderma*) of two species attack Cattle viciously around the legs and flanks, causing them to run wildly with tails in the air. The eggs are laid in rows on the heels or lower part of the belly. The larvae tunnel into the flesh and work their way to the abdominal organs or spinal cord, eventually coming out onto the back where they cut holes in the skin, injuring both the hide and the flesh. They then encyst beneath the hole, forming a sizable swelling. Later they enlarge the hole, emerge, and fall to the ground to pupate. It has been estimated the damage they cause is from $50,000,000 to $120,000,000 a year in the United States; some 75 percent of our domestic Cattle are infested. Bot Flies (*Gastrophilus*) of four species attack Horses. The Horses seem to be frightened by their buzzing, and fight them viciously even though the flies neither sting nor bite. The eggs are glued on to the hairs of the front legs (in the case of the Common Bot Fly) where they mature in 10–14 days but have to wait before hatching (sometimes as long as 100–140 days) for the application of the saliva and warmth of the horse's tongue or lips. On emerging the larvae burrow into the tongue for a month or so before passing into the digestive tract, where they remain for 9–10 months. The eggs of the Chin or Throat Bot are laid in hairs beneath the jaw, causing the Horse to toss its head or to lay it across the shoulder of other Horses in the pasture. The larvae from these eggs hatch by themselves, crawling up to the mouth unaided. The eggs of the Lip Bots are laid on the lips; the emerging larvae burrow through the flesh of the lips to reach the mouth.

950. What bugs attack man? Bedbugs (Cimicidae), Kissing Bugs (Reduviidae), Backswimmers (Notonectidae), and Water Scorpions (Nepidae) are the chief "biting" bugs.

951. Where do Bedbugs breed? They breed throughout the year in cracks of furniture, behind baseboards or wallpaper, wherever their flat bodies can find shelter during the day. Both sexes suck blood;

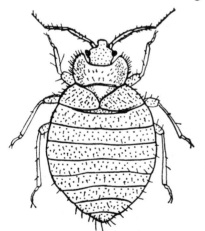

Figure 15. *Climex lectularius,* the Bedbug.

and if no human is available they will feed on Mice, Rabbits, Cattle, Poultry, and Horses. They therefore may breed around such animals, and may be brought into the house from henhouses and barns. They can live without food for several months and, being active migrants on utility wires or in luggage, can become established far from their point of origin.

952. Do bats carry Bedbugs?   No. Bats are infested with a closely related species but these seldom, if ever, attack man. You cannot blame the Bats in the attic for the human Bedbugs in your house.

953. Do Bedbugs carry disease?   Although they have never been proven guilty of actually carrying disease, they may, in cases of serious infestation, reduce a person's vitality to such a degree that he may be made more susceptible to disease. The conditions that are conducive to prolonged Bedbug infestation are also conducive to disease.

954. What caterpillars give one a rash?   Many caterpillars, such as those of Flannel Moths (Megalopygidae), the Saddlebacks (Eucleidae), the Processionaries (Thaumatopoeidae), the Browntail Moth, the White-marked Tussock Moth, and the Io, have long, barbed hairs which cause a local irritation, sometimes very severe. Typical urticating hairs have a poison-filled central cavity. Some hairs irritate because of poisonous fecal matter that has been rubbed onto them in the nest.

955. Are there any adult insects that irritate the skin?   Blister Beetles and Oil Beetles (Meloidae) and a few Rove Beetles (Staphylinidae) have body secretions that have a blistering effect upon the human skin. Adult Tiger Moths (Arctiidae) and some Sphinx Moths have spines and poison glands on the hind legs that are irritating.

956. Do insects ever cause asthma or hayfever?   There are people who are sensitive to the scales of moths and butterflies and to the hairs of Caddisflies. A few cases of asthma have been traced to the cast skins of Mayflies, and to the hairs of Browntail Moths when the infestation is heavy. Doubtless there are other airborne allergies that come from insects.

957. What Lice attack man? Two species of Sucking Lice (Ano-plura) attack man: the Crab or Pubic Louse, *Phthirius pubis,* and the Body and Head Louse, *Pediculus humanus.* The latter may be known as "cootie," "grayback," or "seam squirrel."

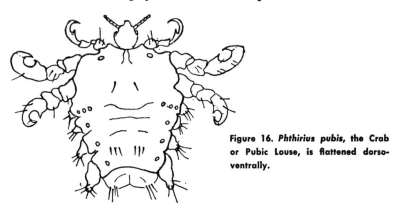

Figure 16. *Phthirius pubis,* the Crab or Pubic Louse, is flattened dorso-ventrally.

958. Where do Lice breed? The Crab Lice, like most Sucking Lice, cement their eggs to the hair of the host and live out their entire life on the host. The Body Lice, however, sometimes scatter their eggs in the seams of clothing or in bedding, although the physiological strain that lives on the head may cement their eggs to the hairs there.

959. How are Lice adapted for their way of life? The body of a Louse is very flat; the spiracles have moved around to the upper sur-face to facilitate respiration. The mouthparts of Sucking Lice are adapted for piercing the skin and sucking blood. The tarsi are armed with a single strong, curved claw that can snap back against a curved hollow on the side of the last tarsal segment and thus form a grasping structure that can cling tenaciously to the hair of the host.

960. Do domestic animals have lice? All do, and some of them have both Biting and Sucking Lice of several varieties.

961. What is the difference between Biting and Sucking Lice? Both are wingless; both are greatly flattened. The Mallophaga, or Biting Lice, do not puncture the skin although they will eat dried blood or drink at a wound. They feed on debris and bits of dried skin, but they irritate the host so greatly that it may easily become weakened and succumb to disease. They are more common on birds, but characteristic species are found on domestic mammals. The most serious pest among them is probably the widespread Chicken Louse, *Menopon pallidum.* The Anoplura, or Siphunculata, the Sucking Lice, are fewer in number but occur on a wide variety of mammals. They pierce the skin to suck blood. Each tarsus has a single, strong, curved claw that snaps back against the curved last segment of the foot to form a strong hair-grasping organ.

962. How do Fleas differ from Lice?   Both suck blood (except the Biting Lice), but in most other ways are different. Fleas have a complete metamorphosis. The larvae are greatly reduced, legless, maggot-like creatures that live as scavengers in the debris in or near the nest of the host. The pupal stage may remain quiescent for long periods

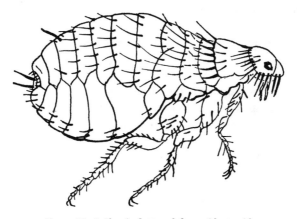

Figure 17. A Flea is flattened from side to side.

of time. The adults are flattened from side to side, instead of dorso-ventrally as are the lice, and thus can run easily between the hairs and feathers of the host, escaping defensive action with great agility, even leaping off the host if necessary. They may live for considerable periods of time away from the host.

963. Is there a specific Flea on humans?   One species, the Human Flea, *Pulex irritans,* is a normal parasite on man the world over. It also attacks many other animals, including Badgers, Skunks, Squirrels, Pigs, and Dogs.

964. Why does man often get three little Flea bites in a row? The presence of several little bites in a row indicates that the individual has been bitten, not by a Human Flea, but by a Flea accustomed to another host species, such as the Dog or Cat. Finding the first bite distasteful, it has tried again, and perhaps again.

965. Do any other Fleas regularly attack man? The Chigoe Flea, *Tunga penetrans,* of the tropics regularly does, and is a serious and, at times, a dangerous pest. The female may become encysted under the skin of a human, especially on the feet, and become greatly swollen with eggs. She must be removed, unruptured, and the wound thoroughly disinfected, else a serious sore may ensue.

966. What are Beach Fleas and Sand Fleas? Mostly these are small Crustacea, living as scavengers in the intertidal beach zone. Widespread popular beliefs to the contrary, they in no way attack or affect man.

967. Where do Dog and Cat Fleas breed? They breed off the animal, which makes their control more difficult. The eggs are laid in dust or dirt, the animal's bedding, or cracks in the floor. The larva, living from one to five weeks, feeds on dried organic matter, even on excreta of the adult Fleas or of Mice. When full grown it forms a small silken cocoon in which it pupates, spending from two weeks to three months, or even as long as two years in that stage.

INSECTS AND DISEASE

968. Why does one refer to insects as transmitting disease, not causing it? An actual infection by insects is rare. Myiasis, an infection by fly larvae, does occur occasionally; so also does Canthariasis, an infection by beetle larvae; and Scoleciasis, an infection by lepidopterous larvae. But all other cases of insect involvement in disease have been due to the insect carrying the organism, either a bacterium, a virus, a fungus, or a Round Worm. These organisms are the true causative agents.

969. How does an insect carry a disease-causing organism? It may carry it mechanically, that is, on its beak, body, or feet, having picked it up accidentally. Individual Houseflies have been known to carry as many as 500,000,000 organisms on the surface of the body at one time, many of them undoubtedly capable of causing disease. Or the insect may carry the disease-causing organism physiologically, in which case passage through its body or intestinal tract is an essential part of the life cycle of the causative agent, as with malaria.

970. What insects transmit disease? Mosquitoes, the Housefly, several other flies, and certain Lice and Fleas transmit disease. Assassin Bugs (Reduviidae) in Central and South America transmit Chagas disease but no North American species does more than inflict an occasional sharp bite.

971. What diseases are transmitted by Mosquitoes? The malarias, called the worst scourge of mankind, causing several million deaths a year, are Mosquito-borne. They are world-wide in tropical, subtropical, and temperate regions, where the protozoans causing them

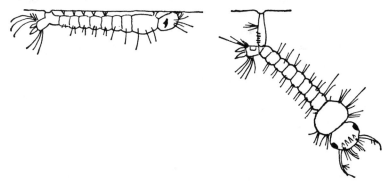

Figure 18. The larvae of Anopheline (left) and Culicine (right) mosquitoes can be distinguished by the way they rest at the surface film.

are carried by some thirty species of Mosquitoes of the genus *Anopheles*. Yellow fever, once the great menace of the tropics, is now fairly well eradicated, although reservations of it are still nurtured in monkeys and rodents. The virus that causes it may be carried by twenty different species of insects, the chief of which is *Stegomyia fasciata* (formerly known as *Aedes aegypti*). Various types of encephalitis are transmitted by species of *Culex* and other genera of Mosquitoes; dengue fever by a species of *Aedes* and by *S. fasciata;* and elephantiasis, caused by a filarial worm, is carried by several species about the world including one, *Wuchereria bancrofti,* which is found in the United States.

972. What disease are transmitted by the Housefly? The Housefly is guilty of transmitting tuberculosis, typhoid, cholera, yaws, bacillary and amoebic dysentery, anthrax, conjunctivitis, and several Cestode and Nematode Worms.

973. What other flies carry diseases? Blackflies (*Simuliidae*) carry a worm infection, onchocerciasis, in Central America, Mexico, and Africa. Deer Flies (*Chrysops*) carry the Filarial Worm, *Loa loa,* in Africa and the West Indies, and may be one of the carriers of tularemia, which is widespread in North America. The Tsetse Flies (*Glossina*) have made large areas of Africa uninhabitable because of their transmission of nagana and of African sleeping sickness. Both of these affect wild and domesticated animals as well as man, and the latter is one of the most serious of human diseases. Sand Flies of the genus *Phlebotomus* (Psychodidae) carry several Leishmania parasites, one of which causes kala-azar, a disease common in the Mediterranean region, Asia, and South America; another causes Oriental sore in Africa, Asia, and South America; and still another causes espundia, of world-wide equatorial distribution. *Phlebotomus* also carries the virus disease pappataci fever of the Mediterranean region, India, and Ceylon; and a Bartonella-caused South American disease, oroya fever. Horseflies (*Tabanus*) transmit anthrax.

974. Do Fleas carry disease? Fleas are dangerous vectors of disease. Normally preferring a single host they will, if deprived of that host, feed upon a variety of others. Thus a Dog or Cat Flea will feed upon man as will the Rat Flea who may previously have been feeding on a large variety of rodents, in this way transmitting disease from species to species. Rat Fleas, and others as well, transmit the bacterium that causes bubonic plague (the Black Death) and that is also carried by several other rodents including Ground Squirrels. Rat Fleas also carry both endemic and epidemic typhus, a world-wide disease of man and rodents, and a Tapeworm that may infest man. The Dog Flea carries a Dog Tapeworm which can also live in man.

975. Do Human Lice carry disease?   Although both species cause physical and mental discomfort, only *Pediculus humanus* transmits disease. It is chiefly important as a vector of typhus and relapsing fevers, both of which may be fatal; and of trench fever, which is no longer the serious menace it was in World War I.

A FEW HARMFUL ARACHNIDA

976. Is a Tick an insect?   No. It is an Arachnid. Ticks have four pairs of legs (although newly hatched larvae sometimes have only three pairs) and no antennae. They differ from Spiders in having the abdomen fused with the cephalothorax, so that the body is made up of one region.

977. Do Ticks carry disease?   Yes. There are two Ticks in the United States that have become important vectors of human diseases. The Spotted Fever Tick of the western states transmits the often fatal Rocky Mountain spotted fever. It also causes a progressive paralysis which, beginning in the legs, may spread to other parts of the body, even causing death. This paralysis seems to be caused by poisons injected by the Tick but only when it feeds at the back of the neck or the base of the skull. This tick also transmits tularemia, a serious rodent disease which also affects man.

The common and widespread Wood Tick or Dog Tick has, within the past few decades, been found to be capable of transmitting Rocky Mountain spotted fever and Tularemia also. Only the adults attack man and dogs, the other stages feeding on rodents.

978. Where do Ticks breed?   The eggs are not laid on the host but in various places in cracks, rubbish, or vegetation. The young larvae climb up on grass and plants to await the passing of a host animal, usually a rodent such as a Meadow Mouse. They may live for a year without feeding but when they find a host, they become filled with blood in a few days. They drop to the ground to molt. Adults may live for three years without feeding. Normally they are about one-sixteenth of an inch long but when filled with blood may become one-half inch long and one-third inch broad. Control is almost impossible. Cutting the underbrush, poisoning off the rodents, and spraying oneself and one's domestic animals and pets with repellent give partial relief. Staying out of all vegetation in spring and summer is often the only answer.

979. What is the difference between a Mite and a Tick? The difference is primarily one of size. The large members of the order Acarina are called Ticks; the small ones, Mites.

980. What are Harvest Mites? These are the "Chiggers" or "Redbugs" that cause man both annoyance and a violent itching which in some people amounts almost to pain. At times they reach an abundance that makes outdoor living nearly impossible without the use of repellents. Their eggs are laid on vegetation close to the ground and the hatching larvae crawl around on the low vegetation until they can attach themselves to a passing vertebrate, preferably a reptile. They stay on the host sucking blood, partly embedding themselves in the flesh, until they have become filled; they then drop off. However, on man, who is not a normal host, they remain embedded in the flesh where they die, often causing painful lesions that may become infected.

981. Do Mites cause or transmit diseases? In parts of Asia and Australia Harvest Mites carry the Rickettsial organism that causes scrub typhus, a disease that caused a large number of casualties in World War II. Itch Mites, which live on organic substances such as cheese, dried meats, flour, and seeds, often get onto man, causing an itching dermatitis known as miller's or grocer's itch. Mites of the family Sarcoptidae attack man and a variety of other animals, burrowing under the skin, causing a severe itching and irritation known as scabies, or sarcoptic mange. These Mites, unlike those that cause the Itch, live their entire life on the host. The eggs are laid in tunnels under the skin, parallel to the surface, by a female who is only one-sixtieth of an inch long. The irritation caused by her tunneling and by the feeding activities of the larvae is difficult to diagnose and may, therefore, last for long periods of time before being brought under control. It is sometimes called the seven-year itch. All victims should be isolated.

982. Are animals other than man bothered by Mites? Sarcoptic Mange Mites attack many animals. In addition there are Mites that get into the hair follicles of mammals; there are Mites that are parasitic upon Hermit Crabs, Louse Flies, Bats, birds, Cattle, and Antelope, often getting into the ears of the Cattle. There are aquatic Mites that are very abundant at times in fresh waters, especially ponds, and that become attached to many aquatic insects; Dragonflies sometimes emerge from the larval skin heavily coated with them. There is one genus of Mites that lives only in the tympanic cavity of moths. These have become so adapted to their specialized environment that they infest only one tympanic cavity on any one individual moth, thus saving their host from total loss of tympanic hearing. The Poultry or Chicken Mite may become so abundant that the perches and litter in the hencoops may appear to be crawling with them and large areas may be sprinkled with the black-and-white dust that is their excreta. They cause listlessness and even death of the fowl. Another mite causes the condition known as scaly leg of poultry.

983. Do Spiders bite? The majority of Spiders are predaceous, that is, they live on living creatures which they kill and devour. The majority are poisonous in that they secrete toxins which they inject into their victims. But Spiders seldom "bite" humans; and the popular attributions to them of each and every casual bite one receives is erroneous and unfounded. There are a few Spiders that do bite and whose bite may be serious, but those species are few in number.

984. What Spiders are noted for inflicting a serious sting? In South America a few of the large Wolf Spiders of the genus *Lycosa,* as well as a few other isolated species whose exact identity is often difficult to establish, inflict a bad sting, the venom of which destroys cells in the vicinity of the wound, making healing slow and difficult. The Wolf Spiders of Europe, long credited with fabulous potentialities for affecting man, are now known to be innocent of the charges. In the United States a few species of *Lycosa* will bite when handled, but the sting subsides within an hour or so, leaving no unpleasant aftereffects. Within the last few years the Brown Recluse, *Loxosceles reclusa,* has become an infamous resident of many Midwestern and Western homes, often hiding behind books, under beds, or in poorly lit corners. It bites with but little provocation and produces a lesion that does not heal but which has to be excised. In addition to these one should be acquainted with Tarantulas and Black Widows.

985. What are Tarantulas? The name Tarantula is used differently by different peoples. In Europe it is used for the large Wolf Spiders, the name having been derived from Taranto, Italy. In America it is used in the broad sense for several families of Spiders and in particular for the very large, hairy Spiders, the Theraphosidae. South American species may be 9½ inches across when the legs are extended. Our own species are not as large but are none the less formidable in appearance. They are sluggish and easily tamed. Although they do bite, and certain South American species can kill a guinea pig in half an hour, their venom has little effect upon man, other than that of the mechanical hurt of the injury.

986. Is the Black Widow dangerous? Yes. But the Black Widow (like most Spiders) is shy. As a rule it attacks man only when it is frightened, cornered, pinched (as when caught in shoes, clothing, bedding, etc.), or when its web is triggered. This reaction, as it lies in wait at the side of its web, is a natural one since the trembling of the web is the signal that a victim has been ensnared. People are frequently attacked in outdoor toilets, or when putting their hands into woodpiles or into vegetation, because of their interference with the web.

There are members of the genus *Latrodectus* in nearly all parts of the world and all are believed to be purveyors of venom that is excessively toxic to man; but they are not responsible for as many fatalities as the newspaper supplements would lead us to believe. However, they should be avoided; and their bite should be given proper medical attention, even though it is seldom fatal except in small children and in very old people.

987. Can the Black Widow always be recognized by its famous red hourglass? The famous red hourglass, if seen, will identify the principal American species, *L. mactans*. However, it is on the ventral surface of the body and not always easily observed. Black Widows are extremely variable in color pattern, immature forms often having additional bright spots and bands, and even mature black ones sometimes having only a very pale hourglass. Another species, the Red

Legged Widow, *L. bishopi,* has many bright markings and bright orange or red legs, but lacks the hourglass spot or has only a partial one. A third species, the Gray Widow, *L. geometricus,* to be found in parts of the South, is usually grayish or light brown and lacks the hourglass. Its venom is not as powerful as that of the other members of the genus.

988. Are there other harmful Arachnids?   Scorpions, members of another order of Arachnids, bear a venomous spine on the tip of the abdomen which is often carried curled forward over the back in striking position. They also have pincers with which to grasp their victims. They do not ordinarily attack man and can be carefully brushed off the body without danger; but if they are suddenly disturbed they may inflict a painful sting. The sting of two species in the United States may even be fatal. Whip Scorpions ("Vinagaroons") and Wind Scorpions (Solpugids) may "bite" but they have no venom. The Harvestmen, or Daddy Longlegs, are of course completely harmless and are even considered beneficial since they feed on many living insects.

HOUSEHOLD PESTS

989. What ants get into the house?   Many species run in and out of houses. The chief troublemakers are the Argentine ant, *Iridomyrmex humilis;* the Little Black Ant, *Monomorium minimum;* Pharaoh's Ant, *M. pharaonis;* the Thief Ant, *Solenopsis molesta;* and the big Carpenter Ant, *Camponotus herculeanus.* They are all a nuisance, swarming over food, especially sweet or fatty foods (except the Thief Ant which prefers proteins, and comes in mainly when the weather is very warm), but do no serious harm. None of them sting, and only the Carpenter Ant bites.

990. What insects injure fabrics?   A few moth and beetle larvae are the chief offenders. The widely publicized Clothes Moths (Tineidae) that eat fabrics of animal origin, such as wool, mohair, and cashmere, as well as felts and furs, are no longer the serious pests that they were at one time. Since they seldom touch fabric that is not soiled with grease, sweat, or other animal substance, modern dry-cleaning facilities and the use of synthetics have reduced their incidence greatly. But they do breed in accumulations of dust or trash of animal origin, so that good housekeeping is essential if they are to be kept under control. The larvae not only chew their way through fabrics, lining their tunnels with silk, but many of them make silken cases in which they live and which they carry about with them.

991. What has replaced the Clothes Moth in importance as a pest on fabrics?   Carpet Beetles and Buffalo Bugs, members of the family Dermestidae, are abundant and destructive on fabrics. They are small oval beetles with a pattern of bright scales. Their larvae may be oval, reddish brown, and bristly (*Anthrenus*) or elongate, golden brown, and silky, with a long tail of hairs (*Attagenus*). They chew not only woolens and furs, but cottons and many synthetic fibers. They will work unseen and unsuspected on the lower surface of carpets or in upholstery. We have found them breeding in the dust and dead insects accumulated inside a globular lightshade suspended from the ceiling, and in a few crumbs in the napkin drawer of the sideboard. They do not spin silk or make cases. They are harder to control than Clothes Moths and are not killed in cedar chests.

992. What insects do damage to books and papers?   Several insects do this: Silverfish (Thysanura), Book Lice (Psocoptera), termites, and occasionally Cockroaches. If the book bindings, papers, boxes, wallpaper, etc., show evidence of large irregular blotches having been eaten, the blame probably lies with the Silverfish who have been eating the paste, glue, or sizing. Their flat, silvery, scaled bodies, characterized by three long tails, slip into cracks of the smallest dimension, so they are seldom seen, especially since they are primarily nocturnal. The Book Lice, or Dust Lice, are tiny, wingless creatures, some of whom live outdoors, feeding on lichens, fungi, and dead plant material in walls, fences, and bird nests; but they often infest houses in large numbers. They feed on paste, glue, and sizing as well as dried organic material, and can reduce valuable papers and books to a powdery dust.

993. What wood-boring insects are serious as household pests?   Termites, Carpenter Ants, and beetles do much damage by working in wood. Termites will enter any wood that is in contact with the soil and work their way up into the house, eating out a beam or sill or wooden article so that nothing remains but the shell. They work in darkness, never breaking through to the air except when they make their colonizing swarms. Carpenter Ants tend to work in stumps and tree trunks, telephone poles and old timbers of buildings, making rather large, irregular tunnels that often open to the outside. Much work that is blamed on termites is done by these big ants.

Beetles of several families bore in wood in houses but their work, though invisible, can be detected by the accumulations of powdery dust that they extrude from the tiny exit holes made by the adult beetles. The Powder Post Beetles (Lyctidae) and the larger Augur Beetles (Bostrichidae), although normally working outdoors in living wood, infest household timbers and furniture, even crates, wine casks, and corks. The Lyctidae are sometimes employed in the faking of antique furniture. Death Watch Beetles (Anobiidae) similarly bore in old wood and furniture.

994. Do termites ever get into wood that is not in contact with the ground? Contrary to popular opinion, some species do, especially the Dry Wood Termite, *Kalotermes minor,* of the western United States. Some species of *Reticulotermes* build tunnels from the soil up over stone foundations and in that way reach the wood.

995. Are termites widespread in the United States? There are fifty-five species of termites in the United States. Although they are more abundant in the tropics, there are species that extend north into Canada and west to the state of Washington. The most widespread in the north are species of *Reticulotermes.*

996. What insects get into stored foods, grains, and cereals? There are many that do this, mostly beetles, although a few moths and an occasional fly do considerable damage. The following table lists some of these:

Larvae	Adult	Food	Name
BEETLES—			
Grubs			
Small, white, hairy	Light-brown, ¹⁄₁₆ in. Wings hairy	Tobacco, drugs, herbs, spices	Cigarette Beetle *Lasioderma serricorne*
Small, white curved	Narrow oval, reddish-brown. Wings striated	Drugs, food, leather	Drugstore Beetle *Sitodrepa panicea*

Larvae	Adult	Food	Name
Hairy, brown. Two curved hooks on last segment	Dark brown, ⅓ in. Yellow band across back	Meats, feathers, skin	Larder Beetle *Dermestes lardarius*
Similar to above	Black above, white beneath, ¼–⅓ in.	Meats, hides, tallow	Hide Beetle *Dermestes vulpinus*
Elongate, slender, purplish, tapering to head	Greenish-blue; red legs; ¼ in. Runs rapidly	Hams, bacon, cheese, dried eggs, fruits, nuts	Red-legged Ham Beetle *Necrobia rufipes*
Smooth, shiny, brownish-yellow	Robust, 1 in.	Anything on pantry shelf	Mealworm *Tenebrio molitor*
Brownish-white	Dark red, narrow, ⅙ in. Active	Flour	Confused Flour Beetle and Red Flour Beetle *Tribolium confusum* and *castaneum*
FLIES— Maggots Yellow. Jump by bending and straightening		Cheese, smoked meats	Cheese Skipper *Piophila casei*
MOTHS— Caterpillars Yellowish-white to pinkish-brown, ⅝ in.	½ in. wing spread. Tips and base of wings dark	Tobacco, nuts, chocolate, dried vegetables	Tobacco Moth *Ephestia elutella*
Whitish, ½ in. Inside kernels	Brownish-gray. Fly and crawl over grain	Wheat and corn. Mostly in mills	Angoumois Grain Moth *Sitotroga cerealella*
White to pinkish, ⅗ in. In silk tubes	Gray, black-marked	Flour. Mostly in mills	Mediterranean Flour Moth *Ephestia kuhniella*
White to greenish-white, ½ in.	Basal half of front wings lighter	Webbing in flour, grain, fruits, nuts, candy.	Indian Meal Moth *Plodia interpunctella*

997. Are Cockroaches harmful? Cockroaches sometimes eat book bindings, magazines, paper-covered boxes, and the like; they certainly nibble on food; and they foul everything over which they run. They are often accused of carrying disease; because of their filthy habits they may be guilty of spreading such diseases as tuberculosis, cholera, leprosy, dysentery, and typhoid. They do not bite.

INSECTS AND THE LAW

998. Are there government controls regulating the collecting of insects? No. But insects should never be collected in nature preserves, or national or state parks, without permission. No species of insects, however, are protected.

999. Are there government controls regulating the transportation of insects? Yes. In 1905, Congress passed the Insect Pest Act, providing authority to regulate the entry and interstate movement of injurious insects. In 1912, the Plant Quarantine Act provided authority to regulate the entry and interstate movement of plant material that might harbor insects. Various amendments have made it possible to set up local quarantines against specific insects, with power to inspect persons, vehicles, and receptacles without a warrant.

1000. Are there postal restrictions regarding the sending of insects through the mails? Yes. No live insects other than Mealworms, Hellgramites, Honeybees, and the true Silkworms may be sent through the mails. All others, regardless of the purpose for which they are intended, must be accompanied by a permit from the Chief of the Bureau of Entomology and Plant Quarantine.

1001. Are these regulations important? They are extremely so, and should be obeyed scrupulously. One careless or wilful introduction of a pest insect can cause the loss of millions upon millions of dollars. Remember the Cabbage Butterfly, Codling Moth, Hessian Fly, Japanese Beetle, Mediterranean Fruit Fly, Mexican Bean Beetle, Cotton Boll Weevil, Cottony Cushion Scale, Gypsy Moth, European Corn Borer, and Asiatic Beetle.

BIBLIOGRAPHY

BORROR, D. J., and DeLONG, D. M. *An Introduction to the Study of Insects.* New York: Rinehart, 1957.

COMSTOCK, J. H. *An Introduction to Entomology.* Ithaca, N.Y.: Comstock, 1940.

DILLON, LAWRENCE S. and ELIZABETH S. *A Manual of Common Beetles of Eastern North America.* Evanston, Ill.: Row, Peterson, 1961.

ESSIG, E. O. *College Entomology.* New York: Macmillan, 1947.

FABRE, J. H. *Souvenirs Entomologique.* 10 vols. Paris: many editions, 1879–91.

FROST, S. W. *General Entomology.* New York: McGraw-Hill, 1942.

GERTSCH, WILLIS J. *American Spiders.* New York: Van Nostrand, 1949.

IMMS, A. D. *A General Textbook of Entomology* (9th ed., revised by O. W. RICHARDS and R. G. DAVIS). London: Methuen; New York: Wiley, 1957.

KLOTS, ALEXANDER B. *A Field Guide to the Butterflies.* Boston: Houghton Mifflin, 1951.

——. *The World of Butterflies and Moths.* New York: McGraw-Hill, 1959.

KLOTS, ALEXANDER B. and ELSIE B. *Living Insects of the World.* New York: Doubleday, 1959.

LUTZ, F. E. *A Field Book of Insects.* New York: Putnam's, 1948.

METCALF, C. L., FLINT, W. P., and METCALF, R. L. *Destructive and Useful Insects.* New York: McGraw-Hill, 1939.

ROEDER, K. D. (ed.). *Insect Physiology.* New York: Wiley, 1953.

SNODGRASS, R. E. *Principles of Insect Morphology.* New York: McGraw-Hill, 1935.

SWAIN, R. B. *The Insect Guide.* New York: Doubleday, 1948.

USINGER, ROBERT L. (ed.). *Aquatic Insects of California.* Berkeley: University of California Press, 1956.

WIGGLESWORTH, V. B. *Principles of Insect Physiology.* London: Methuen; New York: Dutton, 1956.

For Collecting and Preserving Insects

BEIRNE, B. P. *Collecting, Preparing and Preserving Insects.* Ottawa: Canada Department of Agriculture, 1955.

OLDROYD, H. *Collecting, Preserving and Studying Insects.* London: Hutchinson, 1958.

OMAN, P. W., and CUSHMAN, A. D. *Collection and Preservation of Insects.* Washington, D.C.: U. S. Department of Agriculture, 1946.

INDEX

A CATALOG OF SELECTED DOVER
BOOKS IN ALL FIELDS OF INTEREST

DRAWINGS OF REMBRANDT, edited by Seymour Slive. Updated Lippmann, Hofstede de Groot edition, with definitive scholarly apparatus. All portraits, biblical sketches, landscapes, nudes. Oriental figures, classical studies, together with selection of work by followers. 550 illustrations. Total of 630pp. 9⅛ × 12¼.
21485-0, 21486-9 Pa., Two-vol. set $29.90

GHOST AND HORROR STORIES OF AMBROSE BIERCE, Ambrose Bierce. 24 tales vividly imagined, strangely prophetic, and decades ahead of their time in technical skill: "The Damned Thing," "An Inhabitant of Carcosa," "The Eyes of the Panther," "Moxon's Master," and 20 more. 199pp. 5⅜ × 8½. 20767-6 Pa. $3.95

ETHICAL WRITINGS OF MAIMONIDES, Maimonides. Most significant ethical works of great medieval sage, newly translated for utmost precision, readability. Laws Concerning Character Traits, Eight Chapters, more. 192pp. 5⅜ × 8½.
24522-5 Pa. $4.50

THE EXPLORATION OF THE COLORADO RIVER AND ITS CANYONS, J. W. Powell. Full text of Powell's 1,000-mile expedition down the fabled Colorado in 1869. Superb account of terrain, geology, vegetation, Indians, famine, mutiny, treacherous rapids, mighty canyons, during exploration of last unknown part of continental U.S. 400pp. 5⅜ × 8½. 20094-9 Pa. $7.95

HISTORY OF PHILOSOPHY, Julián Marías. Clearest one-volume history on the market. Every major philosopher and dozens of others, to Existentialism and later. 505pp. 5⅜ × 8½. 21739-6 Pa. $9.95

ALL ABOUT LIGHTNING, Martin A. Uman. Highly readable non-technical survey of nature and causes of lightning, thunderstorms, ball lightning, St. Elmo's Fire, much more. Illustrated. 192pp. 5⅜ × 8½. 25237-X Pa. $5.95

SAILING ALONE AROUND THE WORLD, Captain Joshua Slocum. First man to sail around the world, alone, in small boat. One of great feats of seamanship told in delightful manner. 67 illustrations. 294pp. 5⅜ × 8½. 20326-3 Pa. $4.95

LETTERS AND NOTES ON THE MANNERS, CUSTOMS AND CONDITIONS OF THE NORTH AMERICAN INDIANS, George Catlin. Classic account of life among Plains Indians: ceremonies, hunt, warfare, etc. 312 plates. 572pp. of text. 6⅛ × 9¼. 22118-0, 22119-9, Pa. Two-vol. set $17.90

ALASKA: The Harriman Expedition, 1899, John Burroughs, John Muir, et al. Informative, engrossing accounts of two-month, 9,000-mile expedition. Native peoples, wildlife, forests, geography, salmon industry, glaciers, more. Profusely illustrated. 240 black-and-white line drawings. 124 black-and-white photographs. 3 maps. Index. 576pp. 5⅜ × 8½. 25109-8 Pa. $11.95

THE BOOK OF BEASTS: Being a Translation from a Latin Bestiary of the Twelfth Century, T. H. White. Wonderful catalog real and fanciful beasts: manticore, griffin, phoenix, amphivius, jaculus, many more. White's witty erudite commentary on scientific, historical aspects. Fascinating glimpse of medieval mind. Illustrated. 296pp. 5⅜ × 8¼. (Available in U.S. only) 24609-4 Pa. $6.95

FRANK LLOYD WRIGHT: ARCHITECTURE AND NATURE With 160 Illustrations, Donald Hoffmann. Profusely illustrated study of influence of nature—especially prairie—on Wright's designs for Fallingwater, Robie House, Guggenheim Museum, other masterpieces. 96pp. 9¼ × 10¾. 25098-9 Pa. $7.95

FRANK LLOYD WRIGHT'S FALLINGWATER, Donald Hoffmann. Wright's famous waterfall house: planning and construction of organic idea. History of site, owners, Wright's personal involvement. Photographs of various stages of building. Preface by Edgar Kaufmann, Jr. 100 illustrations. 112pp. 9¼ × 10. 23671-4 Pa. $8.95

YEARS WITH FRANK LLOYD WRIGHT: Apprentice to Genius, Edgar Tafel. Insightful memoir by a former apprentice presents a revealing portrait of Wright the man, the inspired teacher, the greatest American architect. 372 black-and-white illustrations. Preface. Index. vi + 228pp. 8¼ × 11. 24801-1 Pa. $10.95

THE STORY OF KING ARTHUR AND HIS KNIGHTS, Howard Pyle. Enchanting version of King Arthur fable has delighted generations with imaginative narratives of exciting adventures and unforgettable illustrations by the author. 41 illustrations. xviii + 313pp. 6⅛ × 9¼. 21445-1 Pa. $6.95

THE GODS OF THE EGYPTIANS, E. A. Wallis Budge. Thorough coverage of numerous gods of ancient Egypt by foremost Egyptologist. Information on evolution of cults, rites and gods; the cult of Osiris; the Book of the Dead and its rites; the sacred animals and birds; Heaven and Hell; and more. 956pp. 6⅛ × 9¼. 22055-9, 22056-7 Pa., Two-vol. set $21.90

A THEOLOGICO-POLITICAL TREATISE, Benedict Spinoza. Also contains unfinished *Political Treatise*. Great classic on religious liberty, theory of government on common consent. R. Elwes translation. Total of 421pp. 5⅜ × 8½. 20249-6 Pa. $6.95

INCIDENTS OF TRAVEL IN CENTRAL AMERICA, CHIAPAS, AND YUCATAN, John L. Stephens. Almost single-handed discovery of Maya culture; exploration of ruined cities, monuments, temples; customs of Indians. 115 drawings. 892pp. 5⅜ × 8½. 22404-X, 22405-8 Pa., Two-vol. set $15.90

LOS CAPRICHOS, Francisco Goya. 80 plates of wild, grotesque monsters and caricatures. Prado manuscript included. 183pp. 6⅝ × 9⅝. 22384-1 Pa. $5.95

AUTOBIOGRAPHY: The Story of My Experiments with Truth, Mohandas K. Gandhi. Not hagiography, but Gandhi in his own words. Boyhood, legal studies, purification, the growth of the Satyagraha (nonviolent protest) movement. Critical, inspiring work of the man who freed India. 480pp. 5⅜ × 8½. (Available in U.S. only) 24593-4 Pa. $6.95

CATALOG OF DOVER BOOKS

ILLUSTRATED DICTIONARY OF HISTORIC ARCHITECTURE, edited by Cyril M. Harris. Extraordinary compendium of clear, concise definitions for over 5,000 important architectural terms complemented by over 2,000 line drawings. Covers full spectrum of architecture from ancient ruins to 20th-century Modernism. Preface. 592pp. 7½ × 9⅜. 24444-X Pa. $15.95

THE NIGHT BEFORE CHRISTMAS, Clement Moore. Full text, and woodcuts from original 1848 book. Also critical, historical material. 19 illustrations. 40pp. 4⅝ × 6. 22797-9 Pa. $2.50

THE LESSON OF JAPANESE ARCHITECTURE: 165 Photographs, Jiro Harada. Memorable gallery of 165 photographs taken in the 1930's of exquisite Japanese homes of the well-to-do and historic buildings. 13 line diagrams. 192pp. 8⅜ × 11¼. 24778-3 Pa. $10.95

THE AUTOBIOGRAPHY OF CHARLES DARWIN AND SELECTED LETTERS, edited by Francis Darwin. The fascinating life of eccentric genius composed of an intimate memoir by Darwin (intended for his children); commentary by his son, Francis; hundreds of fragments from notebooks, journals, papers; and letters to and from Lyell, Hooker, Huxley, Wallace and Henslow. xi + 365pp. 5⅜ × 8. 20479-0 Pa. $6.95

WONDERS OF THE SKY: Observing Rainbows, Comets, Eclipses, the Stars and Other Phenomena, Fred Schaaf. Charming, easy-to-read poetic guide to all manner of celestial events visible to the naked eye. Mock suns, glories, Belt of Venus, more. Illustrated. 299pp. 5¼ × 8¼. 24402-4 Pa. $7.95

BURNHAM'S CELESTIAL HANDBOOK, Robert Burnham, Jr. Thorough guide to the stars beyond our solar system. Exhaustive treatment. Alphabetical by constellation: Andromeda to Cetus in Vol. 1; Chamaeleon to Orion in Vol. 2; and Pavo to Vulpecula in Vol. 3. Hundreds of illustrations. Index in Vol. 3. 2,000pp. 6⅛ × 9¼. 23567-X, 23568-8, 23673-0 Pa., Three-vol. set $41.85

STAR NAMES: Their Lore and Meaning, Richard Hinckley Allen. Fascinating history of names various cultures have given to constellations and literary and folkloristic uses that have been made of stars. Indexes to subjects. Arabic and Greek names. Biblical references. Bibliography. 563pp. 5⅜ × 8½. 21079-0 Pa. $8.95

THIRTY YEARS THAT SHOOK PHYSICS: The Story of Quantum Theory, George Gamow. Lucid, accessible introduction to influential theory of energy and matter. Careful explanations of Dirac's anti-particles, Bohr's model of the atom, much more. 12 plates. Numerous drawings. 240pp. 5⅜ × 8½. 24895-X Pa. $5.95

CHINESE DOMESTIC FURNITURE IN PHOTOGRAPHS AND MEASURED DRAWINGS, Gustav Ecke. A rare volume, now affordably priced for antique collectors, furniture buffs and art historians. Detailed review of styles ranging from early Shang to late Ming. Unabridged republication. 161 black-and-white drawings, photos. Total of 224pp. 8⅜ × 11¼. (Available in U.S. only) 25171-3 Pa. $13.95

VINCENT VAN GOGH: A Biography, Julius Meier-Graefe. Dynamic, penetrating study of artist's life, relationship with brother, Theo, painting techniques, travels, more. Readable, engrossing. 160pp. 5⅜ × 8½. (Available in U.S. only) 25253-1 Pa. $4.95

HOW TO WRITE, Gertrude Stein. Gertrude Stein claimed anyone could understand her unconventional writing—here are clues to help. Fascinating improvisations, language experiments, explanations illuminate Stein's craft and the art of writing. Total of 414pp. 4⅜ × 6⅜. 23144-5 Pa. $6.95

ADVENTURES AT SEA IN THE GREAT AGE OF SAIL: Five Firsthand Narratives, edited by Elliot Snow. Rare true accounts of exploration, whaling, shipwreck, fierce natives, trade, shipboard life, more. 33 illustrations. Introduction. 353pp. 5⅜ × 8½. 25177-2 Pa. $8.95

THE HERBAL OR GENERAL HISTORY OF PLANTS, John Gerard. Classic descriptions of about 2,850 plants—with over 2,700 illustrations—includes Latin and English names, physical descriptions, varieties, time and place of growth, more. 2,706 illustrations. xlv + 1,678pp. 8½ × 12¼. 23147-X Cloth. $75.00

DOROTHY AND THE WIZARD IN OZ, L. Frank Baum. Dorothy and the Wizard visit the center of the Earth, where people are vegetables, glass houses grow and Oz characters reappear. Classic sequel to *Wizard of Oz*. 256pp. 5⅜ × 8. 24714-7 Pa. $5.95

SONGS OF EXPERIENCE: Facsimile Reproduction with 26 Plates in Full Color, William Blake. This facsimile of Blake's original "Illuminated Book" reproduces 26 full-color plates from a rare 1826 edition. Includes "The Tyger," "London," "Holy Thursday," and other immortal poems. 26 color plates. Printed text of poems. 48pp. 5¼ × 7. 24636-1 Pa. $3.50

SONGS OF INNOCENCE, William Blake. The first and most popular of Blake's famous "Illuminated Books," in a facsimile edition reproducing all 31 brightly colored plates. Additional printed text of each poem. 64pp. 5¼ × 7. 22764-2 Pa. $3.50

PRECIOUS STONES, Max Bauer. Classic, thorough study of diamonds, rubies, emeralds, garnets, etc.: physical character, occurrence, properties, use, similar topics. 20 plates, 8 in color. 94 figures. 659pp. 6⅛ × 9¼. 21910-0, 21911-9 Pa., Two-vol. set $15.90

ENCYCLOPEDIA OF VICTORIAN NEEDLEWORK, S. F. A. Caulfeild and Blanche Saward. Full, precise descriptions of stitches, techniques for dozens of needlecrafts—most exhaustive reference of its kind. Over 800 figures. Total of 679pp. 8⅛ × 11. Two volumes. Vol. 1 22800-2 Pa. $11.95
Vol. 2 22801-0 Pa. $11.95

THE MARVELOUS LAND OF OZ, L. Frank Baum. Second Oz book, the Scarecrow and Tin Woodman are back with hero named Tip, Oz magic. 136 illustrations. 287pp. 5⅜ × 8½. 20692-0 Pa. $5.95

WILD FOWL DECOYS, Joel Barber. Basic book on the subject, by foremost authority and collector. Reveals history of decoy making and rigging, place in American culture, different kinds of decoys, how to make them, and how to use them. 140 plates. 156pp. 7⅞ × 10¾. 20011-6 Pa. $8.95

HISTORY OF LACE, Mrs. Bury Palliser. Definitive, profusely illustrated chronicle of lace from earliest times to late 19th century. Laces of Italy, Greece, England, France, Belgium, etc. Landmark of needlework scholarship. 266 illustrations. 672pp. 6⅛ × 9¼. 24742-2 Pa. $14.95

ILLUSTRATED GUIDE TO SHAKER FURNITURE, Robert Meader. All furniture and appurtenances, with much on unknown local styles. 235 photos. 146pp. 9 × 12. 22819-3 Pa. $8.95

WHALE SHIPS AND WHALING: A Pictorial Survey, George Francis Dow. Over 200 vintage engravings, drawings, photographs of barks, brigs, cutters, other vessels. Also harpoons, lances, whaling guns, many other artifacts. Comprehensive text by foremost authority. 207 black-and-white illustrations. 288pp. 6 × 9.
24808-9 Pa. $8.95

THE BERTRAMS, Anthony Trollope. Powerful portrayal of blind self-will and thwarted ambition includes one of Trollope's most heartrending love stories. 497pp. 5⅜ × 8½. 25119-5 Pa. $9.95

ADVENTURES WITH A HAND LENS, Richard Headstrom. Clearly written guide to observing and studying flowers and grasses, fish scales, moth and insect wings, egg cases, buds, feathers, seeds, leaf scars, moss, molds, ferns, common crystals, etc.—all with an ordinary, inexpensive magnifying glass. 209 exact line drawings aid in your discoveries. 220pp. 5⅜ × 8½. 23330-8 Pa. $4.95

RODIN ON ART AND ARTISTS, Auguste Rodin. Great sculptor's candid, wide-ranging comments on meaning of art; great artists; relation of sculpture to poetry, painting, music; philosophy of life, more. 76 superb black-and-white illustrations of Rodin's sculpture, drawings and prints. 119pp. 8⅝ × 11¼. 24487-3 Pa. $7.95

FIFTY CLASSIC FRENCH FILMS, 1912–1982: A Pictorial Record, Anthony Slide. Memorable stills from Grand Illusion, Beauty and the Beast, Hiroshima, Mon Amour, many more. Credits, plot synopses, reviews, etc. 160pp. 8¼ × 11.
25256-6 Pa. $11.95

THE PRINCIPLES OF PSYCHOLOGY, William James. Famous long course complete, unabridged. Stream of thought, time perception, memory, experimental methods; great work decades ahead of its time. 94 figures. 1,391pp. 5⅜ × 8½.
20381-6, 20382-4 Pa., Two-vol. set $23.90

BODIES IN A BOOKSHOP, R. T. Campbell. Challenging mystery of blackmail and murder with ingenious plot and superbly drawn characters. In the best tradition of British suspense fiction. 192pp. 5⅜ × 8½. 24720-1 Pa. $3.95

CALLAS: PORTRAIT OF A PRIMA DONNA, George Jellinek. Renowned commentator on the musical scene chronicles incredible career and life of the most controversial, fascinating, influential operatic personality of our time. 64 black-and-white photographs. 416pp. 5⅜ × 8¼. 25047-4 Pa. $8.95

GEOMETRY, RELATIVITY AND THE FOURTH DIMENSION, Rudolph Rucker. Exposition of fourth dimension, concepts of relativity as Flatland characters continue adventures. Popular, easily followed yet accurate, profound. 141 illustrations. 133pp. 5⅜ × 8½. 23400-2 Pa. $4.95

HOUSEHOLD STORIES BY THE BROTHERS GRIMM, with pictures by Walter Crane. 53 classic stories—Rumpelstiltskin, Rapunzel, Hansel and Gretel, the Fisherman and his Wife, Snow White, Tom Thumb, Sleeping Beauty, Cinderella, and so much more—lavishly illustrated with original 19th century drawings. 114 illustrations. x + 269pp. 5⅜ × 8½. 21080-4 Pa. $4.95

SUNDIALS, Albert Waugh. Far and away the best, most thorough coverage of ideas, mathematics concerned, types, construction, adjusting anywhere. Over 100 illustrations. 230pp. 5⅜ × 8½. 22947-5 Pa. $4.95

PICTURE HISTORY OF THE NORMANDIE: With 190 Illustrations, Frank O. Braynard. Full story of legendary French ocean liner: Art Deco interiors, design innovations, furnishings, celebrities, maiden voyage, tragic fire, much more. Extensive text. 144pp. 8⅞ × 11¾. 25257-4 Pa. $10.95

THE FIRST AMERICAN COOKBOOK: A Facsimile of "American Cookery," 1796, Amelia Simmons. Facsimile of the first American-written cookbook published in the United States contains authentic recipes for colonial favorites—pumpkin pudding, winter squash pudding, spruce beer, Indian slapjacks, and more. Introductory Essay and Glossary of colonial cooking terms. 80pp. 5⅜ × 8½. 24710-4 Pa. $3.50

101 PUZZLES IN THOUGHT AND LOGIC, C. R. Wylie, Jr. Solve murders and robberies, find out which fishermen are liars, how a blind man could possibly identify a color—purely by your own reasoning! 107pp. 5⅜ × 8½. 20367-0 Pa. $2.50

THE BOOK OF WORLD-FAMOUS MUSIC—CLASSICAL, POPULAR AND FOLK, James J. Fuld. Revised and enlarged republication of landmark work in musico-bibliography. Full information about nearly 1,000 songs and compositions including first lines of music and lyrics. New supplement. Index. 800pp. 5⅜ × 8¼. 24857-7 Pa. $15.95

ANTHROPOLOGY AND MODERN LIFE, Franz Boas. Great anthropologist's classic treatise on race and culture. Introduction by Ruth Bunzel. Only inexpensive paperback edition. 255pp. 5⅜ × 8½. 25245-0 Pa. $6.95

THE TALE OF PETER RABBIT, Beatrix Potter. The inimitable Peter's terrifying adventure in Mr. McGregor's garden, with all 27 wonderful, full-color Potter illustrations. 55pp. 4¼ × 5½. (Available in U.S. only) 22827-4 Pa. $1.75

THREE PROPHETIC SCIENCE FICTION NOVELS, H. G. Wells. *When the Sleeper Wakes, A Story of the Days to Come* and *The Time Machine* (full version). 335pp. 5⅜ × 8½. (Available in U.S. only) 20605-X Pa. $6.95

APICIUS COOKERY AND DINING IN IMPERIAL ROME, edited and translated by Joseph Dommers Vehling. Oldest known cookbook in existence offers readers a clear picture of what foods Romans ate, how they prepared them, etc. 49 illustrations. 301pp. 6⅛ × 9¼. 23563-7 Pa. $7.95

SHAKESPEARE LEXICON AND QUOTATION DICTIONARY, Alexander Schmidt. Full definitions, locations, shades of meaning of every word in plays and poems. More than 50,000 exact quotations. 1,485pp. 6½ × 9¼. 22726-X, 22727-8 Pa., Two-vol. set $29.90

THE WORLD'S GREAT SPEECHES, edited by Lewis Copeland and Lawrence W. Lamm. Vast collection of 278 speeches from Greeks to 1970. Powerful and effective models; unique look at history. 842pp. 5⅜ × 8½. 20468-5 Pa. $11.95

THE BLUE FAIRY BOOK, Andrew Lang. The first, most famous collection, with many familiar tales: Little Red Riding Hood, Aladdin and the Wonderful Lamp, Puss in Boots, Sleeping Beauty, Hansel and Gretel, Rumpelstiltskin; 37 in all. 138 illustrations. 390pp. 5⅜ × 8½. 21437-0 Pa. $6.95

THE STORY OF THE CHAMPIONS OF THE ROUND TABLE, Howard Pyle. Sir Launcelot, Sir Tristram and Sir Percival in spirited adventures of love and triumph retold in Pyle's inimitable style. 50 drawings, 31 full-page. xviii + 329pp. 6½ × 9¼. 21883-X Pa. $7.95

AUDUBON AND HIS JOURNALS, Maria Audubon. Unmatched two-volume portrait of the great artist, naturalist and author contains his journals, an excellent biography by his granddaughter, expert annotations by the noted ornithologist, Dr. Elliott Coues, and 37 superb illustrations. Total of 1,200pp. 5⅜ × 8.
Vol. I 25143-8 Pa. $8.95
Vol. II 25144-6 Pa. $8.95

GREAT DINOSAUR HUNTERS AND THEIR DISCOVERIES, Edwin H. Colbert. Fascinating, lavishly illustrated chronicle of dinosaur research, 1820's to 1960. Achievements of Cope, Marsh, Brown, Buckland, Mantell, Huxley, many others. 384pp. 5¼ × 8¼. 24701-5 Pa. $7.95

THE TASTEMAKERS, Russell Lynes. Informal, illustrated social history of American taste 1850's–1950's. First popularized categories Highbrow, Lowbrow, Middlebrow. 129 illustrations. New (1979) afterword. 384pp. 6 × 9.
23993-4 Pa. $8.95

DOUBLE CROSS PURPOSES, Ronald A. Knox. A treasure hunt in the Scottish Highlands, an old map, unidentified corpse, surprise discoveries keep reader guessing in this cleverly intricate tale of financial skullduggery. 2 black-and-white maps. 320pp. 5⅜ × 8½. (Available in U.S. only) 25032-6 Pa. $6.95

AUTHENTIC VICTORIAN DECORATION AND ORNAMENTATION IN FULL COLOR: 46 Plates from "Studies in Design," Christopher Dresser. Superb full-color lithographs reproduced from rare original portfolio of a major Victorian designer. 48pp. 9¼ × 12¼. 25083-0 Pa. $7.95

PRIMITIVE ART, Franz Boas. Remains the best text ever prepared on subject, thoroughly discussing Indian, African, Asian, Australian, and, especially, Northern American primitive art. Over 950 illustrations show ceramics, masks, totem poles, weapons, textiles, paintings, much more. 376pp. 5⅜ × 8. 20025-6 Pa. $7.95

SIDELIGHTS ON RELATIVITY, Albert Einstein. Unabridged republication of two lectures delivered by the great physicist in 1920–21. *Ether and Relativity* and *Geometry and Experience*. Elegant ideas in non-mathematical form, accessible to intelligent layman. vi + 56pp. 5⅜ × 8½. 24511-X Pa. $2.95

THE WIT AND HUMOR OF OSCAR WILDE, edited by Alvin Redman. More than 1,000 ripostes, paradoxes, wisecracks: Work is the curse of the drinking classes, I can resist everything except temptation, etc. 258pp. 5⅜ × 8½. 20602-5 Pa. $4.95

ADVENTURES WITH A MICROSCOPE, Richard Headstrom. 59 adventures with clothing fibers, protozoa, ferns and lichens, roots and leaves, much more. 142 illustrations. 232pp. 5⅜ × 8½. 23471-1 Pa. $3.95

PLANTS OF THE BIBLE, Harold N. Moldenke and Alma L. Moldenke. Standard reference to all 230 plants mentioned in Scriptures. Latin name, biblical reference, uses, modern identity, much more. Unsurpassed encyclopedic resource for scholars, botanists, nature lovers, students of Bible. Bibliography. Indexes. 123 black-and-white illustrations. 384pp. 6 × 9. 25069-5 Pa. $8.95

FAMOUS AMERICAN WOMEN: A Biographical Dictionary from Colonial Times to the Present, Robert McHenry, ed. From Pocahontas to Rosa Parks, 1,035 distinguished American women documented in separate biographical entries. Accurate, up-to-date data, numerous categories, spans 400 years. Indices. 493pp. 6½ × 9¼. 24523-3 Pa. $10.95

THE FABULOUS INTERIORS OF THE GREAT OCEAN LINERS IN HISTORIC PHOTOGRAPHS, William H. Miller, Jr. Some 200 superb photographs capture exquisite interiors of world's great "floating palaces"—1890's to 1980's: *Titanic, Ile de France, Queen Elizabeth, United States, Europa,* more. Approx. 200 black-and-white photographs. Captions. Text. Introduction. 160pp. 8⅞ × 11¾. 24756-2 Pa. $9.95

THE GREAT LUXURY LINERS, 1927–1954: A Photographic Record, William H. Miller, Jr. Nostalgic tribute to heyday of ocean liners. 186 photos of Ile de France, Normandie, Leviathan, Queen Elizabeth, United States, many others. Interior and exterior views. Introduction. Captions. 160pp. 9 × 12. 24056-8 Pa. $10.95

A NATURAL HISTORY OF THE DUCKS, John Charles Phillips. Great landmark of ornithology offers complete detailed coverage of nearly 200 species and subspecies of ducks: gadwall, sheldrake, merganser, pintail, many more. 74 full-color plates, 102 black-and-white. Bibliography. Total of 1,920pp. 8⅜ × 11¼. 25141-1, 25142-X Cloth. Two-vol. set $100.00

THE SEAWEED HANDBOOK: An Illustrated Guide to Seaweeds from North Carolina to Canada, Thomas F. Lee. Concise reference covers 78 species. Scientific and common names, habitat, distribution, more. Finding keys for easy identification. 224pp. 5⅜ × 8½. 25215-9 Pa. $6.95

THE TEN BOOKS OF ARCHITECTURE: The 1755 Leoni Edition, Leon Battista Alberti. Rare classic helped introduce the glories of ancient architecture to the Renaissance. 68 black-and-white plates. 336pp. 8⅜ × 11¼. 25239-6 Pa. $14.95

MISS MACKENZIE, Anthony Trollope. Minor masterpieces by Victorian master unmasks many truths about life in 19th-century England. First inexpensive edition in years. 392pp. 5⅜ × 8½. 25201-9 Pa. $8.95

THE RIME OF THE ANCIENT MARINER, Gustave Doré, Samuel Taylor Coleridge. Dramatic engravings considered by many to be his greatest work. The terrifying space of the open sea, the storms and whirlpools of an unknown ocean, the ice of Antarctica, more—all rendered in a powerful, chilling manner. Full text. 38 plates. 77pp. 9¼ × 12. 22305-1 Pa. $4.95

THE EXPEDITIONS OF ZEBULON MONTGOMERY PIKE, Zebulon Montgomery Pike. Fascinating first-hand accounts (1805–6) of exploration of Mississippi River, Indian wars, capture by Spanish dragoons, much more. 1,088pp. 5⅜ × 8½. 25254-X, 25255-8 Pa. Two-vol. set $25.90

CATALOG OF DOVER BOOKS

A CONCISE HISTORY OF PHOTOGRAPHY: Third Revised Edition, Helmut Gernsheim. Best one-volume history—camera obscura, photochemistry, daguerreotypes, evolution of cameras, film, more. Also artistic aspects—landscape, portraits, fine art, etc. 281 black-and-white photographs. 26 in color. 176pp. 8⅜ × 11¼. 25128-4 Pa. $13.95

THE DORÉ BIBLE ILLUSTRATIONS, Gustave Doré. 241 detailed plates from the Bible: the Creation scenes, Adam and Eve, Flood, Babylon, battle sequences, life of Jesus, etc. Each plate is accompanied by the verses from the King James version of the Bible. 241pp. 9 × 12. 23004-X Pa. $9.95

HUGGER-MUGGER IN THE LOUVRE, Elliot Paul. Second Homer Evans mystery-comedy. Theft at the Louvre involves sleuth in hilarious, madcap caper. "A knockout."—Books. 336pp. 5⅜ × 8½. 25185-3 Pa. $5.95

FLATLAND, E. A. Abbott. Intriguing and enormously popular science-fiction classic explores the complexities of trying to survive as a two-dimensional being in a three-dimensional world. Amusingly illustrated by the author. 16 illustrations. 103pp. 5⅜ × 8½. 20001-9 Pa. $2.50

THE HISTORY OF THE LEWIS AND CLARK EXPEDITION, Meriwether Lewis and William Clark, edited by Elliott Coues. Classic edition of Lewis and Clark's day-by-day journals that later became the basis for U.S. claims to Oregon and the West. Accurate and invaluable geographical, botanical, biological, meteorological and anthropological material. Total of 1,508pp. 5⅜ × 8½.
21268-8, 21269-6, 21270-X Pa. Three-vol. set $26.85

LANGUAGE, TRUTH AND LOGIC, Alfred J. Ayer. Famous, clear introduction to Vienna, Cambridge schools of Logical Positivism. Role of philosophy, elimination of metaphysics, nature of analysis, etc. 160pp. 5⅜ × 8½. (Available in U.S. and Canada only) 20010-8 Pa. $3.95

MATHEMATICS FOR THE NONMATHEMATICIAN, Morris Kline. Detailed, college-level treatment of mathematics in cultural and historical context, with numerous exercises. For liberal arts students. Preface. Recommended Reading Lists. Tables. Index. Numerous black-and-white figures. xvi + 641pp. 5⅜ × 8½.
24823-2 Pa. $11.95

HANDBOOK OF PICTORIAL SYMBOLS, Rudolph Modley. 3,250 signs and symbols, many systems in full; official or heavy commercial use. Arranged by subject. Most in Pictorial Archive series. 143pp. 8⅛ × 11. 23357-X Pa. $6.95

INCIDENTS OF TRAVEL IN YUCATAN, John L. Stephens. Classic (1843) exploration of jungles of Yucatan, looking for evidences of Maya civilization. Travel adventures, Mexican and Indian culture, etc. Total of 669pp. 5⅜ × 8½.
20926-1, 20927-X Pa., Two-vol. set $11.90

DEGAS: An Intimate Portrait, Ambroise Vollard. Charming, anecdotal memoir by famous art dealer of one of the greatest 19th-century French painters. 14 black-and-white illustrations. Introduction by Harold L. Van Doren. 96pp. 5⅜ × 8½.
25131-4 Pa. $4.95

PERSONAL NARRATIVE OF A PILGRIMAGE TO ALMANDINAH AND MECCAH, Richard Burton. Great travel classic by remarkably colorful personality. Burton, disguised as a Moroccan, visited sacred shrines of Islam, narrowly escaping death. 47 illustrations. 959pp. 5⅜ × 8½. 21217-3, 21218-1 Pa., Two-vol. set $19.90

PHRASE AND WORD ORIGINS, A. H. Holt. Entertaining, reliable, modern study of more than 1,200 colorful words, phrases, origins and histories. Much unexpected information. 254pp. 5⅜ × 8½.
20758-7 Pa. $5.95

THE RED THUMB MARK, R. Austin Freeman. In this first Dr. Thorndyke case, the great scientific detective draws fascinating conclusions from the nature of a single fingerprint. Exciting story, authentic science. 320pp. 5⅜ × 8½. (Available in U.S. only)
25210-8 Pa. $6.95

AN EGYPTIAN HIEROGLYPHIC DICTIONARY, E. A. Wallis Budge. Monumental work containing about 25,000 words or terms that occur in texts ranging from 3000 B.C. to 600 A.D. Each entry consists of a transliteration of the word, the word in hieroglyphs, and the meaning in English. 1,314pp. 6⅜ × 10.
23615-3, 23616-1 Pa., Two-vol. set $31.90

THE COMPLEAT STRATEGYST: Being a Primer on the Theory of Games of Strategy, J. D. Williams. Highly entertaining classic describes, with many illustrated examples, how to select best strategies in conflict situations. Prefaces. Appendices. xvi + 268pp. 5⅜ × 8½.
25101-2 Pa. $5.95

THE ROAD TO OZ, L. Frank Baum. Dorothy meets the Shaggy Man, little Button-Bright and the Rainbow's beautiful daughter in this delightful trip to the magical Land of Oz. 272pp. 5⅜ × 8.
25208-6 Pa. $5.95

POINT AND LINE TO PLANE, Wassily Kandinsky. Seminal exposition of role of point, line, other elements in non-objective painting. Essential to understanding 20th-century art. 127 illustrations. 192pp. 6½ × 9¼.
23808-3 Pa. $5.95

LADY ANNA, Anthony Trollope. Moving chronicle of Countess Lovel's bitter struggle to win for herself and daughter Anna their rightful rank and fortune—perhaps at cost of sanity itself. 384pp. 5⅜ × 8½.
24669-8 Pa. $8.95

EGYPTIAN MAGIC, E. A. Wallis Budge. Sums up all that is known about magic in Ancient Egypt: the role of magic in controlling the gods, powerful amulets that warded off evil spirits, scarabs of immortality, use of wax images, formulas and spells, the secret name, much more. 253pp. 5⅜ × 8½.
22681-6 Pa. $4.50

THE DANCE OF SIVA, Ananda Coomaraswamy. Preeminent authority unfolds the vast metaphysic of India: the revelation of her art, conception of the universe, social organization, etc. 27 reproductions of art masterpieces. 192pp. 5⅜ × 8½.
24817-8 Pa. $5.95

CHRISTMAS CUSTOMS AND TRADITIONS, Clement A. Miles. Origin, evolution, significance of religious, secular practices. Caroling, gifts, yule logs, much more. Full, scholarly yet fascinating; non-sectarian. 400pp. 5⅜ × 8½.
23354-5 Pa. $6.95

THE HUMAN FIGURE IN MOTION, Eadweard Muybridge. More than 4,500 stopped-action photos, in action series, showing undraped men, women, children jumping, lying down, throwing, sitting, wrestling, carrying, etc. 390pp. 7⅞ × 10⅝.
20204-6 Cloth. $21.95

THE MAN WHO WAS THURSDAY, Gilbert Keith Chesterton. Witty, fast-paced novel about a club of anarchists in turn-of-the-century London. Brilliant social, religious, philosophical speculations. 128pp. 5⅜ × 8½. 25121-7 Pa. $3.95

A CEZANNE SKETCHBOOK: Figures, Portraits, Landscapes and Still Lifes, Paul Cezanne. Great artist experiments with tonal effects, light, mass, other qualities in over 100 drawings. A revealing view of developing master painter, precursor of Cubism. 102 black-and-white illustrations. 144pp. 8¾ × 6⅝. 24790-2 Pa. $5.95

AN ENCYCLOPEDIA OF BATTLES: Accounts of Over 1,560 Battles from 1479 B.C. to the Present, David Eggenberger. Presents essential details of every major battle in recorded history, from the first battle of Megiddo in 1479 B.C. to Grenada in 1984. List of Battle Maps. New Appendix covering the years 1967–1984. Index. 99 illustrations. 544pp. 6½ × 9¼. 24913-1 Pa. $14.95

AN ETYMOLOGICAL DICTIONARY OF MODERN ENGLISH, Ernest Weekley. Richest, fullest work, by foremost British lexicographer. Detailed word histories. Inexhaustible. Total of 856pp. 6½ × 9¼.
21873-2, 21874-0 Pa., Two-vol. set $17.00

WEBSTER'S AMERICAN MILITARY BIOGRAPHIES, edited by Robert McHenry. Over 1,000 figures who shaped 3 centuries of American military history. Detailed biographies of Nathan Hale, Douglas MacArthur, Mary Hallaren, others. Chronologies of engagements, more. Introduction. Addenda. 1,033 entries in alphabetical order. xi + 548pp. 6½ × 9¼. (Available in U.S. only)
24758-9 Pa. $13.95

LIFE IN ANCIENT EGYPT, Adolf Erman. Detailed older account, with much not in more recent books: domestic life, religion, magic, medicine, commerce, and whatever else needed for complete picture. Many illustrations. 597pp. 5⅜ × 8½.
22632-8 Pa. $8.95

HISTORIC COSTUME IN PICTURES, Braun & Schneider. Over 1,450 costumed figures shown, covering a wide variety of peoples: kings, emperors, nobles, priests, servants, soldiers, scholars, townsfolk, peasants, merchants, courtiers, cavaliers, and more. 256pp. 8⅜ × 11¼. 23150-X Pa. $9.95

THE NOTEBOOKS OF LEONARDO DA VINCI, edited by J. P. Richter. Extracts from manuscripts reveal great genius; on painting, sculpture, anatomy, sciences, geography, etc. Both Italian and English. 186 ms. pages reproduced, plus 500 additional drawings, including studies for *Last Supper, Sforza* monument, etc. 860pp. 7⅞ × 10¾. (Available in U.S. only) 22572-0, 22573-9 Pa., Two-vol. set $31.90

THE ART NOUVEAU STYLE BOOK OF ALPHONSE MUCHA: All 72 Plates from "Documents Decoratifs" in Original Color, Alphonse Mucha. Rare copyright-free design portfolio by high priest of Art Nouveau. Jewelry, wallpaper, stained glass, furniture, figure studies, plant and animal motifs, etc. Only complete one-volume edition. 80pp. 9⅜ × 12¼. 24044-4 Pa. $9.95

ANIMALS: 1,419 COPYRIGHT-FREE ILLUSTRATIONS OF MAMMALS, BIRDS, FISH, INSECTS, ETC., edited by Jim Harter. Clear wood engravings present, in extremely lifelike poses, over 1,000 species of animals. One of the most extensive pictorial sourcebooks of its kind. Captions. Index. 284pp. 9 × 12. 23766-4 Pa. $9.95

OBELISTS FLY HIGH, C. Daly King. Masterpiece of American detective fiction, long out of print, involves murder on a 1935 transcontinental flight—"a very thrilling story"—NY Times. Unabridged and unaltered republication of the edition published by William Collins Sons & Co. Ltd., London, 1935. 288pp. 5⅜ × 8½. (Available in U.S. only) 25036-9 Pa. $5.95

VICTORIAN AND EDWARDIAN FASHION: A Photographic Survey, Alison Gernsheim. First fashion history completely illustrated by contemporary photographs. Full text plus 235 photos, 1840–1914, in which many celebrities appear. 240pp. 6½ × 9¼. 24205-6 Pa. $6.95

THE ART OF THE FRENCH ILLUSTRATED BOOK, 1700–1914, Gordon N. Ray. Over 630 superb book illustrations by Fragonard, Delacroix, Daumier, Doré, Grandville, Manet, Mucha, Steinlen, Toulouse-Lautrec and many others. Preface. Introduction. 633 halftones. Indices of artists, authors & titles, binders and provenances. Appendices. Bibliography. 608pp. 8⅜ × 11¼. 25086-5 Pa. $24.95

THE WONDERFUL WIZARD OF OZ, L. Frank Baum. Facsimile in full color of America's finest children's classic. 143 illustrations by W. W. Denslow. 267pp. 5⅜ × 8½. 20691-2 Pa. $7.95

FRONTIERS OF MODERN PHYSICS: New Perspectives on Cosmology, Relativity, Black Holes and Extraterrestrial Intelligence, Tony Rothman, et al. For the intelligent layman. Subjects include: cosmological models of the universe; black holes; the neutrino; the search for extraterrestrial intelligence. Introduction. 46 black-and-white illustrations. 192pp. 5⅜ × 8½. 24587-X Pa. $7.95

THE FRIENDLY STARS, Martha Evans Martin & Donald Howard Menzel. Classic text marshalls the stars together in an engaging, non-technical survey, presenting them as sources of beauty in night sky. 23 illustrations. Foreword. 2 star charts. Index. 147pp. 5⅜ × 8½. 21099-5 Pa. $3.95

FADS AND FALLACIES IN THE NAME OF SCIENCE, Martin Gardner. Fair, witty appraisal of cranks, quacks, and quackeries of science and pseudoscience: hollow earth, Velikovsky, orgone energy, Dianetics, flying saucers, Bridey Murphy, food and medical fads, etc. Revised, expanded In the Name of Science. "A very able and even-tempered presentation."—The New Yorker. 363pp. 5⅜ × 8. 20394-8 Pa. $6.95

ANCIENT EGYPT: ITS CULTURE AND HISTORY, J. E Manchip White. From pre-dynastics through Ptolemies: society, history, political structure, religion, daily life, literature, cultural heritage. 48 plates. 217pp. 5⅜ × 8½. 22548-8 Pa. $5.95

SIR HARRY HOTSPUR OF HUMBLETHWAITE, Anthony Trollope. Incisive, unconventional psychological study of a conflict between a wealthy baronet, his idealistic daughter, and their scapegrace cousin. The 1870 novel in its first inexpensive edition in years. 250pp. 5⅜ × 8½. 24953-0 Pa. $5.95

LASERS AND HOLOGRAPHY, Winston E. Kock. Sound introduction to burgeoning field, expanded (1981) for second edition. Wave patterns, coherence, lasers, diffraction, zone plates, properties of holograms, recent advances. 84 illustrations. 160pp. 5⅜ × 8¼. (Except in United Kingdom) 24041-X Pa. $3.95

INTRODUCTION TO ARTIFICIAL INTELLIGENCE: SECOND, EN-LARGED EDITION, Philip C. Jackson, Jr. Comprehensive survey of artificial intelligence—the study of how machines (computers) can be made to act intelligently. Includes introductory and advanced material. Extensive notes updating the main text. 132 black-and-white illustrations. 512pp. 5⅜ × 8½. 24864-X Pa. $8.95

HISTORY OF INDIAN AND INDONESIAN ART, Ananda K. Coomaraswamy. Over 400 illustrations illuminate classic study of Indian art from earliest Harappa finds to early 20th century. Provides philosophical, religious and social insights. 304pp. 6⅜ × 9⅜. 25005-9 Pa. $9.95

THE GOLEM, Gustav Meyrink. Most famous supernatural novel in modern European literature, set in Ghetto of Old Prague around 1890. Compelling story of mystical experiences, strange transformations, profound terror. 13 black-and-white illustrations. 224pp. 5⅜ × 8½. (Available in U.S. only) 25025-3 Pa. $6.95

PICTORIAL ENCYCLOPEDIA OF HISTORIC ARCHITECTURAL PLANS, DETAILS AND ELEMENTS: With 1,880 Line Drawings of Arches, Domes, Doorways, Facades, Gables, Windows, etc., John Theodore Haneman. Sourcebook of inspiration for architects, designers, others. Bibliography. Captions. 141pp. 9 × 12. 24605-1 Pa. $7.95

BENCHLEY LOST AND FOUND, Robert Benchley. Finest humor from early 30's, about pet peeves, child psychologists, post office and others. Mostly unavailable elsewhere. 73 illustrations by Peter Arno and others. 183pp. 5⅜ × 8½. 22410-4 Pa. $4.95

ERTÉ GRAPHICS, Erté. Collection of striking color graphics: *Seasons, Alphabet, Numerals, Aces* and *Precious Stones*. 50 plates, including 4 on covers. 48pp. 9⅜ × 12¼. 23580-7 Pa. $7.95

THE JOURNAL OF HENRY D. THOREAU, edited by Bradford Torrey, F. H. Allen. Complete reprinting of 14 volumes, 1837–61, over two million words; the sourcebooks for *Walden*, etc. Definitive. All original sketches, plus 75 photographs. 1,804pp. 8½ × 12¼. 20312-3, 20313-1 Cloth., Two-vol. set $120.00

CASTLES: THEIR CONSTRUCTION AND HISTORY, Sidney Toy. Traces castle development from ancient roots. Nearly 200 photographs and drawings illustrate moats, keeps, baileys, many other features. Caernarvon, Dover Castles, Hadrian's Wall, Tower of London, dozens more. 256pp. 5⅜ × 8¼. 24898-4 Pa. $6.95

CATALOG OF DOVER BOOKS

AMERICAN CLIPPER SHIPS: 1833–1858, Octavius T. Howe & Frederick C. Matthews. Fully-illustrated, encyclopedic review of 352 clipper ships from the period of America's greatest maritime supremacy. Introduction. 109 halftones. 5 black-and-white line illustrations. Index. Total of 928pp. 5⅜ × 8½.
25115-2, 25116-0 Pa., Two-vol. set $17.90

TOWARDS A NEW ARCHITECTURE, Le Corbusier. Pioneering manifesto by great architect, near legendary founder of "International School." Technical and aesthetic theories, views on industry, economics, relation of form to function, "mass-production spirit," much more. Profusely illustrated. Unabridged translation of 13th French edition. Introduction by Frederick Etchells. 320pp. 6⅛ × 9¼. (Available in U.S. only)
25023-7 Pa. $8.95

THE BOOK OF KELLS, edited by Blanche Cirker. Inexpensive collection of 32 full-color, full-page plates from the greatest illuminated manuscript of the Middle Ages, painstakingly reproduced from rare facsimile edition. Publisher's Note. Captions. 32pp. 9⅜ × 12¼.
24345-1 Pa. $4.95

BEST SCIENCE FICTION STORIES OF H. G. WELLS, H. G. Wells. Full novel *The Invisible Man*, plus 17 short stories: "The Crystal Egg," "Aepyornis Island," "The Strange Orchid," etc. 303pp. 5⅜ × 8½. (Available in U.S. only)
21531-8 Pa. $6.95

AMERICAN SAILING SHIPS: Their Plans and History, Charles G. Davis. Photos, construction details of schooners, frigates, clippers, other sailcraft of 18th to early 20th centuries—plus entertaining discourse on design, rigging, nautical lore, much more. 137 black-and-white illustrations. 240pp. 6⅛ × 9¼.
24658-2 Pa. $6.95

ENTERTAINING MATHEMATICAL PUZZLES, Martin Gardner. Selection of author's favorite conundrums involving arithmetic, money, speed, etc., with lively commentary. Complete solutions. 112pp. 5⅜ × 8½.
25211-6 Pa. $2.95

THE WILL TO BELIEVE, HUMAN IMMORTALITY, William James. Two books bound together. Effect of irrational on logical, and arguments for human immortality. 402pp. 5⅜ × 8½.
20291-7 Pa. $7.95

THE HAUNTED MONASTERY and THE CHINESE MAZE MURDERS, Robert Van Gulik. 2 full novels by Van Gulik continue adventures of Judge Dee and his companions. An evil Taoist monastery, seemingly supernatural events; overgrown topiary maze that hides strange crimes. Set in 7th-century China. 27 illustrations. 328pp. 5⅜ × 8½.
23502-5 Pa. $6.95

CELEBRATED CASES OF JUDGE DEE (DEE GOONG AN), translated by Robert Van Gulik. Authentic 18th-century Chinese detective novel; Dee and associates solve three interlocked cases. Led to Van Gulik's own stories with same characters. Extensive introduction. 9 illustrations. 237pp. 5⅜ × 8½.
23337-5 Pa. $4.95

Prices subject to change without notice.
Available at your book dealer or write for free catalog to Dept. GI, Dover Publications, Inc., 31 East 2nd St., Mineola, N.Y. 11501. Dover publishes more than 175 books each year on science, elementary and advanced mathematics, biology, music, art, literary history, social sciences and other areas.